Microsoft®
Excel Macros

Version 4

For Windows™ and the Macintosh®

Step by Step

Microsoft
PRESS®

Steve Wexler and
Julianne Sharer
For WexTech
Systems, Inc.

PUBLISHED BY
Microsoft Press
A Division of Microsoft Corporation
One Microsoft Way
Redmond, Washington 98052-6399

Library of Congress Cataloging-in-Publication Data
Wexler, Steve, 1958–
    Microsoft Excel 4 macros step by step / Steve Wexler, Julianne
Sharer.
       p.   cm.
   Includes index.
   ISBN 1-55615-496-8
   1. Microsoft Excel 4 for Windows. 2. Macro instructions
(Electronic computers) 3. Business--Computer programs.
4. Electronic spreadsheets. 5. Apple computer--Programming.
6. Macintosh (Computer)--Programming. I. Sharer, Julianne, 1960–
. II. Title.
HF5548.4.M523W49   1992
650'.0285'5369--dc20   92-14711
                                        CIP

Printed and bound in the United States of America.

1 2 3 4 5 6 7 8 9 MLML 7 6 5 4 3 2

Distributed to the book trade in Canada by Macmillan of Canada,
a division of Canada Publishing Corporation.

Distributed to the book trade outside the United States and
Canada by Penguin Books Ltd.

Penguin Books Ltd., Harmondsworth, Middlesex, England
Penguin Books Australia Ltd., Ringwood, Victoria, Australia
Penguin Books N.Z. Ltd., 182-190 Wairau Road, Auckland 10, New Zealand

British Cataloging-in-Publication Data available.

Apple and Macintosh are registered trademarks of Apple Computer, Inc.
1-2-3 and Lotus are registered trademarks of Lotus Development Corporation.
Microsoft is a registered trademark and Windows is a trademark of Microsoft
Corporation. Paintbrush is a trademark of ZSoft Corporation.

Contents

About This Book

Just as Microsoft Excel macros help you do your work faster, *Microsoft Excel Macros Step by Step* has been written to help you learn how to use macros faster. While we are now very comfortable with developing complex applications using Microsoft Excel, it's not all that long ago that we were grappling to understand how to use macros. In this book we will show you the essential things we wish somebody had shown us several years ago when we first started out.

The Microsoft Excel Function Reference *is an indispensable tool for writing macros. One of the goals of this book is to make you comfortable with using this reference.*

In *Microsoft Excel Macros Step by Step* we will cover the topics that are most important to using macros efficiently and effectively. This book will not be a substitute for the *Microsoft Excel Function Reference*, but will instead explain why you would want to use a particular function and how a particular function can solve a common problem.

In addition to sample macros and lesson files, the *Microsoft Excel Macros Step by Step* disk also comes with a full, working Client Tracking System written using Microsoft Excel Macros. This custom application manages mail lists, generates invoices and produces reports.

Microsoft Excel Macros Step by Step is written to appeal to a wide audience, including the novice programmer, the power user, the Lotus 1-2-3 convert and the professional programmer.

The Novice Programmer

Many novices are intimidated by the idea of programming, believing that since "power users" write macros, the Microsoft Excel macro language is only for power users. This is a little bit like saying that since great artists use brushes, brushes should only be used by great artists.

Like the autosum tool, the Microsoft Excel macro language is a tool—a very powerful tool—that both the novice and the professional can exploit to meet their needs. In *Microsoft Excel Macros Step by Step* we will take the cryptic phrase "macro language," reveal its remarkable power (and accessibility), and above all make it useful, even to the casual user.

The Power User

Microsoft Excel comes with a bevy of powerful features, but if you're like most sophisticated users, you probably feel that there's at least one important feature that is missing or isn't implemented in an ideal fashion. In *Microsoft Excel Macros Step by Step* we will show that macros allow you to do a lot more than just create shortcuts; you can actually customize Microsoft Excel to enhance and extend its basic functionality. In other words, if you want Microsoft Excel to behave differently, using the macro language you can change Microsoft Excel so that it works the way you want.

The Lotus 1-2-3 User

While your Lotus 1-2-3 version 2.01 macros will indeed run under Microsoft Excel, the Microsoft Excel native macro language has capabilities that far surpass 1-2-3's. In *Microsoft Excel Macros Step by Step* we will show you, the 1-2-3 macro user, how to take full advantage of the Microsoft Excel macro facility.

The Professional Programmer

To many professional programmers and developers, the term "macro language" connotes a keystroke-oriented facility for automating very simple, repetitive tasks. The Microsoft Excel macro language is much more than that; it is a mature development environment that allows you to create robust, mission-critical applications. In *Microsoft Excel Macros Step By Step* we will explore the programming tools available for developing and integrating complex applications.

Microsoft Excel for Windows vs. Microsoft Excel for the Macintosh

With but a few exceptions, Microsoft Excel for Windows works and "looks" like Microsoft Excel for the Macintosh. (Indeed, this cross-platform compatibility is one of the unique features of Microsoft Excel.) Except for where the products behave differently (or display different options or dialog boxes) we will present examples created in Microsoft Excel for Windows.

A small number of the procedures we set forth will work in both environments except for one step. In these cases, we offer two versions of the same step number, with Macintosh and Windows icons in the left margin to distinguish them. An even smaller number of the procedures had to be presented twice in full, once for Windows and once for the Macintosh. Again, these are identified by the appropriate icons in the left margin.

Prerequisites

About the only prerequisite for working with this book is comfort with using Microsoft Excel on an intermediate level. You do not need to know anything about programming; in fact, a sophisticated programming background (while certainly welcome) will not substitute for hands-on knowledge of Microsoft Excel. The macro language is driven by the user interface, in that you must choose particular commands in a particular order to achieve desired results. In other words, if you don't know how to sort a range of cells, you're certainly going to have a hard time writing a macro to do the same.

How This Book Is Organized

If you work through all the lessons in this book you will be able to build sophisticated applications using Microsoft Excel. Lessons One through Three focus on building simple, but useful, utilities that will help you in your day-to-day use of Microsoft Excel. Lesson Four covers replacing the built-in Sort command with an enhanced, friendlier version.

Lesson Five introduces a custom Client Tracking System built using Microsoft Excel. The Client Tracking application manages client lists, generates invoices, and tracks invoices using several reports generated with the Microsoft Excel Crosstab utility. Lessons Six and Seven take you through the steps needed to build the Client Tracking application.

In the appendix, we cover the basics of Dynamic Data Exchange.

Conventions Used in This Book

Keyboard Conventions

- Names of keys are in small capital letters; for example, ENTER and SHIFT.

- A plus sign (+) between two keynames means that you must press those keys at the same time. For example, "Press CTRL + d" means that you hold down the CTRL key while you press d.

Icons

Throughout this book, icons in the left margin draw your attention to examples in the text that can be found on the accompanying diskette or highlight information of special interest to Lotus 1-2-3 users, Microsoft Windows users and Apple Macintosh users, as follows:

Icon	Meaning
	A disk icon will appear next to the examples that can be found on the sample diskette.
	This icon will appear next to text that is of particular interest to Lotus 1-2-3 users.
	A Microsoft Windows icon will appear next to text that is of particular interest to Windows users.
	A Macintosh icon will appear next to text that is of particular interest to Apple Macintosh users.

Getting Ready

Before you begin the lessons you will need to install the lesson files and the Client Tracking System files. Inside this book you'll find two disks named "Practice Files for *Microsoft Excel Macros Step by Step*." One disk is for Microsoft Excel for Windows and the other is for Microsoft Excel for the Macintosh. The files and directories contained on these disks should be copied onto your hard drive into a directory called XLMSTEP.

 ## Installing the Practice Files (Windows)

While you can employ a number of techniques to transfer the files and directories to your hard drive, we recommend you use the Windows File Manager. Using the File Manager, you'll be able to transfer the files and the directories contained on the disk in one step.

For this example we will copy the files from the A drive to a directory called XLMSTEP on the C drive.

To Install the Practice Files Using the Windows File Manager

1 From the Program Manager, load the File Manager by double-clicking the File Manager icon.

2 With the File Manager active, click the C drive icon and click the root directory as shown in Figure 1.

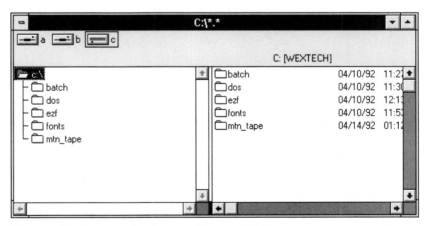

Figure 1 File Manager showing root directory of C drive

3 Put the Practice Disk in the A drive and click the A drive icon. Your screen should look like the one shown in Figure 2.

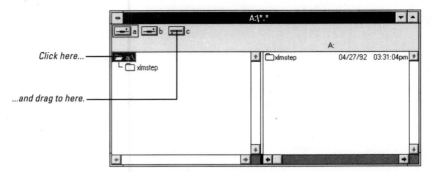

Click here...

...and drag to here.

Figure 2   File Manager showing root directory of Practice Disk

4   Click the A drive root directory folder and drag it over the C drive icon.

5   If you are asked whether you want to copy selected files and directories to C:\, click Yes.

Windows will copy the files and directories from the A drive to a directory called XLMSTEP on the C drive.

Installing the Practice Files (Macintosh)

For the instructions that follow, the Finder has been set to display files by name.

To Install the Practice Files

1 Place the Practice Disk in the disk drive and activate the Finder. Your screen should look like the one shown in Figure 3.

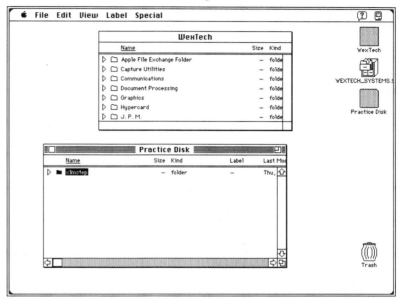

Figure 3 Macintosh Finder

2 Drag the XLMSTEP folder from the Practice Disk window to the window that represents your hard drive.

The Finder will copy the files and directories from the Practice Disk to a folder called XLMSTEP on the hard drive.

What's on the Disk

The XLMSTEP directory contains directories and files as described below.

LESSONS Directory

The LESSONS directory (contained in the XLMSTEP directory) has the following files:

File	Description
CHDIR.XLM	Macros for changing directories and opening files used in Lesson 3
CHDIR2.XLM	Macros for changing directories and creating custom commands used in Lesson 3
CLUSTERS.XLS	Practice worksheet used in Lesson 2
COMX.XLM	Sample macros used in Lesson 2
COMXDONE.XLM	Completed version of COMX.XLM
DIALOG.XLM	Macro sheet template for dialog boxes used in Lesson 3
MORETOOL.XLM	Utility macros used in Lesson 3
PRINT_ME.XLS	Practice worksheet used in Lesson 1
ROUNDTO.XLM	Custom macro function for rounding numbers used in Lesson 2
SMALBASE.XLS	Sample database used in Lesson 4
SMRTSORT.XLM	Macro sheet for improving the Data Sort command used in Lesson 4
SPELLOUT.XLA	Custom Function Add-In for spelling out numbers used in Lesson 2
TOOLS.XLM	Utility macro sheet that contains macros that help you write macros, used in Lesson 3
TROUBLE.XLM	Dialog box example used in Lesson 3

TRACKING Directory

The TRACKING directory (contained in the XLMSTEP directory) has the following files:

File	Description
CATEGORY.XLS	Client Tracking System report worksheet used in Lessons 5, 6 and 7
EXEC.XLS	Client Tracking System EIS front panel used in Lessons 5 and 7
INVOICE.XLS	Client Tracking System invoice database used in Lessons 5 and 7
LETTER.DOT	Word for Windows letter template used in Lesson 5 (on Windows disk only)
MAILLIST.XLS	Client Tracking System Mail List used in Lessons 5 and 7
OUSTAND.XLS	Client Tracking System report worksheet used in Lessons 5, 6 and 7
TRACKING.XLS	Client Tracking System tracking database used in Lessons 5 and 7
YTD.XLS	Client Tracking System report worksheet used in Lessons 5, 6 and 7

FINISHED Directory

The FINISHED directory (contained in the TRACKING directory) has the following files:

File	Description
EXEC.XLA	Completed EIS Add-In used in Lesson 5
TRACKING.XLA	Completed Client Tracking System Add-In used in Lesson 5

LESSON6 Directory

The LESSON6 directory (contained in the TRACKING directory) has the following file:

File	Description
TRACKING.XLA	Incomplete Client-Tracking System Add-In used in Lesson 6

LESSON7 Directory

The LESSON7 directory (contained in the TRACKING directory) has the following files:

File	Description
TRACKING.XLA	Incomplete Client-Tracking System Add-In used in Lesson 7
EXEC.XLA	Incomplete EIS Add-In used in Lesson 7

 ## XLDDE Directory (Windows Only)

The XLDDE directory (contained in the XLMSTEP directory) has the following files:

File	Description
DDETEST.DOC	Word for Windows sample DDE document
DDETEST.XLM	Microsoft Excel sample DDE macro sheet

Getting Started with Microsoft Excel Macros

A macro, in virtually all computer applications, is simply a method of automating a task or a series of tasks into a single, user-defined, easily accessible command. The word is short for *macroinstruction* and has been in use since the days of punch cards.

In a sense, all computer programs are organized collections of macros. This is an over-simplification, of course, but from the perspective of someone typing numbers into a worksheet or characters into a word processor, the various functions found behind menus or attached to keystroke shortcuts are basically "internal" macros written and structured by a programmer.

In the same way that Microsoft Excel has assembled these "macros" in a logical fashion and made them accessible through menus, you, too, can assemble and combine various functions and commands into routines that help you perform tasks better and faster.

This lesson explains how to do the following:

- Record and edit macros
- Assign shortcut keys to macros
- Work with global macros
- Understand the difference between worksheets and macro sheets
- Hide and save macro sheets
- Assign macros to tools
- Create custom tools and toolbars

Types of Macros

The types of macros you can create fall into three basic categories:

- **Utility Macros**—Macros that are so helpful in your day-to-day use of Microsoft Excel that you want them available all the time, no matter what type of worksheet or chart you are working with.

- **Task-Specific Macros**—Macros that aid in accomplishing a particular task or function and are only needed with certain types of worksheets or charts.

- **Full Application Macros**—Macros that, when combined with custom menus, dialog boxes and toolbars, create a comprehensive, standalone application.

Creating Macros

You create macros either by *recording* or by *editing*. Recording is the simplest way to create a macro. The Microsoft Excel macro recorder records keystrokes, commands, dialog check box states, and so on. It does not record mouse pointer movement, although it will record the results of a mouse action, such as clicking an option button or selecting a range of cells.

Editing a macro is more complex but gives you much more control over what the macro will accomplish. In many cases you will record then edit a macro. You record the macro to transcribe its basic shape and function, then edit the macro to test and perfect it.

Let's begin problem solving using Microsoft Excel macros.

Recording Your First Macro

Problem: Microsoft Excel has many tools and shortcut keys, but there isn't a tool or shortcut for placing a double border around cells.

Solution: Use the macro recorder to record the steps needed to place a double border around cells.

To Record the Double Border Macro

1   If you have not already done so, load Microsoft Excel with a blank worksheet.

2   Select a small range of cells; any range will do.

3   From the Macro menu, choose Record. The Record Macro dialog box will appear.

4   Change the macro name to **DoubleBorder** and shortcut key to CTRL+ d (for double border), as shown in Figure 1.1.

The use of a small "d" for the shortcut key is intentional. Using a capital "d" would require that you hold down the SHIFT key as well as the CTRL key.

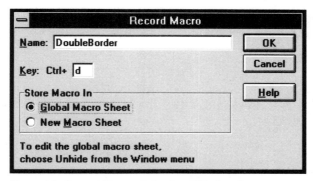

Figure 1.1   Record Macro dialog box (Windows)

4   Change the macro name to **DoubleBorder** and shortcut key to OPTION + COMMAND + d (for double border), as shown in Figure 1.2.

The use of a small "d" for the shortcut key is intentional. Using a capital "d" would require that you hold down the SHIFT key as well as the OPTION and COMMAND keys.

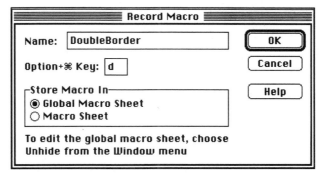

Figure 1.2   Record Macro dialog box (Macintosh)

5   With Global Macro Sheet selected (we'll discuss what that means in a moment), click OK. The word "Recording" will appear in the status bar at the bottom of your screen.

6   From the Format menu, choose Border. The Border dialog box will appear.

7   Select double border style and choose Outline, as shown in Figure 1.3.

Figure 1.3   Format Border dialog box

8   Click OK. Microsoft Excel will apply a double border to the selected cells.

9   From the Macro menu, choose Stop to turn the macro recorder off.

To see the results, click outside the selected area. You have just created a macro called DoubleBorder which you can run to apply a double border around cells. Because the macro was recorded as a *global* macro, the double border will be available whenever you use Microsoft Excel, no matter what worksheet you happen to be working with. In other words, in creating a global macro you have extended the basic functionality of Microsoft Excel to include a new formatting shortcut.

 You don't need to be as careful when you use the Microsoft Excel macro recorder as when you use the Lotus 1-2-3 recorder. Unlike the Lotus 1-2-3 recorder, where every keystroke is recorded (including all the pressings of ESCAPE and BACKSPACE to remedy an error while recording), the Microsoft Excel recorder just transcribes the completed actions.

Running the Macro

As we mentioned earlier, the DoubleBorder macro is available for you to use on any worksheet at any time. You can run this macro using either of the following procedures:

To Execute the Macro Using the Macro Run Command

1   From the Macro menu, choose Run. A dialog box similar to the one shown in Figure 1.4 will appear.

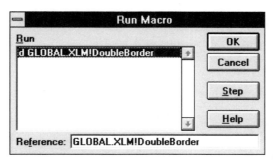

Figure 1.4   Run macro dialog box

2   Choose the macro you want to run, in this case DoubleBorder, and click OK.

To Execute the Macro with a Shortcut Key

▶   In Microsoft Excel for Windows, press CTRL + d. In Microsoft Excel for the Macintosh, press OPTION + COMMAND + d.

Where Do Macros Live?

In the same fashion you used to record the DoubleBorder macro, you can create additional macros that are stored on the *global macro sheet*. At this point you may be wondering what a macro sheet is, let alone a global macro sheet.

Unlike some other worksheet applications, such as Lotus 1-2-3, Microsoft Excel does not store macros on the worksheet you are currently editing, but instead maintains macros on separate *macro sheets*. Like worksheets and chart files, as many macro sheets may be open as will fit into available memory—you're not constrained to working with only one macro sheet at a time.

Macro sheets in Microsoft Excel are similar to the macro library in Lotus 1-2-3 where you create macros that can be used with any worksheet. However, unlike working with the Lotus 1-2-3 macro library, when working with Microsoft Excel you can have more than one macro sheet loaded at one time and can edit macro sheets without having to close the active worksheet.

Examining the Macro Sheet

Before we go any further, let's look "under the hood" and examine the global macro sheet.

When you create global macros, Microsoft Excel adds the macros to a hidden macro sheet called GLOBAL.XLM.

When you create global macros, Microsoft Excel adds the macros to a hidden macro sheet called "Global Macros."

To Examine the Global Macro Sheet

1   From the Window menu, choose Unhide.

2   When the Unhide dialog box appears, choose the global macro sheet ("GLOBAL.XLM" in Windows, "Global Macros" for the Macintosh) and click OK. Your screen should look like the one shown in Figure 1.5.

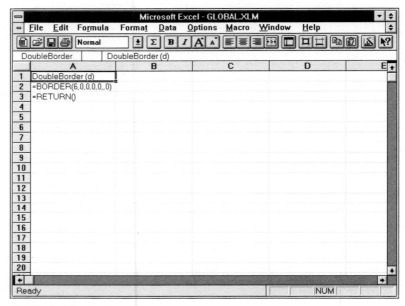

Figure 1.5   Global Macro Sheet

The Differences Between Worksheets and Macro Sheets

The first obvious difference is that in macro sheets the columns are a little wider and, in Microsoft Excel for Windows, macro sheets have an XLM extension. The columns are wider because, by default, Microsoft Excel displays formulas instead of values in macro sheets, and formulas take up more real estate than values. Just as there are probably times when editing worksheets that you want to see all the cells' underlying formulas, there will definitely be occasions when editing a macro sheet that you'll want to see cell values.

To See Macro Sheet Values

We'll explore the ramifications of these TRUE values a bit later on.

1 With the global macro sheet active, press CTRL + ` (accent grave—it's located underneath the tilde). On the Macintosh COMMAND + ` will work, too. Microsoft Excel will display macro sheet values (in this case the value TRUE in cells A2 and A3). Notice also that the columns are now narrower.

2 Press CTRL + ` again to display formulas.

Note   You can also view formulas through the Options Display dialog box.

In addition to a default display of formulas instead of values, macro sheets also handle recalculation differently. On macro sheets Microsoft Excel doesn't recalculate the entire sheet at once, but instead evaluates each cell of a macro in succession as the macro is executed.

To review, the major differences between macro sheets and worksheets are:

- By default, macro sheets have an XLM extension (Windows version only).

- By default, formulas are displayed on macro sheets instead of values.

- Microsoft Excel doesn't recalculate the entire macro sheet, but instead evaluates one cell of a macro at a time while the macro is running.

Named Areas

Before examining the "guts" of the macro, let's first observe that Microsoft Excel has created a named area on the sheet called DoubleBorder that refers to cell $A$1.

To Examine the Names on the Macro Sheet

1 From the Formula menu, choose Define Name. The Define Name dialog box will appear.

2 In the Names in Sheet list box, click DoubleBorder. The dialog box should look like the one shown in Figure 1.6.

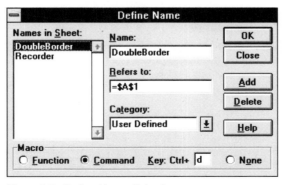

Figure 1.6   Define Name dialog box

Note Notice, in the Define Name dialog box, that DoubleBorder refers to cell $A$1, is a command macro of the User Defined category, and has been assigned the shortcut CTRL + d (OPTION + COMMAND + d on the Macintosh). Also notice that a second area called Recorder exists. Whenever you record a macro, the macro recorder will designate a record area unless you use the Set Recorder command from the Macro menu to specify a range into which Microsoft Excel should place the recorded macro.

3 Click OK.

Understanding the DoubleBorder Macro

When you recorded the macro, Microsoft Excel placed the following entries into cells A1:A3.

	A
1	DoubleBorder (d)
2	=BORDER(6,0,0,0,0,,0)
3	=RETURN()

Figure 1.7 Recorded DoubleBorder macro

The first line of the macro

```
DoubleBorder (d)
```

All macro statements are formulas, therefore they must begin with an equal sign.

was created by Microsoft Excel solely for our benefit as Microsoft Excel ignores macro cell entries that don't begin with an equal sign. The cell is a label that tells us the name of the macro and the shortcut key to which it has been assigned. The cell can be erased or modified and the macro will still work.

The next line

```
=BORDER(6,0,0,0,0,,0)
```

tells Microsoft Excel to format the selected cells with a double border. But where did this "6" come from and what do all the zeros and commas mean?

As we mentioned in the introduction, one of the goals of this book is to make you comfortable with using the *Microsoft Excel Function Reference*, so now is as good a time as any to crack the binding and take a look at what's written about the BORDER command.

According to the *Microsoft Excel Function Reference*, the correct way to designate the BORDER command, that is to say, the "syntax" of the BORDER command, is

BORDER(*outline,left,right,top,bottom,shade,outline_color,left_color, right_color,top_color,bottom_color*)

where *outline, left, right, top* and *bottom* are numbers from 0 to 7 corresponding to the line styles in the Format Border dialog box, as shown in the following table:

Value	Line Type
0	No Border
1	Thin Line
2	Medium Line
3	Dashed Line
4	Dotted Line
5	Thick Line
6	Double Line
7	Hairline

Outline_color, left_color, right_color, top_color and *bottom_color* are numbers from 0 to 16 corresponding to the Color box in the Format Border dialog box. Zero corresponds to automatic color.

So, here's what the second line of the macro means:

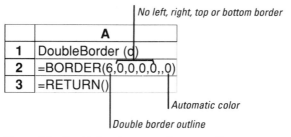

Figure 1.8   DoubleBorder macro (annotated)

The final line of the macro

=RETURN( )

terminates the macro and returns control back to the caller of the macro, in this case Microsoft Excel itself. There will be cases in which one macro (the main routine) calls another macro (the subroutine). We'll see how this works a little later on.

Optional Arguments

Notice that in the example shown above, the value for shading has not been specified (hence the two commas). This means that shading should be left unchanged as opposed to being explicitly turned on or off. As with the BORDER command, most Microsoft Excel functions have *optional arguments*, that is, items that can be left out. For example, let's say you want to place a thick left border in the selected region, but not change any border settings which already exist. You could do this by employing the following variation of the BORDER command:

```
=BORDER(,5)
```

What's an "Argument"?

Throughout this book we will use the term *argument* (also called a *parameter*). While the term itself may seem foreign to you, you use the "idea" behind arguments in your everyday speech. For example, if you go to a pharmacy, you might say to the druggist "I would like to buy a large bottle of mint-flavored antacid." In this case the *function* is that you "want to buy" and the *arguments* are antacid, large, and mint. In Microsoft Excel, you might express this as

```
=I.WANT.TO.BUY("Antacid","Large","Mint")
```

and if you don't care about the flavor, you might express this as

```
=I.WANT.TO.BUY("Antacid","Large")
```

Editing the Macro

Problem: I've changed my mind. I'd rather have a solid blue border instead of a double border.

Solution: Edit the macro, changing the arguments of the BORDER command so that cells are formatted with a solid blue border.

Now that we understand how the BORDER command works, all we have to do is edit the macro so that it looks like this.

	A
1	DoubleBorder (d)
2	=BORDER(2,0,0,0,0,,5)
3	=RETURN()

Figure 1.9   Modified DoubleBorder macro

The "2" indicates that we want a medium solid line and the "5" indicates that we want the fifth color option from the Color box in the Format Border dialog box.

Before continuing   Reactivate the worksheet and try running the DoubleBorder macro by pressing CTRL + d. When you are finished, reactivate the macro sheet and change the "2" back to a "6" and the "5" back to a "0."

Lotus 1-2-3 macro mavens are often surprised that the label at the top of the macro doesn't produce a macro error. Consider the example shown in Figure 1.10.

	A
1	DoubleBorder (d)
2	=BORDER(2,0,0,0,0,,5)
3	This won't hurt a thing
4	
5	=RETURN()

Figure 1.10   Macro with comments

Again, macro statements are formulas.

When you execute the macro shown in Figure 1.10, Microsoft Excel will simply ignore the label in cell A3 and the empty entry in cell A4. The Microsoft Excel macro language is command-oriented, not keystroke oriented—it doesn't try to run a macro one keystroke at a time but instead evaluates the results of an entire statement. Since cell A3 doesn't begin with an equal sign and since cell A4 is blank, Microsoft Excel ignores these cells when it executes the macro.

Solving More Problems

Quick and Dirty Printing

Problem: I'd like to print a selected area without having to set the Print Area and wade through the File Print dialog box.

Solution: Use the macro recorder to transcribe the actions needed to print a selected area.

___

Before continuing   Open PRINT_ME.XLS. Your screen should look like the one shown in Figure 1.11.

___

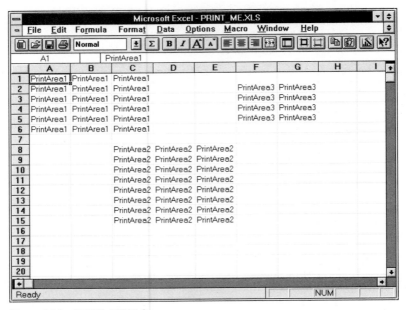

Figure 1.11   PRINT_ME.XLS

To Record the PrintSelection Macro

1 Select the area you want to print, in this case A1:C6.

2 From the Macro menu, choose Record. The Record Macro dialog box will appear.

 3 Change the macro name to PrintSelection and assign the shortcut key CTRL + p, as shown in Figure 1.12.

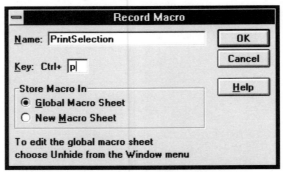

Figure 1.12   Record Macro dialog box (Windows)

 3 Change the macro name to PrintSelection and assign the shortcut key OPTION + COMMAND + p, as shown in Figure 1.13.

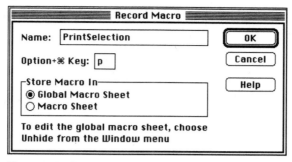

Figure 1.13   Record Macro dialog box (Macintosh)

4   Click OK. The word "Recording" will appear in the status bar.

5   From the Options menu, choose Set Print Area.

6   From the File menu, choose Print. The Print dialog box will appear.

7   For this example (so as not to waste paper) make sure Print Preview is checked and click OK. Microsoft Excel will display the print preview window.

8   In the preview window, click the Close button.

9   From the Macro menu, choose Stop Recorder.

Let's see if this thing works by printing a different selection.

To Run the PrintSelection Macro

1   Select the area you want to print, in this case C8:E15.

2   Run the macro by pressing either CTRL + p within Windows or OPTION + COMMAND + p on the Macintosh. The preview window will appear on your screen.

3   In the preview window, click Close.

Examining the PrintSelection Macro

When you activate the global macro sheet (by selecting that file from the Window menu) you'll see that Microsoft Excel transcribed the following entries.

	B
1	PrintSelection (p)
2	=SET.PRINT.AREA()
3	=PRINT(1,,,1,FALSE,TRUE,1,FALSE,1)
4	=RETURN()

Figure 1.14   PrintSelection macro

The first line of the macro

```
PrintSelection (p)
```

is a label that tells us the name of the macro and the shortcut key to which it has been assigned. The cell can be erased or modified and the macro will still work. The line

```
=SET.PRINT.AREA()
```

was recorded when you chose Set Print Area from the Options menu. The line

```
=PRINT(1,,,1,FALSE,TRUE,1,FALSE,1)
```

represents the values recorded in the Print dialog box. Again, a visit to the *Microsoft Excel Function Reference* shows that the syntax for this command is

PRINT(*Range_num,from,to,copies,draft,preview,print_what,color, feed,quality,v_quality*)

Color and feed are only available on Microsoft Excel for the Macintosh.

where *range_num* is either equal to 1 (meaning print all the pages) or 2 (meaning print a specified range). The *from* and *to* arguments are ignored unless *range_num* equals 2. The final line

```
=RETURN()
```

ends the macro.

What it Means to Be "Global"

At this point the global macro sheet contains two macros, DoubleBorder and PrintSelection, which will be available as long as the global macro sheet is loaded. But you can have other macros on other macro sheets that are always available, too. As long as the macro sheet is open, all of the macros contained on that sheet will be available.

Let's illustrate this by creating a very simple macro (in this case a macro that just beeps) on a different macro sheet.

To Write the Beeper Macro

1   From the File menu, choose New. When the dialog box appears, choose Macro Sheet and click OK.

2   Make the cell entries shown in Figure 1.15.

Enter formulas in a macro sheet in lower case. If you type a valid formula, Microsoft Excel will convert the formula to upper case.

	A
1	Beeper (b)
2	=BEEP()
3	=RETURN()

Figure 1.15   Beeper macro

3   Select cells A1:A3 and choose Define Name from the Formula menu. The Define Name dialog box will appear.

4   Change the macro name to Beeper and indicate that you want this to be a command macro with the shortcut key CTRL + b (OPTION + COMMAND + b on the Macintosh), as shown in Figure 1.16.

Notice that in this example, BEEPER refers to a range instead of an individual cell. While not necessary (you only need to name the first cell in a macro) this certainly won't hurt anything.

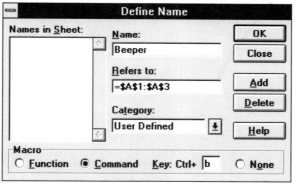

Figure 1.16   Define Name dialog box

5   Click OK.

To Run the Beeper Macro

1   Activate PRINT_ME.XLS.

2   Press CTRL + b (or OPTION + COMMAND + b) to run the Beeper macro.

To further illustrate that all the macros from both the new macro sheet (currently named Macro1) and the global macro sheet are available, choose Run from the Macro menu. The dialog box similar to the one shown in Figure 1.17 will appear.

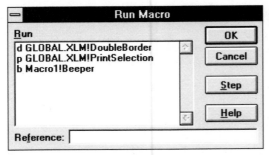

Figure 1.17   Run Macro dialog box with macros from different macro sheets

Before continuing   Click Cancel.

So, What Makes the Global Macro Sheet "Global"?

If you come from a Microsoft Word for Windows environment you may be a bit confused because Microsoft Word has only one global template, called NORMAL.DOT. What makes the global macro sheet "global" is not that it has macros that can always be available; what makes it global is that

- By default, GLOBAL.XLM is saved in the Microsoft Excel startup directory (XLSTART, located beneath the directory where Microsoft Excel has been installed). *Any* macro sheet (or worksheet, for that matter) saved in this directory will load automatically whenever you start Microsoft Excel.

- By default, "Global Macros" is saved in the Excel Startup Folder (4), located within the Preferences folder (which, in turn, is located within the System folder). *Any* macro sheet (or worksheet, for that matter) saved in this directory will load automatically whenever you start Microsoft Excel.

- Microsoft Excel automatically transcribes any recorded macros on the global macro sheet when you indicate that the macro you want to record is a global macro.

Saving the New Macro Sheet (Windows)

For this next example, let's save the new macro sheet in the XLSTART directory so that the macro sheet will load automatically whenever you start Microsoft Excel.

To Save the Macro Sheet

1   From the Window menu, choose the window you want to work with, in this case Macro1.

2   From the File menu, choose Save.

3   When the dialog box appears, change the filename to **scratch** and change to the XLSTART directory, as shown in Figure 1.18.

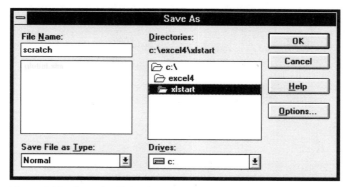

Figure 1.18   Save As dialog box

4   Click OK. Microsoft Excel will automatically append the extension .XLM to the macro sheet name.

 ## Saving the New Macro Sheet (Macintosh)

For this next example, let's save the new macro sheet in the Excel Startup Folder (4) so that the macro sheet will load automatically whenever you start Microsoft Excel.

To Save the Macro Sheet

1   From the Window menu, choose the window you want to work with, in this case Macro1.

2   From the File menu, choose Save.

3   When the dialog box appears, change the filename to **scratch.xlm** and change to the Excel Startup Folder (4), as shown in Figure 1.19.

You do not need to give the file an extension of .XLM. We're adding an extension in this example to be consistent with the Windows example.

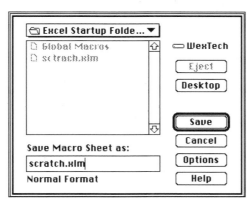

Figure 1.19   Save As dialog box

Before continuing   Activate and save the global macro sheet.

Let's see if saving a macro sheet in this fashion works.

To See if the Global Macro Sheet and SCRATCH.XLM Will Load Automatically

1   Exit Microsoft Excel. When asked if you want to save PRINT_ME.XLS or the blank worksheet, click No.

2   Load Microsoft Excel. SCRATCH.XLM and the global macro sheet will load automatically.

Hiding Macro Sheets: Part One

We will write a macro to save a hidden window in the next lesson.

Except when you are actively editing macro sheets, you'll probably want to keep your macro sheets hidden, either to keep your workspace tidy or to prevent those who use your macros from accidentally changing something. Unfortunately, if you hide a macro sheet there is no easy way to directly save that macro sheet. If you hide both the global macro sheet and SCRATCH.XLM, the Save option is not available under the File menu. There is, however, a simple work-around.

To Save a Macro Sheet as a Hidden Window

1   Activate SCRATCH.XLM.

2   From the Window menu, choose Hide. This will hide SCRATCH.XLM and leave the global macro sheet active.

3   From the Window menu, choose Hide. This will hide the global macro sheet.

New Worksheet Icon

4   Create a new worksheet by clicking the New Worksheet icon (or by choosing New from the File menu and choosing Worksheet).

5   While holding down the SHIFT key, click File and choose Close All.

6   When prompted to save SCRATCH.XLM, click Yes.

You may be wondering why Microsoft Excel didn't ask you about the global macro sheet. When you select Close All from the File menu, Microsoft Excel does not close the global macro sheet. The only way to close the global macro sheet without exiting Microsoft Excel is to unhide it and then close it. However, when you exit Microsoft Excel, you are prompted to save your changes to the global macro sheet.

Before continuing   Open PRINT_ME.XLS.

Toolbars

So far we've looked at two different ways of running macros: using shortcut keys and the Macro Run dialog box. In the next series of exercises we'll see how you can assign macros to one of the seven built-in toolbars as well as create your own custom toolbar.

For this next example we will assign the DoubleBorder macro to the Standard toolbar.

To Assign a Macro to the Standard Toolbar

1   Make sure the macro sheet that contains the macro you want to assign is loaded (in this case the global macro sheet, which should still be loaded).

2   From the Options menu, choose Toolbars.

3   When the Toolbar dialog box appears, make sure Standard is selected and click Customize.

Note   You can also access the Customize dialog box using the Toolbar shortcut menu. To access the Toolbar shortcut menu in Windows, click the right mouse button in the Standard Toolbar. To access the Toolbar shortcut menu on the Macintosh, hold down the OPTION and COMMAND keys and click the Standard Toolbar.

---

4   When the Customize dialog box appears, click Custom in the categories list box, as shown in Figure 1.20.

If the Customize dialog box is obscuring the toolbar, click in the Customize title bar and drag the dialog box to another location.

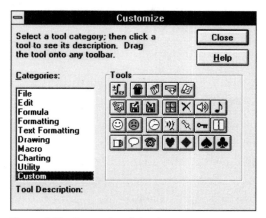

Figure 1.20   Customize dialog box

5   Click the tool you want to use (we'll see how to create your own icons later) and drag the tool to the right of the autosum icon on the Standard toolbar. The Assign to Tool dialog box will appear, as shown in Figure 1.21.

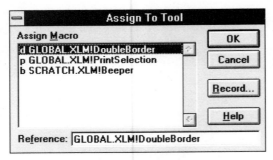

Figure 1.21   Assign to Tool dialog box

6   Click the macro you want to assign, in this case DoubleBorder, and click OK. The Standard toolbar should look like the one shown in Figure 1.22.

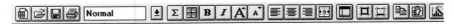

Figure 1.22   Customized (and crowded) toolbar

7   Click Close to close the Customize dialog box.

Making the Toolbar Less Crowded

A good candidate for tool removal is the Shrink Font tool. Holding down the SHIFT key while clicking the Grow Font tool performs the same function as clicking the Shrink Font tool.

If you are working in standard VGA resolution (640 x 480), your toolbar may be a bit crowded. There's a little more room on the Macintosh. You can remedy this crowding by

- Removing a tool
- Changing the spacing between tools
- Narrowing the width of the Style tool

In this case we'll narrow the width of the Style tool.

To Narrow the Width of the Style Tool

1   Click the right mouse button in the Standard toolbar and choose Customize. The Customize dialog box will appear.

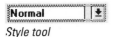

Style tool

2   Ignoring the Customize dialog box, click in the Style tool in the Standard toolbar.

3   Move the mouse pointer to the right of the drop-down arrow so that the mouse pointer changes to a double arrow.

4   Drag the mouse about 1/4-inch to the left.

5   Close the Customize dialog box.

Creating Your Own Tools

While Microsoft Excel comes with a set of custom tools, you can also create your own tools using whatever drawing or paint package you favor. In fact, any image you create that can be copied to the Clipboard can be made into a tool. In the example shown below, we will demonstrate how to copy a tool that was created using Windows Paintbrush.

To Copy a Tool from a Draw or Paint Application

1   Activate the paint or drawing software application you want to use and open the file that contains the image you want to use (an example using Windows Paintbrush is shown in Figure 1.23).

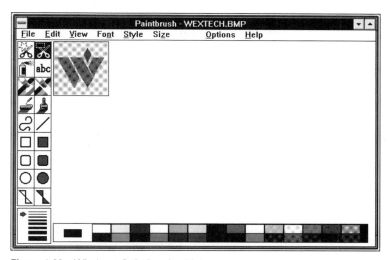

Figure 1.23   Windows Paintbrush with image

2   Copy the image to the Clipboard using the Edit Copy command.

3   Activate Microsoft Excel, click the right mouse button in the Standard toolbar and choose Customize.

3   Activate Microsoft Excel. While pressing the OPTION and COMMAND keys, click in the Standard toolbar and choose Customize.

4   Ignoring the Customize dialog box, click the tool in the Standard toolbar you want to change.

5   From the Edit menu, choose Paste Tool Face.

6   Close the Customize dialog box. The toolbar should look similar to the one shown in Figure 1.24.

Figure 1.24   Toolbar with custom tool

Microsoft Excel Macros Step by Step

Resetting the Standard Toolbar

Resetting will restore the toolbar to its original arrangement.

Let's suppose you decide that instead of crowding the Standard toolbar with new tools, you'd rather reset the Standard toolbar and create a completely new custom toolbar.

To Reset the Standard Toolbar

1   Acesss the Toolbar shortcut menu (see note on page 19) and choose Toolbars. The Toolbars dialog box will appear.

2   With Standard selected in the Show Toolbars list box, click Reset.

3   Click Close.

Creating a Custom Toolbar

In addition to the Standard toolbar, Microsoft Excel comes with six built-in toolbars that facilitate formatting, drawing, and so on. You can also create your own custom toolbars that contain any Microsoft Excel built-in tools as well as custom tools assigned to macros. In this next example we will create a toolbar called MyBar that contains tools for running the DoubleBorder and PrintSelection macros.

To Create a Custom Toolbar

1   Acesss the Toolbar shortcut menu (see note on page 19) and choose Toolbars. The Toolbars dialog box will appear.

2   Change the Toolbar Name to MyBar, as shown in Figure 1.25.

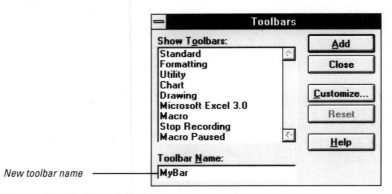

New toolbar name

Figure 1.25   Toolbars dialog box

3   Click Add. A very small, empty toolbar will appear in the upper left corner of the screen, along with the Customize dialog box.

4   In the Customize dialog box, click Custom in the categories list box.

5   Click one of the custom tools and drag it into the MyBar toolbar.

6   When the Assign to Tool dialog box appears, choose DoubleBorder and click OK.

7   Repeat steps 5 and 6 to assign the PrintSelection macro to the MyBar toolbar.

8   Close the Customize dialog box.

A Note on Toolbars

Microsoft Excel stores information on which toolbars you have and how the toolbars are configured in the EXCEL.XLB file. If you will be developing applications that contain custom toolbars, you cannot simply distribute your copy of EXCEL.XLB to your end users as doing so will wipe out whatever toolbar customization and personalization the end user may have made.

Microsoft Excel stores information on which toolbars you have and how the toolbars are configured in the Excel Toolbars file, located in the Preferences folder. If you will be developing applications that contain custom toolbars, you cannot simply distribute your copy of Excel Toolbars to your end users as doing so will wipe out whatever toolbar customization and personalization the end user may have made.

Note   If your application has a custom toolbar, this toolbar should be created anew every time the application is run using special toolbar macro commands, and dismantled when the application is closed. This will leave your end user's toolbar settings intact. Using these commands will provide the added benefit of allowing you to associate a meaningful description to the tool when the user clicks on it. (Right now when you click on a custom tool the status bar reads "Blank tool for assigning a macro".) Creating custom toolbars is discussed on page 120.

Lesson Summary

In this section we have covered the fundamental principles of creating macros in Microsoft Excel. We have used the macro recorder to create macros and have edited the macros on the macro sheet. We have worked with global macros (macros stored in GLOBAL.XLM) and have created macros that are stored on a different macro sheet (the Beeper macro stored in SCRATCH.XLM). We have seen that you can get macros to load automatically by placing macro sheets in the XLSTART directory and have implemented one solution for saving macros in a hidden state. We've also assigned macros to the Standard toolbar and have created our own toolbar from scratch.

In this section we have covered the fundamental principles of creating macros in Microsoft Excel. We have used the macro recorder to create macros and have edited the macros on the macro sheet. We have worked with global macros (macros stored in the macro sheet "Global Macros") and have created macros that are stored on a different macro sheet (the Beeper macro stored in SCRATCH.XLM). We have seen that you can get macros to load automatically by placing macro sheets in the Excel Startup Folder (4) folder and have implemented one solution for saving macros in a hidden state. We've also assigned macros to the Standard toolbar and have created our own toolbar from scratch.

Preview of the Next Lesson

In the next lesson, you will improve the macros you created in this lesson using informational functions, Microsoft Excel control structures and subroutines. You will also learn to use various debugging tools and how to communicate with the user.

Before continuing   Close Microsoft Excel and delete the file SCRATCH.XLM.

Communicating with Microsoft Excel

In the previous lesson, we explored the basic mechanisms behind creating, editing and saving macros. What we did not explore was how we can communicate with Microsoft Excel and have Microsoft Excel communicate with a user. That is, we have not explored what makes Microsoft Excel macros a programming *language*.

In this section we will learn how to communicate with Microsoft Excel and in so doing create more complex—and more useful—macros.

This lesson explains how to do the following:

- Format the macro sheet in three-column style
- Work with informational functions such as GET.WINDOW and GET.DOCUMENT
- Work with conditional branching statements
- Work with the Macro toolbar and the Single Step dialog box
- Communicate with the user using Alert boxes and status bar messages
- Work with Add-Ins
- Work with function macros
- Use R1C1 cell references
- Create subroutines
- Work with the OFFSET and SET.NAME functions

Completed versions of the macros discussed in this section can be found in COMXDONE.XLM.

First, Some House Cleaning

Open the file COMX.XLM. Your screen should look like the one shown in Figure 2.1.

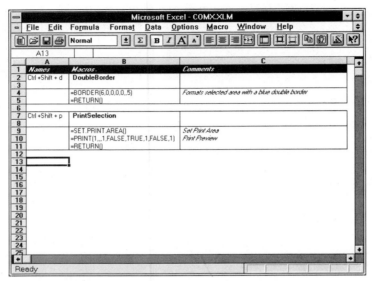

Figure 2.1   COMX.XLM

In case you're coming in late, COMX.XLM is a modified version of the global macro sheet created in the previous lesson. In this version we are employing a three-column format to help us maintain macros. The first column contains names and shortcut keys, the second column contains the macro commands and the third column contains comments about how the macros work. Unless you want to make your life truly miserable (not to mention the lives of those who may have to maintain your code) you should make sure you add comments to your macros. You'll be very glad you did several months from now when you need to make a change to the product of today's 3A.M. inspiration.

The Macro Sheet's "Look"

In creating COMX.XLM we have employed a number of formatting techniques that make the macro sheet easier to work with. Specifically, we have turned off the display of gridlines, placed borders around both macros and, for the Windows version, reduced the font size to 8 point. While not necessary, these steps will help keep the macro sheet neat and organized.

Note   Macintosh users don't need to change the font size as 10 point type in Microsoft Excel for the Macintosh is sufficiently small to see all three columns. Windows users should reduce macro sheet font size by redefining Normal style using the Format Style command.

A Note on Methodology

Depending on your personality, your macro sheets can either be organized or chaotic. Microsoft Excel invites organization in that you can "see" all the components of your program, as well as label and format these components. By the same token, Microsoft Excel invites chaos in that you can put code just about anywhere you want and name macros just about anything you want. Chaos is fine if your projects are simple, but if you plan to develop complex applications, you should employ some type of structured methodology.

The methodology used in this book is a simplified version of the EDJ methodology developed by the Tompkins Group. Many of the best Microsoft Excel developers and consultants use the EDJ methodology to develop and maintain complex applications. Developers interested in learning about this system can take the course *Application Development Using Microsoft Excel* presented by Microsoft University.

Note   So as not to conflict with the global macro sheet created in the previous chapter, the shortcut keys for DoubleBorder and PrintSelection in COMX.XLM have been reassigned to CTRL + SHIFT + d and CTRL + SHIFT + p in Windows, and OPTION + COMMAND + SHIFT + d and OPTION + COMMAND + SHIFT + p on the Macintosh.

Changing the Microsoft Excel Display: Toggle Gridlines

Problem: Microsoft Excel does not have an easy way to toggle gridlines on and off.

Solution: Create a macro that determines whether or not gridlines are displayed and then changes the gridlines setting.

Before we explore how to determine the current sheet's gridlines settings, let's see what Microsoft Excel transcribes when we turn gridlines off using the Options Display command.

Rather than let Microsoft Excel determine where it should record the macro, we can determine where the recorded macro should be transcribed using the *Macro Set Recorder* command.

To Set the Recorder

1   Make sure COMX.XLM is the active document.

2   Select cell B13.

3   From the Macro menu, choose Set Recorder.

To Record the Change in Gridlines

1   From the Macro menu, choose Start Recorder to start the macro recorder.

2   From the Options menu, choose Display. The dialog box shown in Figure 2.2 will appear.

Notice that the second option refers to gridlines.

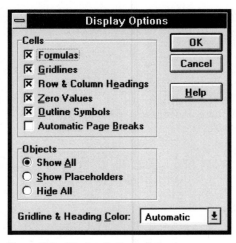

Figure 2.2   Display Options dialog box

3   Make sure the gridlines option is unchecked and click OK.

4   Turn the macro recorder off. Microsoft Excel will have transcribed the macro shown in Figure 2.3.

	B
13	=DISPLAY(TRUE,FALSE,TRUE,TRUE,0,,TRUE,FALSE,1)
14	=RETURN()

Figure 2.3   Display Options recorded macro

Which Argument Stands for Gridlines?

At this point, we need only concern ourselves with the gridlines component of the DISPLAY command. (In fact, we don't want our macro to inadvertently change one of the other display settings.) But which of the TRUEs and FALSEs refers to gridlines? Logic dictates that since the second argument in the Display dialog box concerns gridlines, the second argument in the DISPLAY command should also concern gridlines.

Working without the *Function Reference*

While a quick glance at the *Function Reference* will show that our assumption is correct, there is another way we can check out our hunch: the *Paste Function* command.

The Paste Function command gives you quick access to all the Microsoft Excel built-in functions and provides information on each function's arguments (components). In this next example we'll use the Paste Function command to get a list of arguments for the DISPLAY command.

To Use Paste Function to List Arguments for the DISPLAY Command

1 Select cell B13.

2 From the Formula menu, choose Paste Function. The Paste Function dialog box will appear.

3 With Commands selected in Function Category, scroll down in the Paste Function list box until you get to DISPLAY, as shown in Figure 2.4.

The Paste Function command allows you to view available functions by category.

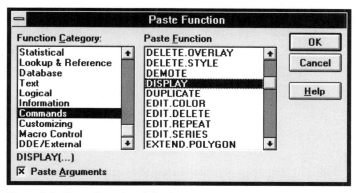

Figure 2.4   Paste Function dialog box

4 With Paste Arguments checked, click OK.

Since DISPLAY is a function that takes different arguments based on whether the current window is a sheet or a special Info window, a special Paste Function dialog box will appear, as shown in Figure 2.5.

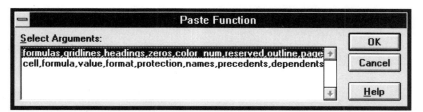

Figure 2.5   Special Paste Function dialog box

5 Click the first choice and click OK. The formula bar in your macro sheet should look as follows:

=DISPLAY(formulas,gridlines,headings,zeros,color_num,reserved,outline,
page_breaks,object_num)

Figure 2.6   Formula Bar

6 Press ESCAPE or click the X in the formula bar.

So, now we know that we need only concern ourselves with the DISPLAY function's second argument. In other words, the macro

```
=DISPLAY(,TRUE)
```

will turn gridlines on, while the macro

```
=DISPLAY(,FALSE)
```

will turn gridlines off.

Let's verify that this is true.

To Edit and Run the Gridlines Macro

1 Edit the macro so that it looks like this.

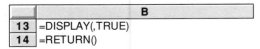

	B
13	=DISPLAY(,TRUE)
14	=RETURN()

Figure 2.7 Edited macro

Tip Remember, you should enter formulas in a macro sheet in lower case. If you type the formula correctly, Microsoft Excel will convert the formula to upper case.

---

2 From the Macro menu, choose Run. The Run Macro dialog box will appear.

−or−

Click the right mouse button in cell B13—this will display the macro sheet shortcut menu. Choose Run to display the Run Macro dialog box.

While pressing the OPTION and COMMAND keys, click the mouse in cell B13—this will display the macro sheet shortcut menu. Choose Run to display the Run Macro dialog box.

3 As we haven't yet given this macro a name, click in the cell that contains the macro you want to run, in this case B13, as shown in Figure 2.8.

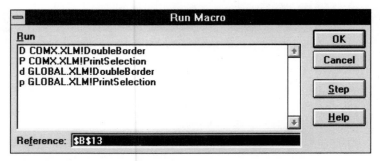

Figure 2.8 Run Macro dialog box

4   Click OK. Microsoft Excel will display gridlines.

Getting Information About Microsoft Excel: GET.WINDOW

We now know how to turn gridlines on and off. What we don't know is whether they should be turned on or off. We can determine whether gridlines are displayed using the GET.WINDOW command. GET.WINDOW is one of several built-in informational commands that let you peer into the "psyche" of Microsoft Excel. For example, you can use the GET.WINDOW command to determine the name of the document in a window, whether the window is hidden, and so on. Likewise, you can use the GET.WORKSPACE function to determine the operating environment, the scroll settings, whether the formula bar is displayed, and so forth. These "GET" functions (along with many other informational functions) can be found by choosing the Information category in the Paste Function dialog box.

According to the *Function Reference*, the syntax for the GET.WINDOW function is

GET.WINDOW(*type_num*,*window_text*)

where *type_num* is a number that specifies what type of window information you want and *window_text* is the name of the window about which you want information. (If *window_text* is omitted, Microsoft Excel provides information about the active window.)

In our case, =GET.WINDOW(9) will return a TRUE value if gridlines are displayed and a FALSE value if gridlines are turned off. Let's add this information-gathering function to the macro:

	B
13	=GET.WINDOW(9)
14	=DISPLAY(,TRUE)
15	=RETURN()

Figure 2.9   Modified Display macro

Why Macro Functions Return Values

Now we're starting to see why macro functions' returning values is so useful—you can have the macro behave differently based upon what a macro function returns. Indeed, if you run the macro shown directly above and toggle values on by pressing CTRL + ` (COMMAND + ` on the Macintosh), you will see that cells B13:B15 return Boolean values (true or false values).

Conditional Branching—Macro Flow Control Structures

An important part of any programming language is its ability to react to circumstances. This is called *conditional branching*. There are several different *control structures* for managing conditional branching that we'll examine, the simplest being the IF command. The general syntax for this command is

IF(*logical text, value_if_true,value_if_false***)**

In our gridlines macro, we want to say something like this:

```
IF(Gridlines are on,Turn them off,Turn them on)
```

The macro that accomplishes this task is shown in Figure 2.10.

	B
13	=GET.WINDOW(9)
14	=IF(B13=TRUE,DISPLAY(,FALSE),DISPLAY(,TRUE))
15	=RETURN()

Figure 2.10   Modified Macro

Understanding the Macro

As we discussed earlier, the line

```
=GET.WINDOW(9)
```

will return a TRUE if gridlines are on and a FALSE if gridlines are off. The line

```
=IF(B13=TRUE,DISPLAY(,FALSE),DISPLAY(,TRUE))
```

turns gridlines off if the value in cell B13 is TRUE, and turns them on if the value is FALSE.

Naming and Formatting the Macro

While the macro is certainly functional, accessing the macro is impractical as the macro has neither a name nor a shortcut key assigned to it.

To Assign a Name and Shortcut Key to the Macro

1   Select cells A13:C14.

2   From the Edit menu, choose Insert.

3   When the Insert dialog box appears, select shift cells down.

4   In the now blank cell B13, type **ToggleGridlines**.

5   Click the Bold tool to format the newly entered name in bold.

6   With cell B13 still selected, choose Define Name from the Formula menu.

 7   When the dialog box appears, make sure the name is ToggleGridlines and the shortcut key is CTRL + t, as shown in Figure 2.11.

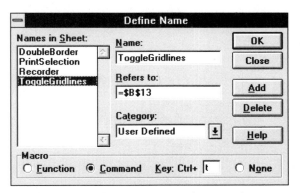

Figure 2.11   Define Name dialog box (Windows)

 7   When the dialog box appears, make sure the name is ToggleGridlines and the shortcut key is OPTION + COMMAND + t, as shown in Figure 2.12.

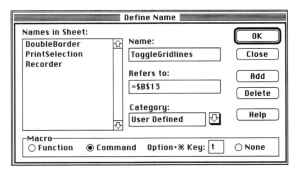

Figure 2.12   Define Name dialog box (Macintosh)

8 Click OK.

To Format the Macro on the Macro Sheet

1 Select cells A13:C17.

2 From the Format menu, choose Border.

3 When the Border dialog box appears, choose outline and left and click OK.

4 Select cells A13:C14.

5 Repeat the border formatting by choosing Repeat Border from the Edit menu. Your screen should look like the one shown in Figure 2.13.

The STEP command can be entered into the blank cell below the macro name when you are debugging the macro and want to force it into Single Step execution. Single Step execution will be discussed later in this book.

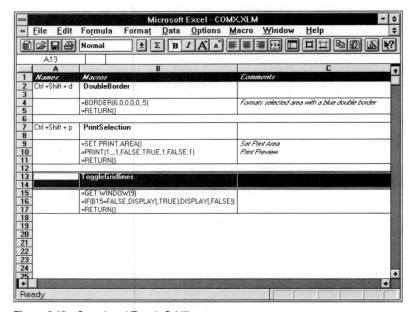

Figure 2.13   Completed ToggleGridlines macro

On Writing Efficient Code

Some programmers may recoil in horror over the inefficient use of the IF function in the ToggleGridlines macro. Indeed it is possible (and often desirable) to write a shorter, faster macro employing the NOT function. Basically, the NOT function, when used with a Boolean argument, returns TRUE if the initial argument is false, and FALSE if the initial argument is true. That is

```
=NOT(TRUE)
```

returns FALSE, and

```
=NOT(FALSE)
```

returns TRUE. Therefore, we can rewrite the ToggleGridlines macro as follows:

	B
13	**ToggleGridlines**
14	
15	=GET.WINDOW(9)
16	=DISPLAY(,NOT(B15))
17	=RETURN()

Figure 2.14   Modified ToggleGridlines macro

In fact, you can nest functions to produce an even more streamlined macro, as shown in Figure 2.15

	B
13	**ToggleGridlines**
14	
15	=DISPLAY(,NOT(GET.WINDOW(9)))
16	=RETURN()

Figure 2.15   Modified ToggleGridlines macro with function nesting

While substituting NOTs for IFs in the ToggleGridlines example will not make the macro run significantly faster, in larger macros writing more efficient code can

- reduce the amount of disk space used by the macro,
- decrease the time it takes to load the macro, and
- make the macro execute faster.

Probing Deeper: Improving PrintSelection

The current region is a rectangular range of cells bounded by blank rows and columns.

Problem: I wish the PrintSelection macro were smarter so that if I only have one cell selected, the macro will print the current region, not just the one cell.

Solution: Modify the PrintSelection macro so that if only one cell is selected, Microsoft Excel selects and prints the current region.

Before continuing   Open PRINT_ME.XLS and, using the Window Arrange command, arrange the windows so that PRINT_ME.XLS and COMX.XLM are both visible, as shown in Figure 2.16.

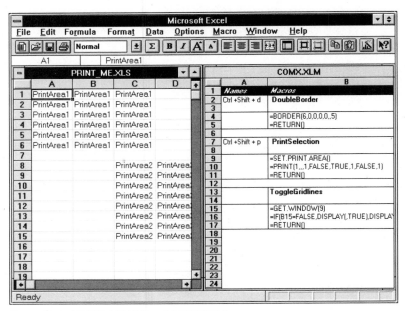

Figure 2.16   PRINT_ME.XLS and COMX.XLM

Using Select Special

Using the Formula Select Special command, you can select a rectangular range around the active cell. The range selected will be an area bounded by blank rows and columns.

Let's see what is transcribed when we record the Formula Select Special command.

To Record Formula Select Special

1   Make COMX.XLM the active window and select cell B19.

2   From the Macro menu, choose Set Recorder.

3   Activate PRINT_ME.XLS and select cell B3.

4   From the Macro menu, choose Start Recorder.

Because this macro will later become a part of the PrintSelection macro, we don't need to name it.

5   From the Formula menu, choose Select Special. The Select Special dialog box will appear.

6   In the Select Special dialog box, choose Current Region and click OK. Notice that Microsoft Excel highlights the current region and transcribes =SELECT.SPECIAL(5) in cell B19 of the macro sheet.

7   Turn the macro recorder off.

Making a Game Plan—Flowcharting

Many people find it useful to diagram a program's flow before writing its actual code. The process of creating a diagram is called flowcharting. A flowchart for the modified PrintSelection macro looks like this:

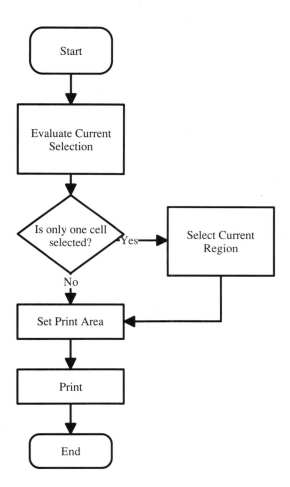

Figure 2.17   PrintSelection flowchart

Determining if Only One Cell Is Selected—the SELECTION Function

*For more information
on the SELECTION
function, See the
Microsoft Excel
Function Reference.*

You use the SELECTION function to return information about the current selection. In our case, we want to determine whether one cell is selected by using SELECTION in combination with the AREAS, ROWS and COLUMNS functions.

Let's see how this works by creating a simple, two-line macro that employs the SELECTION command.

To Create and Run a Macro that Uses the SELECTION Command

1   Type the macro shown below in cells B22 and B23 of COMX.XLM.

	B
22	=SELECTION()
23	=RETURN()

Figure 2.18   Selection macro

2   Activate PRINT_ME.XLS and select cell B3.

3   From the Macro menu, choose Run.

4   When the Run Macro dialog box appears, activate COMX.XLM (by clicking in it) and select cell B22, as shown in Figure 2.19.

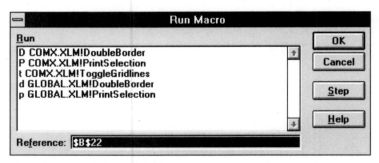

Figure 2.19   Run Macro dialog box

5   Click OK.

6   Activate COMX.XLM.

7   Press CTRL + ` (COMMAND + ` on the Macintosh) to reveal the underlying values, as shown in Figure 2.20.

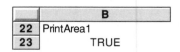

	B
22	PrintArea1
23	TRUE

Figure 2.20   Values returned after running the macro

Unfortunately, this isn't what we want. The SELECTION function is returning the contents of the cell in the active worksheet, not a cell reference.

AREAS, ROWS and COLUMNS

If more than one area is selected, then more than one cell is selected.

The first step in determining whether more than one cell is selected is to determine how many areas are selected. We can do this by nesting the SELECTION function within the AREAS function, as the statement

```
=AREAS(SELECTION())
```

returns the number of areas that are currently selected. If executing this statement returns a value of 1, we determine whether only one cell is selected using the ROWS and COLUMNS functions. The syntax of the ROWS function is

ROWS(*array*)

where *array* is an array, an array formula or (in our case) a reference to a range of cells. Thus the statement

```
=ROWS(SELECTION())
```

will return the number of rows currently selected. The COLUMNS() function has a similar syntax. We can determine whether one cell is selected by multiplying ROWS(SELECTION()) by COLUMNS(SELECTION()). A modified version of the PrintSelection macro is shown in Figure 2.21.

	A	B	C
7	Ctrl +Shift + p	**PrintSelection**	
8			
9		=IF(AREAS(SELECTION())=1)	*If more than one area is selected*
10		= IF(ROWS(SELECTION())*COLUMNS(SELECTION())=1)	*If only one cell in that one area is selected*
11		= SELECT.SPECIAL(5)	*Then select the current region*
12		= END.IF()	
13		=END.IF()	
14		=SET.PRINT.AREA()	*Set Print Area*
15		=PRINT(1,,,1,FALSE,TRUE,1,FALSE,1)	*Print Preview*
16		=RETURN()	

Figure 2.21   Modified PrintSelection macro

IF...END.IF

In this macro we're using a variation of the IF statement we looked at earlier. Since we want the macro to perform more than one action if the first condition is met (the actions being evaluate another condition and select the current region) we need to use an END.IF combined with the IF function. This control structure has the following syntax:

```
=IF(Logical_test)
        commands...
        commands...
        commands...
=END.IF()
```

The indentations (also known as "blocking") of the commands underneath the IF statement in the macro make the logic of the macro stand out more easily. You can produce the indentations by pressing the spacebar after typing the equal sign.

Tools for Debugging Macros

If you have any experience programming, you know that a large part of programming involves trying to figure out why something isn't working correctly. This process of methodically working through each component of a program is called *debugging*.

Fortunately, Microsoft Excel provides two extremely useful and intuitive tools for developing and debugging macros: The *Macro Toolbar* and the *Single Step* dialog box.

The Macro Toolbar

The Macro Toolbar contains tools that allow you to record, run, pause and step through macros.

To Activate the Macro Toolbar

1   Click the right mouse button in the Standard toolbar.

2   When the shortcut menu appears, click Macro. This will activate the Macro Toolbar, as shown in Figure 2.22.

Figure 2.22   Macro Toolbar

Single Step Mode

While the PrintSelection macro does not contain any errors, you can still employ single step mode to see how Microsoft Excel evaluates macro statements. This ability to execute a macro in "slow motion" is particularly useful when trying to figure out why a macro isn't working correctly. So get comfortable with the Single Step dialog box; you'll use it often.

To Run the PrintSelection Macro in Single Step Mode

1 Activate PRINT_ME.XLS and select cell B3.

2 From the Macro menu, choose Run. The Run dialog box will appear.

3 Choose COMX.XLM!PrintSelection and click Step. The Single Step dialog box will appear.

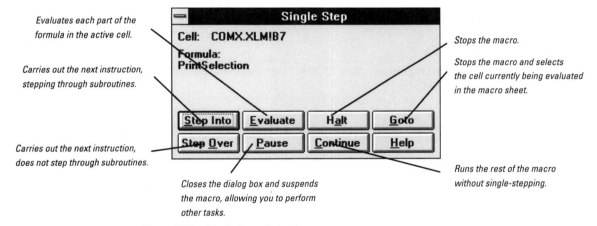

Evaluates each part of the formula in the active cell.

Carries out the next instruction, stepping through subroutines.

Carries out the next instruction, does not step through subroutines.

Stops the macro.

Stops the macro and selects the cell currently being evaluated in the macro sheet.

Closes the dialog box and suspends the macro, allowing you to perform other tasks.

Runs the rest of the macro without single-stepping.

Figure 2.23   Single Step dialog box

4 Click the Evaluate button twice. Notice that the formula in the Single Step dialog box now reads =IF(AREAS(SELECTION())=1).

5 Click Evaluate again. Microsoft Excel will further parse the formula down to =IF(AREAS(PRINT_ME.XLS!$B$3)=1).

6 Click Evaluate again. The Single Step dialog box will display =IF(TRUE).

7 Click Evaluate again. The Single Step dialog box will display TRUE.

8 Click Halt to stop the macro.

Recalculating Part of a Formula

Another extremely useful technique is to recalculate a portion of a formula by selecting that portion in the formula bar and pressing function key F9, the Recalculation key.

To Recalculate Part of a Formula

1   If it is not already selected, select cell B10 in COMX.XLM.

2   In the formula bar, select the portion of the formula you want to evaluate, as shown in Figure 2.24.

```
= IF(ROWS(SELECTION())*COLUMNS(SELECTION())=1)
```

Figure 2.24   Recalculating part of a formula

3   Press function key F9 to evaluate the selected area.

4   Press the ESCAPE key to cancel your editing.

Before continuing   Close PRINT_ME.XLS, then activate COMX.XLM and erase cells B24:B30.

Communicating with the User: ToggleRecalc

Problem: I wish Microsoft Excel had an easy way to toggle between automatic and manual recalculation.

Solution: Write a macro that changes the current mode of recalculation.

A quick look at the *Microsoft Excel Function Reference* reveals that the two functions we'll need to write this macro are GET.DOCUMENT and CALCULATION.

The syntax for GET.DOCUMENT is

GET.DOCUMENT(*type_num*,*name_text*)

where *type_num* is a number that specifies what type of information about the document you want and *name_text* is the name of an open document. If you omit *name_text*, Microsoft Excel returns information about the current document.

On further examining the *Function Reference*, we see that

```
=GET.DOCUMENT(14)
```

The function will return 2 if the document is set for automatic except tables.

returns 1 if the document is set for automatic recalculation and 3 if the document is set for manual recalculation. The syntax for the CALCULATION function is

CALCULATION(*type_num*,*iter*,*max_num*,*max_change*,*update*,*precision*, *date_1904*,*calc_save*,*save_values*)

The only argument we're concerned with is *type_num*. If *type_num* is equal to 1, recalculation is set to automatic; if *type_num* is equal to 3, recalculation is set to manual.

To Create the ToggleRecalc Macro

1   Enter the formulas and labels as shown in Figure 2.25.

	A	B	C
24	Ctrl + r	**ToggleRecalc**	
25			
26	RecalcMode	=GET.DOCUMENT(14)	*Get recalc state*
27		=IF(RecalcMode=1,CALCULATION(3),CALCULATION(1))	*Change recalc state*
28		=RETURN()	

Figure 2.25   ToggleRecalc macro

2   Using the Formula Define Name command, assign cell B24 the command macro name ToggleRecalc with the shortcut key CTRL + r (OPTION + COMMAND + r on the Macintosh).

3   Select cells A26:B26.

4   From the Formula menu, choose Create Names. The Create Names dialog box will appear.

This method of applying names is particularly useful when you have many names to create.

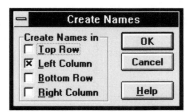

Figure 2.26   Create Names dialog box

5   With Left Column checked, click OK. This will assign the name RecalcMode to cell B26.

Notice that in this example we assigned the name RecalcMode to cell B26 because using a name instead of a cell reference makes the formula in cell B27 less cryptic.

Note   While we could combine B26 and B27 into one macro statement, keeping B26 as a separate statement will prove useful later on when we modify the ToggleRecalc macro.

Tell Me What's Going On

Pressing CTRL + r will run the macro, but how can we tell if the macro worked? Unlike the ToggleGridlines macro, where the results are immediately visible, the only way you can tell whether ToggleRecalc worked is to bring up the Options Calculation dialog box.

Indeed, the problem with ToggleRecalc in its current state is that it doesn't let the user know what's going on. We can remedy this using the ALERT function.

The syntax for the ALERT function is

ALERT(*message_text*,*type_num*)

where message_text is the message displayed in the resulting dialog box and type_num is a number from 1 to 3 signifying what type of dialog box is desired. If you omit the second argument, Microsoft Excel assumes type_num to be 2.

Some Examples

```
=ALERT("Are you sure you want to do that?",1)
```

produces a dialog box that looks like this in Microsoft Excel for Windows:

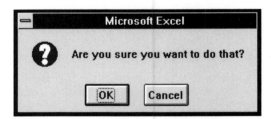

Figure 2.27   Alert box with two choices (Windows)

and produces a dialog box that looks like this in Microsoft Excel for the Macintosh:

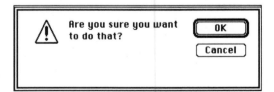

Figure 2.28   Alert box with two choices (Macintosh)

Clicking OK will make the ALERT function return a TRUE, while clicking Cancel will return a FALSE.

The statement

```
=ALERT("I'm sorry, but I can't do that, Dave.",2)
```

will display this dialog box in Windows:

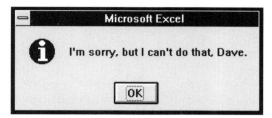

Figure 2.29   Default Alert box (Windows)

and this dialog box on the Macintosh:

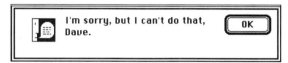

Figure 2.30   Default Alert box (Macintosh)

Clicking OK will return a TRUE value. Finally,

```
=ALERT("I'm sorry, but I can't do that, Dave.",3)
```

produces a dialog box almost identical to the ones shown in Figures 2.29 and 2.30, except with an exclamation or hand icon, as shown in Figures 2.31 and 2.32.

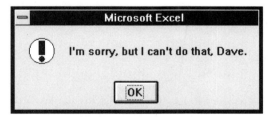

Figure 2.31   Alert box with exclamation icon (Windows)

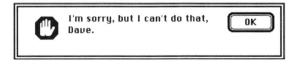

Figure 2.32   Alert box with hand icon (Macintosh)

Clicking OK will also return a TRUE.

The table below summarizes the different types of Alert boxes.

Type_num	Windows Icon	Macintosh Icon	Use
1	Question mark (?)	Exclamation point (!)	Choice (OK,Cancel)
2	Information icon (i)	Mouth	Information/Message
3	Exclamation point (!)	Hand	Error response

So, now we want to do two things after the current recalculation state is determined: we want to change the recalculation state and display an Alert box. A flowchart for this macro looks like this:

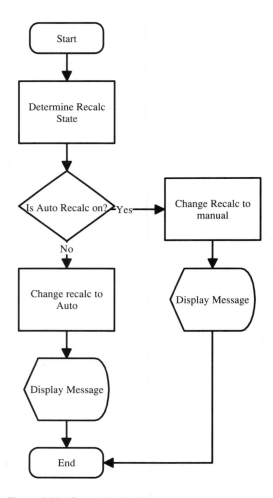

Figure 2.33   Recalculation flowchart

Before continuing   Modify the macro so that it looks like the one shown in Figure 2.34. Then run the macro several times by pressing CTRL + r (COMMAND + r on the Macintosh).

	A	B	C
24	Ctrl + r	**ToggleRecalc**	
25			
26	RecalcMode	=GET.DOCUMENT(14)	*Get recalc state*
27		=IF(RecalcMode=1)	*If recalc is automatic...*
28		= CALCULATION(3)	
29		= ALERT("Calculation is now set to Manual.",2)	
30		=ELSE()	*If recalc is manual...*
31		= CALCULATION(1)	
32		= ALERT("Calculation is now set to Automatic.",2)	
33		=END.IF()	
34		=RETURN()	

Figure 2.34   Modified ToggleRecalc macro using Alert Boxes

IF...ELSE.IF...ELSE...END.IF

In this macro we're using a variation of the IF statement we looked at earlier. Since we want to perform more than one action if a condition is met (the actions being change the calculation mode and display an Alert box) we need to use an ELSE function combined with an END.IF function. This control structure has the following syntax:

```
=IF(Logical_test)
        commands...
        commands...
=ELSE.IF(Logical_test)
        commands...
        commands...
=ELSE()
        commands...
        commands...
=END.IF()
```

The indentations (also known as "blocking") of the commands underneath the IF and ELSE statements in the macro make the logic of the macro stand out more easily. You can produce the indentations by pressing the spacebar after typing the equal sign.

Aren't the Alert Boxes Intrusive?

Yes. Needing to click OK every time you use this macro will grow tiresome, so we need to find a way to display a message that isn't as intrusive as the Alert box. One solution is to employ MESSAGE function, which displays a message in the status bar. The syntax for this command is

MESSAGE(*logical*,*text*)

If *logical* is TRUE, Microsoft Excel displays *text* in the status bar. If *logical* is FALSE, Microsoft Excel removes any user-created message and returns the status bar to normal.

Before continuing   Modify the macro so that it looks like the one shown in Figure 2.35 and then run the macro.

	A	B	C
24	Ctrl + r	**ToggleRecalc**	
25			
26	RecalcMode	=GET.DOCUMENT(14)	*Get recalc state*
27		=IF(RecalcMode=1)	*If recalc is automatic...*
28		= CALCULATION(3)	
29		= MESSAGE(TRUE,"Calculation is now set to Manual.")	
30		=ELSE()	*If recalc is manual...*
31		= CALCULATION(1)	
32		= MESSAGE(TRUE,"Calculation is now set to Automatic.")	
33		=END.IF()	
34		=RETURN()	

Figure 2.35   Modified ToggleRecalc macro using status messages

How to Get the Message to Go Away

The message displayed by the MESSAGE function in cells B29 and B32 won't go away until you execute a macro that contains the command =MESSAGE(FALSE). Unfortunately, you cannot simply place the MESSAGE(FALSE) command after the END.IF command as then the informational message (the one that displays the current calculation mode) will only appear for a split second. We can however, get the message to appear for a specified period of time, and then clear the message with the ON.TIME command.

The syntax for the ON.TIME command is

ON.TIME(*time*,*macro_text*,*tolerance*,*insert_logical*)

where *time* is the time and date (entered as a serial number) when the macro should be executed and *macro_text* is the name of the macro you want to run.

An example:

```
=ON.TIME("8:00:00 AM","WAKEUP")
```

runs a macro called WAKEUP when the system clock reaches 8:00 A.M. (If Microsoft Excel is not in READY mode, either because another macro is being run or a cell is being edited, Microsoft Excel will wait to run the macro. You can control how long Microsoft Excel will wait using the *tolerance* argument. For more information, see "ON.TIME" in the *Microsoft Excel Function Reference*.)

How You Say Five Seconds from Now

If you've worked with any of the Microsoft Excel date and time functions, you probably know that the NOW function returns the current date and time as a serial number. You can get Microsoft Excel to display five seconds from now by typing

```
=NOW()+"00:00:05"
```

which translates as "now, plus zero hours, zero minutes and five seconds." Thus, the macro

```
=ON.TIME(NOW()+"00:00:05","ClearMessage")
```

will execute a macro called ClearMessage five seconds after the ON.TIME command is executed.

Before continuing   Modify the macro as shown in Figure 2.36 and assign the name ClearMessage to cell B37.

	A	B	C
24	Ctrl + r	**ToggleRecalc**	
25			
26	RecalcMode	=GET.DOCUMENT(14)	*Get recalc state*
27		=IF(RecalcMode=1)	*If recalc is automatic...*
28		= CALCULATION(3)	
29		= MESSAGE(TRUE,"Calculation is now set to Manual.")	
30		=ELSE()	*If recalc is manual...*
31		= CALCULATION(1)	
32		= MESSAGE(TRUE,"Calculation is now set to Automatic.")	
33		=END.IF()	
34		=ON.TIME(NOW()+"00:00:05","ClearMessage")	*Run ClearMessage in 5 sec.*
35		=RETURN()	
36			
37		**ClearMessage**	
38			
39		=MESSAGE(FALSE)	
40		=RETURN()	

Figure 2.36   ToggleRecalc macro using ON.TIME command

Hiding Macro Sheets: Part Two

In the previous chapter we looked at a workaround for saving hidden macro sheets (or worksheets, for that matter). While useful, the technique was a bit cumbersome.

Using some of the functions we've just looked at (and some new ones) we can create a simple utility that hides and saves the current document.

To Create the HideAndSave Macro

1 Type the formulas and labels shown in Figure 2.37.

	A	B	C
42	Ctrl + h	**HideAndSave**	
43			
44	DocName	=GET.DOCUMENT(1)	*Get current document name*
45		=HIDE()	*Hide current document*
46		=ACTIVATE(DocName)	*Activate hidden document*
47		=SAVE()	*Save*
48		=RETURN()	

Figure 2.37 HideAndSave macro

2 Using the Formula Define Name command, assign cell B42 the command name HideAndSave and the shortcut key CTRL + h (COMMAND + h on the Macintosh).

3 Assign cell B44 the name DocName.

Before continuing Try running the macro—this will hide and save COMX.XLM. To unhide the document, choose Unhide from the Window menu.

Understanding the Macro

The line

```
=GET.DOCUMENT(1)
```

returns the name of the active document. The line

```
=HIDE()
```

produces the same result as if you had chosen Hide from the Window menu: it hides the active document. The line

```
=ACTIVATE(DocName)
```

If we don't activate the hidden window, we will save the window that is visible.

activates the document contained in the cell DocName, that is, the name returned by the GET.DOCUMENT(1) function. Please note that this activates a window; it does not unhide the window. The line

```
=SAVE()
```

saves the active (and now hidden) document.

As useful as the HideAndSave macro is, there is a technique for hiding and saving macros that is even more useful, friendlier and safer: it allows you to distribute your macros without fear that someone may inadvertently change them. The way you do this is to save your macros not on a macro sheet, but as *Add-Ins*.

Note   GET.DOCUMENT(1) will cause an error on an Add-In sheet. GET.CELL(32,$A$1) works for both macro sheets and Add-Ins. For more information, see "GET.CELL" in the *Microsoft Excel Function Reference*.

Add-Ins: A Transparent Extension of Microsoft Excel

Whether you're an occasional user or an experienced developer, you'll appreciate the power and transparent nature of Microsoft Excel Add-In macros. Basically, an Add-In is just a macro sheet that has been saved in an Add-In file format. When you open an Add-In using the File Open command, Microsoft Excel will show the load status in the upper left corner of the screen, just as it would for any other file. However, after loading, the only way you can tell that you've loaded an Add-In is to enjoy enhanced functionality (such as new menu options, functions, etc.); you cannot examine the contents of an Add-In when the Add-In is opened in a normal fashion.

You can get Microsoft Excel to load the Add-In automatically if you place this file in the Microsoft Excel Startup directory XLSTART in Windows and the Excel Startup Folder 4 on the Macintosh. Alternatively, you can use the Microsoft Excel Add-In Manager (available by choosing Add-In from the Options menu) to manage your Add-Ins.

Differences Between Add-Ins and Macros

The three main differences between an Add-In and a regular macro are as follows:

It is possible to edit an Add-In after it has been loaded. We'll see how to do this on page 53.

- Once an Add-In is loaded it cannot be examined easily. The Add-In will remain loaded until you exit Microsoft Excel. This means developers don't have to worry about hiding the macro sheet or protecting it from curious users. (Note: An Add-In can be made to close itself in a custom application.)

- Command macros on the Add-In do not appear in the Macro Run dialog box.

- Function macros on the Add-In appear in alphabetical order within the Paste Function list box and are not preceded by the Add-In's file name. This is a particularly welcome feature in that custom functions truly become an integral part of Microsoft Excel and no longer require any special attention.

Let's see how Add-Ins work by making COMX.XLM into an Add-In.

To Save a Macro Sheet as an Add-In (Windows)

1   From the File menu, choose Save As.

2   From the Save File as Type drop-down list, choose Add-In, as shown in Figure 2.38.

Notice that extension has been changed to .XLA.

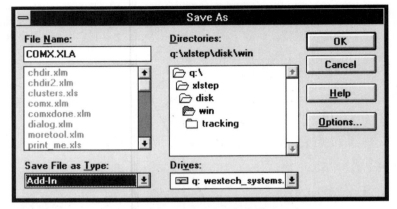

Figure 2.38   Saving a macro sheet as an Add-In (Windows)

3   Click OK.

4   From the File menu, choose Close.

To Save a Macro Sheet as an Add-In (Macintosh)

1   From the File menu, choose Save As.

2   In the Save As dialog box, click the Options button. The Save Options dialog box will appear.

3   Change the File Format to Add-In, as shown in Figure 2.39.

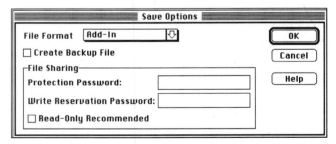

Figure 2.39   Saving a macro sheet as an Add-In (Macintosh)

4   Click OK.

5   To be consistent with the Windows example, change the file extension to .XLA, as shown in Figure 2.40.

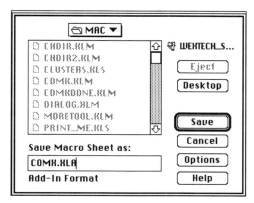

Figure 2.40   Adding an extension

6   Click Save.

7   From the File menu, choose Close.

To Load an Add-In

1   From the File menu, choose Open.

2   When the dialog box appears, choose the file you want to open, in this case COMX.XLA. Microsoft Excel will display the load status in the upper left corner.

Right now the only way you can access this Add-In's macros is using shortcut keys; the macros—DoubleBorder, ToggleGridlines, PrintSelection, ToggleRecalc and HideAndSave—will not be available from the Macro Run dialog box.

Editing an Add-In

Holding down the SHIFT key will also prevent any auto-executing macros from running.

One would think from our overview of Add-Ins that once you save and close an Add-In, the Add-In cannot be edited or modified. In fact, it is very easy to edit an Add-In: simply hold down the SHIFT key when you select the Add-In from the File Open list dialog box.

To Edit an Add-In That Has Already Been Loaded

1   From the File menu, choose Open.

2   While holding down the SHIFT key, select the file you want to edit (in this case COMX.XLA) and click OK. The dialog box shown in Figure 2.41 will appear.

Figure 2.41   Revert dialog box

3   Click OK.

4   From the Window menu, choose Unhide.

5   When the Unhide dialog box appears, choose COMX.XLA.

Protecting Add-Ins

The fact that Add-Ins can be opened and edited so easily leads to the following question: How do you prevent unauthorized users from examining and changing the contents of an Add-In?

You protect an Add-In the same way you protect a worksheet: by locking and hiding individual cells using the *Format Cell Protection* command and then by protecting the entire document using the *Options Protect Document* command.

To Protect an Add-In

1   Select the cells you want to protect.

2   From the Format menu, choose Cell Protection. The Cell Protection dialog box will appear.

3   Make sure Locked and Hidden are checked and click OK.

Note   This action, by itself, doesn't protect the cells; it just marks which cells can and cannot be changed and examined when the document is protected.

---

4   From the Options menu, choose Protect Document. The Protect Document dialog box will appear.

5   Type in a password and click OK.

6   When the confirmation dialog box appears, reenter your password and click OK. Microsoft Excel will hide and lock all cells you marked for protection in steps 2 and 3.

Before continuing   Unprotect the document by choosing Unprotect Document from the Options menu, and entering your password.

Function Macros

So far we've looked at macros that perform tasks. These are called *command macros*. You can also use macros to create custom functions. These macros are called *function macros*.

A function macro differs from a command macro in the way it is run. Function macros do not appear in the Macro Run dialog box, but instead appear in the Paste Function dialog box because you use function macros as you would regular worksheet functions. Also, most function macros differ from command macros in that you need to specify an *argument* (also called a *parameter*) when you use a function macro. (For more information, see the discussion of arguments on page 10).

Using a Custom Function

Open the file SPELLOUT.XLA. This Add-In contains a function called SPELLOUT which "spells out" numbers in a worksheet.

To Use the Spellout Function

1   With SPELLOUT.XLA loaded, create a new worksheet.

2   In cell B2, type **4123.56**.

3   In cell C2, type **=SPELLOUT(B2)** and press the ENTER key. Your screen should look like the one shown in Figure 2.42.

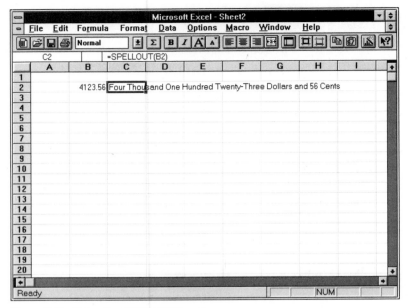

Figure 2.42 Using the SPELLOUT function

Because the custom function was saved in an Add-In, SPELLOUT is a transparent extension of Microsoft Excel, behaving as though it were a built-in function, accessible from the Paste Function dialog box.

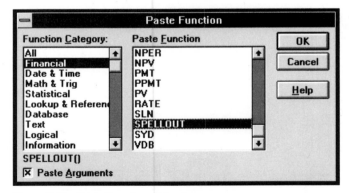

Figure 2.43 Paste Function dialog box

Writing a Versatile Rounding Function

Problem: I know Microsoft Excel has a ROUND function that will round numbers off to the units place, tens place, hundreds, etc., but sometimes I need to round numbers to the nearest 500 or 250.

Solution: Create a custom function that allows you to specify the precision of rounding.

Before tackling the macro, let's first determine the algorithm we use to round numbers. Let's suppose you want to round the number 560 off to the nearest hundred. While most people will produce the answer "600" without giving it a second thought, we must give the process thought if we're going to program Microsoft Excel to do rounding for us.

How We Round

First, let's determine if we have to round the number off at all by dividing the number (560) by the number we want to round to (100) and determining the remainder. Taking 560 and dividing by 100 produces a remainder of 60. So, do we round up or do we round down? We know from elementary school that you're supposed to round up if the amount is greater than or equal to 50. Another way of saying this is if the remainder (60) is greater than or equal to the number we want to round to divided by 2 (100/2), then round up.

Before we can write the custom function, we need to understand the ARGUMENT function.

ARGUMENT

You tell Microsoft Excel what "thing" you want the custom function to act upon using the ARGUMENT function. The syntax is

ARGUMENT(*name_text,data_type_num*)

where *name_text* is the name of the argument—the name will behave much like a range name—and *data_type_num* is a number that determines what type of value the custom function accepts for the argument. The table below lists the different data types. (If you omit *data_type_num*, Microsoft Excel assumes 7.)

Data_type_num	Type of value
1	Number
2	Text
4	Logical
8	Reference
16	Error
64	Array

Note   *Data_type_num* can be the sum of different numbers. For example, if *data_type_num* equals 5 then the function will accept either a number (1) or a logical value (4).

Consider the following somewhat contrived example:

```
StickTogether
=ARGUMENT("FirstThing",2)
=ARGUMENT("SecondThing",2)
=RETURN(FirstThing&" and "&SecondThing)
```

You concatenate, or stick together, text arguments with an ampersand (&).

The first two lines tell the custom function StickTogether to expect two text arguments. The last line of the macro tells the function to return the first argument, concatenate the word "and," and concatenate the second argument. Thus, entering the formula

```
=StickTogether("Jack","Jill")
```

will return

```
Jack and Jill
```

Understanding ROUNDTO

Open the file ROUNDTO.XLM, which contains the following macro.

	A	B	C
1		**ROUNDTO**	
2			
3		=ARGUMENT("Num")	*First Argument*
4		=ARGUMENT("RoundedTo")	*Second Argument*
5	Remainder	=MOD(Num,RoundedTo)	*Determine remainder*
6	RoundingPoint	=RoundedTo/2	*Determine rounding point*
7		=IF(Remainder=0)	*Already rounded*
8		= RETURN(Num)	*Return original number*
9		=ELSE.IF(Remainder<RoundingPoint)	*If remainder < rounding point*
10		= RETURN(Num-Remainder)	*Round Down*
11		=ELSE()	
12		= RETURN(Num+(RoundedTo-Remainder))	*Round Up*
13		=END.IF()	

Figure 2.44   ROUNDTO function macro

The first two lines

```
=ARGUMENT("Num")
=ARGUMENT("RoundedTo")
```

The ARGUMENT function creates the names "Num" and "RoundedTo" when the macro is executed. You can see these names in the Define Name dialog box.

declare two numeric arguments, Num and RoundedTo. (In this case, "Num" is the number we want to round and "RoundedTo" specifies the precision in rounding.) The next line

```
=MOD(Num,RoundedTo)
```

returns the remainder when Num is divided by RoundedTo. Notice that the cell that contains this formula has been assigned the name "Remainder." The line

```
=RoundedTo/2
```

Microsoft Excel Macros Step by Step

returns the value that determines whether the number should be rounded up or down. As with the previous formula, this cell has been assigned a name (in this case, "RoundingPoint").

The first set of conditions

```
=IF(Remainder=0)
   =RETURN(NUM)
```

determines that if the remainder equals 0 (meaning that Num is evenly divisible by RoundedTo) then the number is already rounded. The next set of conditions

```
=ELSE.IF(Remainder<RoundingPoint)
   =RETURN(Num-Remainder)
```

determines that if the Remainder is less than the RoundingPoint, then we should round down; otherwise

```
=ELSE()
   =RETURN(Num+(RoundedTo-Remainder))
=END.IF()
```

we should round up.

Using the Function

Create a new worksheet and type the number **117** in cell A1. Now, let's say we want to round this number to the nearest 25. While it might be tempting to type =ROUNDTO(A1,25) in cell B1, doing so will produce a #NAME? error.

To access any custom function that isn't saved on an Add-In, you must specify the macro sheet name as shown in Figure 2.45.

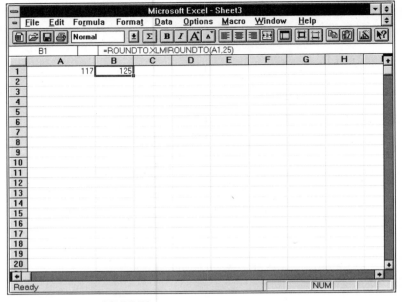

Figure 2.45 Using ROUNDTO

You can also access the ROUNDTO function using the Paste Function command, as shown in Figure 2.46.

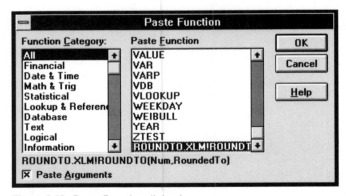

Figure 2.46 Paste Function dialog box

Macro sheet custom functions appear at the bottom of the Paste Function list box; Add-In custom functions appear alphabetically.

References: Recording Cell Selection

Microsoft Excel uses R1C1 cell references in recorded macros instead of the familiar A1-style reference. In R1C1 notation, the row number follows the "R" and the column number follows the "C." The equivalent of cell IV16384 in R1C1 notation is R16384C256.

A reference expressed in R1C1 notation may be relative, absolute, or mixed, depending on the use of brackets around the row or column number. So, for example, R3C2 is the same as cell $B$3, but R[3]C[2] means go three cells down and two cells to the right of the current cell. Likewise, R[-3]C[-2] means go three cells up and two cells to the left.

Most worksheet users don't realize that relative references are more complicated than absolute references. They think absolute references are complicated because absolute references require dollar signs.

The macro recorder employs R1C1 style because RIC1 notation is definitive. While most users prefer to use A1-style references in their worksheets, A1-style references can be confusing in a macro. For example, "R[3]C[2]" always means down 3 over 2, no matter where your starting cell is. However, "C4" means over 3 down 2 if starting in cell A1, and something completely different if you're starting in a different cell.

Let's see how R1C1 works.

Before continuing   Open CLUSTERS.XLS. Your screen should look like the one shown in Figure 2.47.

	A	B	C	D	E	F	G	H	I
1									
2									
3		Heading	Heading	Heading	Heading	Heading			
4	Labels	10	15	20	25	30			
5	Labels	15	20	25	30	35			
6	Labels	20	25	30	35	40			
7	Labels	25	30	35	40	45			
8	Labels	30	35	40	45	50			
9	Subtotal	100	125	150	175	200			
10									
11									
12		Heading	Heading	Heading					
13	Labels	10	15	20					
14	Labels	15	20	25					
15	Labels	20	25	30					
16	Subtotal	45	60	75					
17									
18									
19		Heading	Heading	Heading	Heading	Heading	Heading		
20	Labels	10	15	20	25	30	35		

Figure 2.47   CLUSTERS.XLS worksheet

Problem: I've been asked by my boss to take all the department's worksheets and format all the subtotal rows so that they are in currency format.

Solution: Write a macro that selects the last row in each block and applies currency format.

As with many of the previous examples, we'll get a jump-start on this macro using the Microsoft Excel macro recorder. However, unlike the previous examples where we created general purpose utilities, here we will be creating a macro to perform a one-time-only task. So, instead of placing this macro on a macro sheet that will always be loaded (such as an auto-loading Add-In, or the global macro sheet) let's create a separate, dedicated macro sheet which we will want to close when we're finished.

We will also record cell selection relative to the current cell selection using the macro recorder's Relative Record option.

To Create a New Macro Sheet

1   From the File menu, choose New.

2   When the New dialog box appears, choose macro sheet.

3   Save the macro sheet as CLUSTERS.XLM.

4   Type the label **FormatBottom** in cell B1.

5   Activate cell B2.

6   From the Macro menu, choose Set Recorder.

7   From the Macro menu, choose Relative Record.

To Record the FormatBottom Macro

1   Make CLUSTERS.XLS the active window.

2   Select cell A3.

3   From the Macro menu, choose Start Recorder.

4   Press CTRL + DOWN ARROW (COMMAND + DOWN ARROW on the Macintosh) to move to the first non-blank cell.

5   Press CTRL + DOWN ARROW to move to the last row.

6   Select the cells you want to format, in this case B9:F9.

7   From the Format menu, choose Number.

8   When the Number Format dialog box appears, choose Currency from the category list and $#,##0_);($#,##0) from the Format Codes list box, as shown in Figure 2.48.

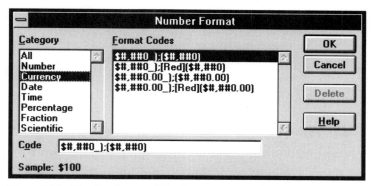

Figure 2.48   Number Format dialog box

9   Click OK.

10   From the Macro menu, choose Stop Recorder.

Before continuing   Activate CLUSTERS.XLM and widen column B so that you can see all of the transcribed macro. Also, assign the name FormatBottom to cell B1 with the shortcut key CTRL + f (OPTION + COMMAND + f on the Macintosh) and format the macro as shown in Figure 2.49.

	A	B	C
1	Ctrl + f	**FormatBottom**	
2			
3		=SELECT.END(4)	*Ctrl down arrow*
4		=SELECT.END(4)	*Ctrl down arrow*
5		=SELECT("RC[1]:RC[5]")	*Select five cells to the right*
6		=FORMAT.NUMBER("$#,##0_);($#,##0)")	*Apply Formatting*
7		=RETURN()	

Figure 2.49   FormatBottom macro

Understanding the Macro

The lines

```
=SELECT.END(4)
=SELECT.END(4)
```

are the transcription of pressing CTRL + DOWN ARROW twice. These two lines of code will always activate the last cell in a column block assuming the first cell was blank and that the column has no gaps in it. The line

```
=SELECT("RC[1]:RC[5]")
```

selects the cell one cell to the right and extends the selection five cells to the right. The line

```
=FORMAT.NUMBER("$#,##0_);($#,##0)")
```

formats the selection in currency notation.

Microsoft Excel Macros Step by Step

Making the Macro Smarter

The macro in its current state is only useful if the width of the block to be formatted is the same as the block used when we recorded the macro. To make the macro work with any size block, we need to determine how wide the block is. We can do this using the SELECT.SPECIAL and COLUMNS functions.

Creating a Subroutine

As we may need to determine the width of a block of cells from within other macros as well, the portion of the macro which performs this task should be written as a separate, reusable unit, called a *subroutine*.

Guidelines for Creating Subroutines

- The name of the macro should suggest its function. An appropriate name in this case is GetBlockSize.

- The subroutine should be limited to the task implied by its name.

- Intermediate calculations performed by the subroutine which will be used by other macros should be given range names. In this example we give the cell that calculates the width of the selected region the name BlockWidth.

To Create the GetBlockSize Subroutine

1   Enter the following in cells A9:C13.

	A	B	C
9		**GetBlockSize**	
10			
11		=SELECT.SPECIAL(5)	*Select whole block*
12	BlockWidth	=COLUMNS(SELECTION())	*Return number of columns*
13		=RETURN()	

Figure 2.50   GetBlockSize macro

2   Using the Formula Define Name command, assign the name GetBlockSize to cell B9. Click the Command option button when you define the name so that the macro can be run (and therefore tested) separately from the main routine.

3   Name the cells which will be referred to by other macros. In this case assign the name BlockWidth to cell B12.

How the Subroutine Works

The line

```
=SELECT.SPECIAL(5)
```

selects the current region (see "Using Select Special" on page 36). The line

```
=COLUMNS(SELECTION())
```

returns the number of columns in the selection.

Calling Subroutines

Calling a subroutine in a Microsoft Excel macro is simple and straightforward. All you need to do is type the name of the macro you want to call, followed by a pair of parentheses. In our case we want to run or "call" the GetBlockSize macro before anything else.

To Modify the FormatBottom Macro to Call GetBlockSize

1   Insert a blank row at row 3.

2   In cell B2 type =**GetBlockSize**().

Function of the Gods—OFFSET

While we could employ R1C1 to select the desired cells using a messy string formula that looks like this:

```
=SELECT("RC[1]:RC["&BlockWidth-1&"]")
```

we can avoid the quotes and the ampersands altogether by utilizing what is perhaps the most powerful macro and worksheet function in Microsoft Excel: OFFSET.

OFFSET doesn't move any cells or change the selection, it just returns a reference. For more information, see "OFFSET" in the Microsoft Excel Function Reference.

Basically, the OFFSET function allows you to reference an area based on its relationship to another area. The syntax for this function is

OFFSET(*reference,rows,columns,height,width*)

where *reference* is the starting point, *rows* is the number of rows, up or down, traversed to reach the destination area, *columns* is the number of columns, up or down, traversed, *height* is the number of rows you want the returned reference to have and *width* is the number of columns you want the returned reference to have. If height or width is omitted, Microsoft Excel assumes the returned reference should be the same height or width of the original *reference*.

We can employ the OFFSET function to select the bottom row of a block (less the first cell) by typing the following:

Figure 2.51 Annotated OFFSET function

The completed macro is shown in Figure 2.52.

	A	B	C
1	Ctrl + f	**FormatBottom**	
2			
3		=GetBlockSize()	
4		=SELECT.END(4)	Ctrl down arrow
5		=SELECT.END(4)	Ctrl down arrow
6		=SELECT(OFFSET(SELECTION(),0,1,1,BlockWidth-1))	Select cells to the right
7		=FORMAT.NUMBER("$#,##0_);($#,##0)")	Apply Formatting
8		=RETURN()	
9			
10		**GetBlockSize**	
11			
12		=SELECT.SPECIAL(5)	Select whole block
13	BlockWidth	=COLUMNS(SELECTION())	Return number of columns
14		=RETURN()	

Figure 2.52 FormatBottom and GetBlockSize

Before continuing Activate CLUSTERS.XLS and try running FormatBottom on several blocks. Remember to select the blank cell where the first row and column of each block intersect before running the macro.

Formatting the Whole Worksheet

While the FormatBottom macro makes it much easier to format the entire worksheet, we are still working too hard. With just a few lines of code, we can create a macro that will format the entire worksheet, not just one block at a time.

To accomplish this, we need a macro to do the following:

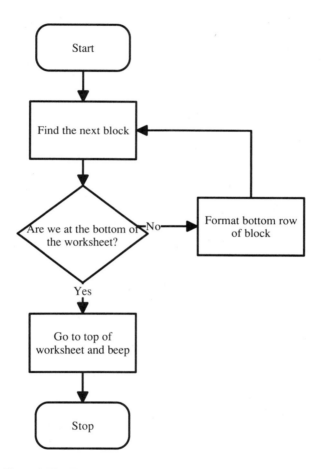

Figure 2.53 Flowchart for formatting the whole worksheet

Rather than modify the FormatBottom macro to perform these additional tasks, we will use FormatBottom as a subroutine to another macro. This preserves FormatBottom for use in other circumstances.

Loops

Microsoft Excel also provides a FOR.CELL control structure which we will examine in the next lesson.

Microsoft Excel has two types of loop control structures: FOR-NEXT and WHILE-NEXT. The FOR-NEXT loop performs an action or a group of actions a specified number of times. The WHILE-NEXT loop performs an action or group of actions until a specified condition is no longer true. We will use the WHILE-NEXT construct.

The syntax of the WHILE-NEXT loop is as follows:

```
=WHILE(logical_test)
    Commands...
    Commands...
=NEXT()
```

The FormatWorksheet Macro

A macro that would format the entire worksheet is shown in Figure 2.54.

	A	B	C
16	Ctrl + w	**FormatWorksheet**	
17			
18		=SELECT("R1C1")	*Select A1*
19		=SELECT.END(4)	*Find first block*
20		=WHILE(NOT(ROW(ACTIVE.CELL())=16384))	*While current row <> last row*
21		= FormatBottom()	
22		= SELECT.END(4)	*Find next block*
23		=NEXT()	
24		=BEEP()	*Signal when done*
25		=SELECT("R1C1")	*Go back to A1*
26		=RETURN()	

Figure 2.54   FormatWorksheet macro

The ROW worksheet function returns the row number from the reference returned by the macro function ACTIVE.CELL. In this case, ACTIVE.CELL is preferable to SELECTION because it returns one cell reference, rather than a range.

Before continuing   Create the macro shown in Figure 2.54 and assign cell B16 the command name FormatWorksheet with the shortcut key CTRL + w (OPTION + COMMAND + w on the Macintosh). Then activate CLUSTERS.XLS and run the macro.

Making the Macro Polite—SET.NAME

A programming purist might argue that we have written a "rude" macro in that the macro leaves the user in cell A1. A "polite" macro would activate whichever cell was active when the macro was started. We can make our macro polite using the SET.NAME function.

The SET.NAME function defines a name on the macro sheet to refer to a value or reference. While the function is particularly useful for storing values while the macro is running, we will use it to mark a placeholder to which we will return after the macro has been run. The syntax for the SET.NAME function is

SET.NAME(*name_text,value*)

where *name_text* is the name you want to assign to *value*. If *value* is omitted, the name *name_text* is deleted. If *value* is a reference, *name_text* is defined to refer to that reference. For more information, see "SET.NAME" in the *Microsoft Excel Function Reference*.

A modified (and more polite) version of the FormatWorksheet macro is shown in Figure 2.55.

	A	B	C
16	Ctrl + w	**FormatWorksheet**	
17			
18		=SET.NAME("PlaceHolder",SELECTION())	
19		=SELECT("R1C1")	*Select A1*
20		=SELECT.END(4)	*Find first block*
21		=WHILE(NOT(ROW(ACTIVE.CELL())=16384))	*While current row <> last row*
22		= FormatBottom()	
23		= SELECT.END(4)	*Find next block*
24		=NEXT()	
25		=BEEP()	*Signal when done*
26		=FORMULA.GOTO(PlaceHolder)	*Go back to A1*
27		=SET.NAME("PlaceHolder")	
28		=RETURN()	

Figure 2.55   "Polite" version of the FormatWorksheet macro

The line

```
=SET.NAME("PlaceHolder",SELECTION())
```

creates a named area called "PlaceHolder" that refers to the current selection. The statement

```
=FORMULA.GOTO(PlaceHolder)
```

activates "PlaceHolder" after the main part of the macro has been completed. The statement

```
=SET.NAME("PlaceHolder")
```

deletes the no-longer-needed named area. While this statement isn't absolutely necessary, it is a nice example of good macro hygiene. Maintaining the named area PlaceHolder would take up memory and add the overhead of requiring Microsoft Excel to keep track of the link between the macro sheet and the worksheet ("PlaceHolder" is a name maintained on the macro sheet that refers to an area on the worksheet).

Lesson Summary

In this section we saw how we could use the macro language to communicate with Microsoft Excel, that is, how to read and then modify many Microsoft Excel settings. We also examined conditional branching and looked at the IF, IF...END.IF, IF...ELSE...END.IF, and WHILE-NEXT control structures. We looked at several development and debugging aids, including the Macro Toolbar, the Single Step dialog box, and the ability to recalculate a portion of a formula. We also discussed ways to communicate with the user using Alert boxes and the MESSAGE function.

In this section we also looked at transparently extending the functionality of Microsoft Excel by saving macro sheets as Add-In sheets, as well as by creating custom macro functions.

Preview of the Next Lesson

In the next lesson, we will explore ways of acquiring information from the user (and acting upon this information) using input boxes and custom dialog boxes. We'll also look at error handling, custom menus and commands, and some useful tools for creating macros and previewing dialog boxes.

Beyond the Basics

In the previous section we looked at ways of communicating with Microsoft Excel, yet our conversations have been very one-sided. We have issued commands to get Microsoft Excel to say something to the user, but we have not looked at ways for getting the user to say something to Microsoft Excel.

In this section we will examine how to get information from the user, and how to act upon that information.

This lesson explains how to do the following:

- Create input boxes
- Handle macro errors
- Create and control custom dialog boxes
- Use the Dialog Editor
- Create dynamic dialog boxes and multiple-selection list boxes
- Create custom commands and menus
- Work with special tools that make macro creation easier

INPUT

While the ALERT and MESSAGE functions can be useful in complex macros, even more important is the ability to ask a question of the user, get a response, then act based upon this response. You get user input either by creating a custom dialog box or by using the INPUT function.

The syntax for INPUT is

INPUT(*message_text*,*type_num*,*title_text*,*default*,*x_pos*,*y_pos*)

Message_text is the prompt you want displayed (or the question you want to ask).

Type_num is a number specifying the type of data that will be entered, as follows:

Type_num	Data type
0	Formula
1	Number
2	Text
4	Logical
8	Reference
16	Error
64	Array

Note   You can add numbers to allow for multiple data types. For example, if type_num equals 3, then the input box will accept either numbers (1) or text (2).

Title_text is text that appears in the input box's title bar. If this argument is omitted, the word "Input" will appear in the title bar.

Default specifies a value to be shown in the edit box when the input box is initially displayed. If this is omitted, the edit box will be empty.

X_pos,y_pos specify the horizontal and vertical position of the input box in points (one point equals 1/72 of an inch). If these arguments are omitted, the input box will be centered.

Some Examples

The macro

	B
2	=INPUT("Please enter the term, in years:",1,"Term",30)
3	=RETURN()

Figure 3.1   Input box macro code

will display an input box that looks like this in Microsoft Excel for Windows:

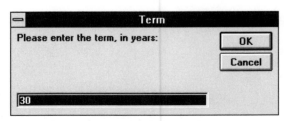

Figure 3.2   Input dialog box (Windows)

and displays an input box that looks like this in Microsoft Excel for the Macintosh:

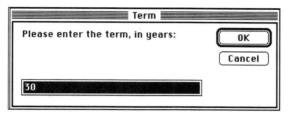

Figure 3.3   Input dialog box (Macintosh)

The macro

	B
2	=INPUT("Please enter the starting date:",2,"Date",TEXT(NOW(),"mmmm d, yyyy"))
3	=RETURN()

Figure 3.4   Another Input box macro

displays this input box in Windows:

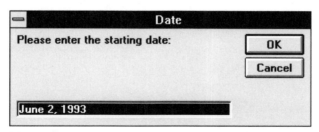

Figure 3.5   Another Input dialog box (Windows)

and this input box on the Macintosh:

Figure 3.6   Another Input dialog box (Macintosh)

If the user chooses OK, the INPUT function will return the default value or the value entered by the user; if the user chooses Cancel, the function will return FALSE.

Before continuing   Create a new macro sheet.

A Change Directory Macro

Problem: I'd like to change the working directory without having to access the File Open dialog box.

Solution: Create a macro that prompts you for the directory name and then changes to that directory using the DIRECTORY function.

Important   Throughout this section we will be working with macros that help facilitate navigating through directories and accessing files. While the macro functions themselves are identical on both Microsoft Excel for Windows and the Macintosh, some of the arguments used with these functions are different. When specifying these arguments, make sure to indicate drive names, paths (folders) and filenames that are applicable to your operating environment.

The Change Directory Macro

1   In the empty macro sheet, type the following:

	A	B
1		**ChangeDir**
2		
3	Choice	=INPUT("Change to w hat directory?",2,"Change Directory","C:\EXCEL")
4		=IF(Choice=FALSE,HALT())
5		=DIRECTORY(Choice)
6		=RETURN()

Figure 3.7   ChangeDir Macro (Windows)

1   In the empty macro sheet, type the following:

	A	B
1		**ChangeDir**
2		
3	Choice	=INPUT("Change to what directory?",2,"Change Directory","WexTech:Excel")
4		=IF(Choice=FALSE,HALT())
5		=DIRECTORY(Choice)
6		=RETURN()

Figure 3.8   ChangeDir Macro (Macintosh)

2   Give cell B1 the command name ChangeDir and assign cell B3 the name Choice.

3   Run the macro.

4   Type a valid pathname in the edit box of the input box and click OK.

Microsoft Excel will change to the new directory. You can verify this by choosing Open from the File menu.

How the Macro Works

The line

```
=INPUT("Change to what directory",2,"Change Directory","C:\EXCEL")
```

displays an input box that accepts text, with C:\EXCEL as the default entry. The line

```
=IF(Choice=FALSE,HALT())
```

determines that if the INPUT function returns FALSE (meaning Cancel was selected) then the macro should be halted; otherwise,

```
=DIRECTORY(Choice)
```

changes the working directory to that which was entered via the input box.

Error Checking

This macro works fine if the directory specified is valid, but if the directory is not valid, a dialog box like the one shown in Figure 3.9 will appear.

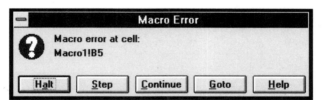

Figure 3.9   Macro Error dialog box

This is Microsoft Excel telling you, in a rather unfriendly way, that it cannot execute the command in cell B5. You can suppress this message—and display a friendlier one—using the ERROR function.

The macro statement

```
=ERROR(FALSE)
```

will suppress the display of error messages. If error checking is turned off and an error is encountered while running a macro, Microsoft Excel ignores the error and continues running. Error checking is turned back on by RETURN at the end of the macro, or by an ERROR(TRUE) statement.

How We Can Check for Errors—ISERROR

We know that the statement that may give us a problem is =DIRECTORY(Choice), but how can we tell, with error checking off, that the statement worked or not? In this case, we can check for success (or failure) using the ISERROR function.

ISERROR(value) returns TRUE if value contains an error, and FALSE if it does not. Thus, we can modify the ChangeDir macro as shown in Figure 3.10.

	A	B	C
1		**ChangeDir**	
2			
3	Choice	=INPUT("Change to what directory?",2,"Change Directory","C:\EXCEL")	*Display input box*
4		=IF(Choice=FALSE,HALT())	*If cancelled, halt*
5		=ERROR(FALSE)	*Supress errors*
6	NewDir	=DIRECTORY(Choice)	*Change to new directory*
7		=IF(ISERROR(NewDir))	*If error in changing...*
8		= ALERT("Directory is not valid.",2)	*Display message*
9		= GOTO(Choice)	*Try again*
10		=END.IF()	
11		=RETURN()	

Figure 3.10   ChangeDir macro that checks for valid directory

How the Macro Works

The lines

```
=INPUT("Change to what directory",2,"Change Directory","C:\EXCEL")
=IF(Choice=FALSE,HALT())
```

display an input box and halt the macro if the user chooses Cancel. The line

```
=ERROR(FALSE)
```

turns error checking off. The statement

```
=DIRECTORY(Choice)
```

changes to the directory specified via the input box. The lines

```
=IF(ISERROR(NewDir))
        =ALERT("Directory is not valid",2)
        =GOTO(Choice)
=END.IF()
```

will, if there is an error in NewDir (cell B6), display an alert box and continue executing macro statements back at Choice (cell B3). Do not confuse GOTO with FORMULA.GOTO. The FORMULA.GOTO statement actually moves the cell pointer while GOTO redirects macro flow.

Dialog Boxes

A custom dialog box can have most of the same "features" and options as the built-in dialog boxes presented by Microsoft Excel. These options include

- Display text
- Text input
- Option buttons grouped within boxes
- Check boxes
- List boxes
- Drop-down list boxes
- Combo boxes
- Pushbuttons
- Pictures

Before examining a dialog box macro, be forewarned: it will look much more complex than it is. Custom dialog box creation seems complicated because most of the statements that define a dialog box item require a set of four numbers that determine its size and position, and the logic of these numbers isn't intuitive.

This is especially true if you are accustomed to character-based applications which measure screen display in terms of rows and columns. The normal text screen is 25 lines high and 80 characters wide. If you want to draw a box on the screen in a character-based application, you would simply specify how many characters across and how many rows down.

Since Windows and the Macintosh are graphical environments that run on different displays with varying degrees of resolution, Microsoft Excel cannot use lines and characters as a standard measurement for placing text on the screen. A line on an EGA monitor is much larger than a line on a SuperVGA or a Macintosh monitor. Instead, the position of an item within a dialog box and the overall placement of a dialog box is measured using screen units.

 In Microsoft Excel for Windows, one horizontal screen unit is 1/8 of the width of one character in the system font, and one vertical screen unit is 1/12 of the height of one character in the system font. That is, the system font is the standard for determining the location of your specific display.

 In Microsoft Excel for the Macintosh, vertical and horizontal screen units are measured in points (one point equals 1/72 inch).

DIALOG.BOX (Windows)

You produce a custom dialog box using the DIALOG.BOX function. The syntax is

DIALOG.BOX(*dialog_ref*)

where *dialog_ref* is a reference to the *dialog box definition table*. The definition
table contains information on how large the dialog box should be, where it should be
positioned, what components should be in the dialog box, and so on.

Consider the example shown in Figure 3.11.

	E	F	G	H	I	J	K
1	Item	x	y	width	height	text	init/ result
2							
3							
4				262	70		
5	5	10	6			This is a simple dialog box	
6	1	31	30	88		OK	
7	2	138	30	88		Cancel	

Figure 3.11 Dialog box definition table (Windows)

here the DIALOG.BOX function displays a dialog box like the one shown in Figure
3.12, according to the information contained in cells E4:K7, the dialog box definition
table.

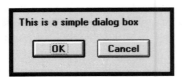

Figure 3.12 Simple dialog box (Windows)

The first line of the table (E4:K4) determines the size and position of the dialog box.
In this case the width of 262 and the height of 70 define a dialog box which is
approximately 262/8 characters wide and 70/12 characters tall. The absence of x and
y coordinates indicates that the dialog box should be centered on the screen.

The next line of the table determines that the first item in the dialog box will be
static text, in this case the text "This is a simple dialog box". This is indicated by the
"5" in cell E5. Each type of dialog box element is identified by a different number.
For example, a "1" indicates an OK button, a "12" indicates an option button, and so
on (see "DIALOG.BOX" in the *Microsoft Excel Function Reference*). The "10" and
the "6" entered in cells F5:G5 indicate that the static text should appear 10 screen
units to the right of and 6 screen units down from the upper left corner of the dialog
box.

The next two lines define the placement of the OK and Cancel buttons (items 1 and
2, respectively). A height coordinate has not been specified, so the buttons will
appear in a standard size.

DIALOG.BOX (Macintosh)

You produce a custom dialog box using the DIALOG.BOX function. The syntax is

DIALOG.BOX(*dialog_ref*)

where *dialog_ref* is a reference to the *dialog box definition table*. The definition table contains information on how large the dialog box should be, where it should be positioned, what components should be in the dialog box, and so on.

Consider the example shown in Figure 3.13.

	E	F	G	H	I	J	K
1	**Item**	**x**	**y**	**width**	**height**	**text**	**init/result**
2							
3							
4				214	87		
5	5	9	9			This is a simple dialog box	
6	1	31	42	64		OK	
7	2	123	42	64		Cancel	

Figure 3.13   Dialog box definition table (Macintosh)

Here the DIALOG.BOX function displays a dialog box like the one shown in Figure 3.14, according to the information contained in cells E4:K7, the dialog box definition table.

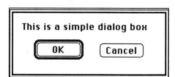

Figure 3.14   Simple dialog box (Macintosh)

The first line of the table (E4:K4) determines the size and position of the dialog box. In this case the width of 214 and the height of 87 define a dialog box which is 214 points wide and 87 points tall. The absence of x and y coordinates indicates that the dialog box should be centered on the screen.

The next line of the table determines that the first item in the dialog box will be static text, in this case the text "This is a simple dialog box". This is indicated by the "5" in cell E5. Each type of dialog box element is identified by a different number. For example, a "1" indicates an OK button, a "12" indicates an option button, etc. (see "DIALOG.BOX" in the *Microsoft Excel Function Reference*). The "9" and the "9" entered in cells F5:G5 indicate that the static text should appear 9 points to the right of and 9 points down from the upper left corner of the dialog box.

The next two lines define the placement of the OK and Cancel buttons (items 1 and 2, respectively). A height coordinate has not been specified, so the buttons will appear in a standard size.

Using the Dialog Editor

Before continuing Open DIALOG.XLM.

While you can certainly create and edit dialog boxes by changing values and attributes in the dialog box definition table, it is much easier (and faster) to use the Microsoft Excel Dialog Editor.

The Dialog Editor is a specialized drawing application that allows you to "draw" and position specific objects such as buttons, list boxes, group boxes, and so on. For this example, you will create a dialog box similar to the one shown on page 79.

To Load the Dialog Editor (Windows)

1 Click in the Control Box in the upper left corner of the Microsoft Excel window and choose Run from the Control menu.

2 When the Run dialog box appears, choose Dialog Editor and click OK. Your screen should look like the one shown in Figure 3.15.

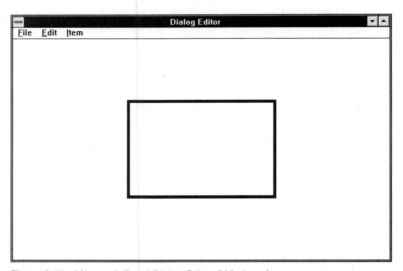

Figure 3.15 Microsoft Excel Dialog Editor (Windows)

To Load the Dialog Editor (Macintosh)

1 Access the Finder and open the folder that contains Microsoft Excel.

2 Double-click the Dialog Editor icon. Your screen should look like the one shown in Figure 3.16.

If you are using system software version 7.0 or higher, you may want to unclutter your screen by choosing Hide Others from the Finder menu.

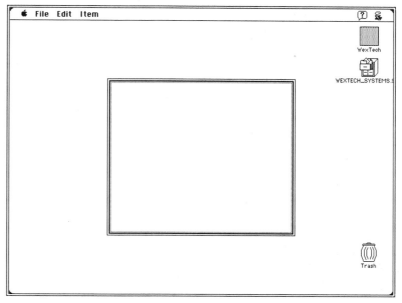

Figure 3.16   Microsoft Excel Dialog Editor (Macintosh)

To Create a Simple Dialog Box

1   From the Item menu, choose Text. The word "text" will appear in the upper left corner.

2   With the word "text" selected, type **This is a simple dialog box**. Your screen should look like the one shown in Figure 3.17.

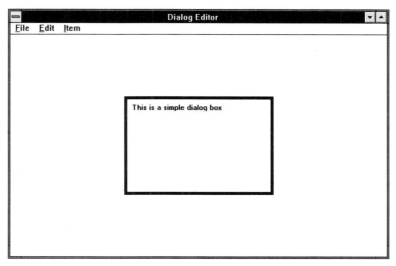

Figure 3.17   Dialog Box beginning

3 From the Item menu, choose Button. The following dialog box will appear.

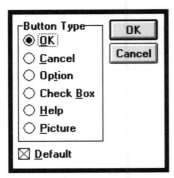

Figure 3.18   Button Type dialog box

4 Choose OK as the button type and click OK.

5 With the OK button selected, press the ENTER key. A Cancel button will appear directly below the OK button. Your screen should look like the one shown in Figure 3.19.

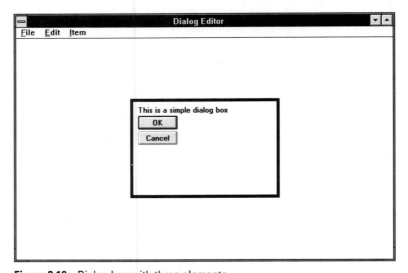

Figure 3.19   Dialog box with three elements

6 Click in the center of the Cancel button (your mouse pointer shape will change), and drag the Cancel button so that it is about one button width to the right of the OK button.

7 Drag the OK button a little to the right. Your screen should look like the one shown in Figure 3.20.

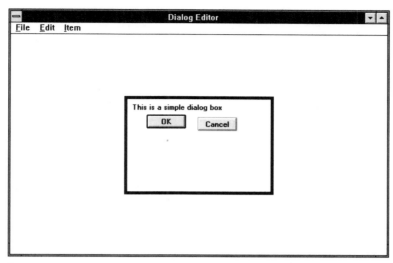

Figure 3.20   Modified dialog box

Aligning and Resizing

While the dialog box is certainly functional, its appearance leaves much to be desired. Specifically, there's too much space at the bottom of the dialog box and the OK and Cancel buttons don't line up.

While we can try to get the buttons to line up by sight, for this next example we will determine the coordinates of the Cancel button, then change the coordinates of the OK button so the OK button lines up with the Cancel button.

To Align the OK and Cancel Buttons

1   Double-click the Cancel button. The following dialog box will appear.

The coordinates in your dialog box may be different.

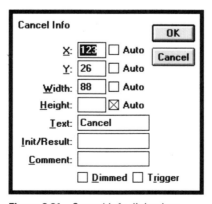

Figure 3.21   Cancel Info dialog box

2   Note the y coordinate and click on Cancel.

3 Double-click the OK button.

4 When the Information dialog box appears, change the y coordinate so it is the same as the y coordinate for the Cancel button and click OK. The OK and Cancel buttons will now be aligned.

To Resize the Dialog Box

1 Move the mouse pointer to the bottom right border of the dialog box. A two-headed arrow will appear.

2 Drag the border up and to the left. Notice that the dialog box shrinks and expands proportionately.

Why the Dialog Box Resizes Proportionately

Unless you specify otherwise, Microsoft Excel will center dialog boxes on the screen. You can change this by explicitly setting the x and y positions for the dialog box.

To Set the Position of the Dialog Box

1 Double-click in an empty portion of the dialog box (do not click on a button or the static text). A dialog box like the one shown in Figure 3.22 will appear.

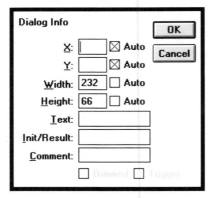

Figure 3.22   Dialog Info dialog box

2 Change the x position to **30** and the y position to **40** and click OK. Your screen should look like the one shown in Figure 3.23.

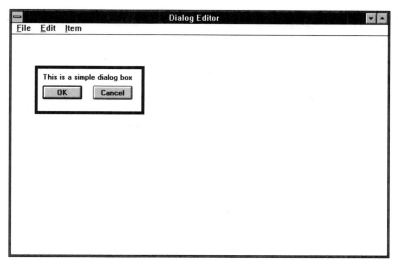

Figure 3.23   Dialog box positioned explicitly

Copying the Dialog Box to the Macro Sheet

You do not save a dialog box file, but instead copy the dialog box into a Microsoft Excel macro sheet using the standard Edit Copy/Edit Paste commands.

To Copy the Dialog Box to the Macro Sheet

1   Make sure the Dialog Editor is the active application.

2   From the Edit menu, choose Select Dialog.

3   From the Edit menu, choose Copy.

4   Activate Microsoft Excel and click in cell E4 in DIALOG.XLM.

5   From the Edit menu, choose Paste. Your screen should look like the one shown in Figure 3.24.

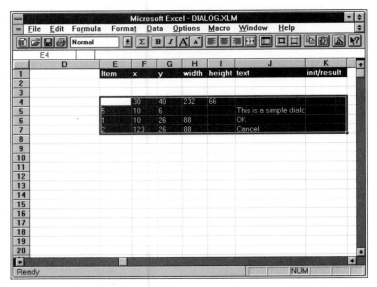

Figure 3.24   A dialog box copied into a macro sheet

6   Using the Formula Define Name command, assign the name Simple to cells E4:K7.

7   From the Format menu, choose Border. The Border dialog box will appear.

8   Choose Outline and Left and click OK.

Note   If you are using Microsoft Excel for the Macintosh, the coordinates in your dialog box definition table will be different. Also, the border command used in step seven is for cosmetic purposes only.

To Display the Dialog Box

1   Type the following in cells B1:B3.

	B
1	**SimpleDialog**
2	
3	=DIALOG.BOX(Simple)
4	=RETURN()

Figure 3.25   SimpleDialog macro

2   Using the Formula Define Name command, assign the name SimpleDialog to cell B1.

3   Run the SimpleDialog macro.

4   When the dialog box appears, click Cancel.

What the DIALOG.BOX Function Returns

If you press CTRL + ` (or choose Display from the Options menu and turn off Formulas) you will see that cell B2 contains a FALSE, indicating that the Cancel key was chosen. But does this mean TRUE will be returned if OK is chosen?

The answer, surprisingly, is no. Clicking OK does not return TRUE but instead returns a number, and this number depends on which row of the definition table contains the OK button definition.

In our example (represented in Figure 3.26) the OK button has been placed in row number two, so running the macro and clicking OK would return 2.

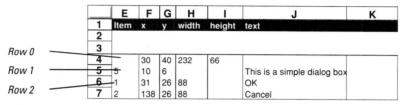

	E	F	G	H	I	J	K
1	Item	x	y	width	height	text	
2							
3							
4		30	40	232	66		
5	5	10	6			This is a simple dialog box	
6	1	31	26	88		OK	
7	2	138	26	88		Cancel	

Row 0 — (points to row 4)
Row 1 — (points to rows 5–6)
Row 2 — (points to row 7)

Figure 3.26   DIALOG.BOX returns values equal to row numbers on definition table

The fact that the DIALOG.BOX function returns a number means that we can have multiple pushbuttons in a dialog box. We'll see how this works in "Dynamic Dialog boxes" on page 101.

More Complicated Dialog Boxes: A Better Change Directory Macro

Problem: I'd like to be able to change the directory by choosing an option from a dialog box, instead of typing the drive and pathname.

Solution: Create a dialog box that looks like the ones shown in Figures 3.27 or 3.28, in which choosing Reports changes the directory to C:\Reports (DiskName:Reports on the Macintosh), choosing Payables changes the directory to C:\Pay, and choosing Receivables changes the directory to C:\Receive.

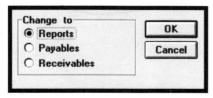

Figure 3.27   Change Directory dialog box (Windows)

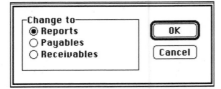

Figure 3.28 Change Directory dialog box (Macintosh)

Tip If you run into trouble creating dialog boxes, see "TroubleDialog " on page 116.

To Create the Dialog Box

1 Activate the Dialog Editor.

2 From the File menu, choose New.

3 From the Item menu, choose Group Box.

4 With the group box selected, type **Change to:** and press the ENTER key. Your screen should look like the one shown in Figure 3.29.

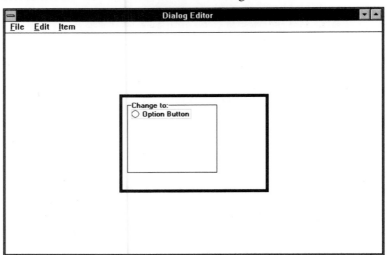

Figure 3.29 Dialog box with group box

5 With the option button selected, type **Reports** and press the ENTER key. A second option button will appear below the first.

6 Type **Payables** and press the ENTER key.

7 Type **Receivables**.

8 From the Item menu, choose Button.

9 When the Button type dialog box appears, select OK and click OK.

10 Drag the OK button to the right of the Change to: group box.

11 With the OK button selected, press the ENTER key to produce a Cancel button. Your screen should look like the one shown in Figure 3.30.

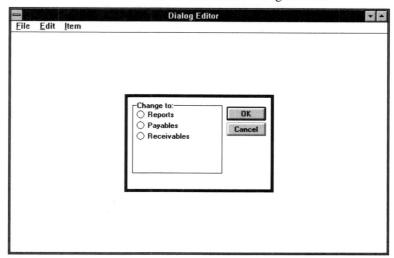

Figure 3.30   Dialog box under construction

Some Fine Tuning

While functional, this dialog box lacks polish for the following reasons:

- The option buttons are missing keyboard accelerators. (This applies to Microsoft Excel for Windows.)

- The group box is too wide and too tall.

- The entire dialog box is too wide and too tall.

To Add Accelerators (Windows)

1 Double-click the Reports button.

2 When the Option Button Info dialog box appears, type an ampersand (&) in front of the "R" in the text edit box as shown in Figure 3.31. The "&" will place an underscore under the "R" in the dialog box.

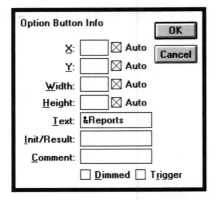

Figure 3.31 Option Button Info dialog box

3 Click OK.

4 Repeat steps 2 and 3, typing an ampersand in front of the "P" in Payables and in front of the "c" in Receivables.

To Add Finishing Touches

1 Make the group box shorter and narrower by clicking in the bottom right corner of the group box and dragging up and to the left.

2 Click the OK button and, while holding down the SHIFT key, click the Cancel button. Both buttons are now selected, and moving one of them will move the other.

3 Drag the two buttons to the left.

4 Make the dialog box smaller by dragging the bottom right corner up and to the left. Your screen should look like the one shown in Figure 3.32.

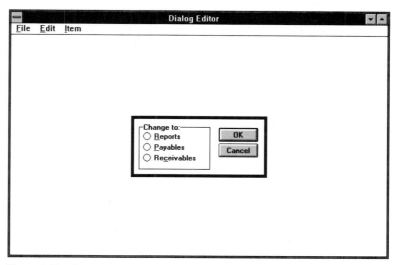

Figure 3.32   Completed dialog box

To Copy the Dialog Box to the Macro Sheet

1   From the Edit menu, choose Select Dialog.

2   From the Edit menu, choose Copy.

3   Activate Microsoft Excel and select cell E10 in DIALOG.XLM.

4   From the Edit menu, choose Paste.

5   Assign cells E10:K17 the name CD_Dialog1 and apply an outline and left border.
The dialog definition table should look similar to the one shown in Figure 3.33.

*The coordinates will
be different in
Microsoft Excel for
the Macintosh.*

	D	E	F	G	H	I	J	K
1		Item	x	y	width	height	text	init/ result
2								
10	CD_Dialog1				290	86		
11		14	10	6	159	71	Change to:	
12		11						
13		12					&Reports	
14		12					&Payables	
15		12					Re&ceivables	
16		1	188	13			OK	
17		2	188	37			Cancel	

Figure 3.33   CD_Dialog1 definition table

*Remember, the first
row of the table is
row zero.*

If things go as expected, executing a macro that contains the statement
DIALOG.BOX(CD_Dialog1) should return FALSE if Cancel is selected and 6 if OK
is selected because the OK button is in row six of the definition table.

To Display the Dialog Box

1 Type the following in cells B6:B9.

	B
6	**ChangeDir1**
7	
8	=DIALOG.BOX(CD_Dialog1)
9	=RETURN()

Figure 3.34   ChangeDir1 macro

2 Assign the command name ChangeDir1 to cell B6.

3 Run the ChangeDir1 macro to display the following dialog box.

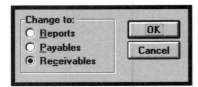

Figure 3.35   Dialog box produced by running ChangeDir1 macro

4 Choose Receivables and click OK.

Analyzing the Results

If you were to display values (by pressing CTRL + `, COMMAND + ` on the Macintosh) you would see that the DIALOG.BOX function does indeed return 6. But where are the button choices stored? If you examine the dialog box definition table, you will see that Microsoft Excel has placed a 3 in cell K12, indicating that the third button in the option group was selected.

Check box and option group results appear in the seventh column of the definition table, the Init/Result column.

	E	F	G	H	I	J	K
1	Item	x	y	width	height	text	init/result
2							
10				290	86		
11	14	10	6	159	71	Change to:	
12	11						3
13	12					&Reports	
14	12					&Payables	
15	12					Re&ceivables	
16	1	188	13			OK	
17	2	188	37			Cancel	

Figure 3.36   Dialog box definition table after running the macro

Before continuing   Assign cell K12 the name CD_Dialog1Choice.

Changing Directories and Presenting the File Open Dialog Box

We can now modify the macro so that it acts upon the results placed in CD_Dialog1Choice (cell K12), changes the directory accordingly, then displays the File Open dialog box.

To Modify the Macro

1   Type the following in the macro sheet. Make sure you enter valid pathnames in cells B11, B13 and B15.

	A	B	C
6		**Change Dir 1**	
7			
8	Result1	=DIALOG.BOX(CD_Dialog1)	*Display dialog box*
9		=IF(Result1=FALSE,HALT())	*If Cancelled...*
10		=IF(CD_Dialog1Choice=1)	*If first button...*
11		= SET.NAME("New Dir","C:\Reports")	
12		=ELSE.IF(CD_Dialog1Choice=2)	*If second button...*
13		= SET.NAME("New Dir","C:\Pay")	
14		=ELSE()	*If third button...*
15		= SET.NAME("New Dir","C:\Receive")	
16		=END.IF()	
17		=DIRECTORY(New Dir)	*Change directory*
18		=OPEN?()	*Display file open dialog*
19		=RETURN()	

Figure 3.37   Modified ChangeDir1 macro

Note   The OPEN? function displays the File Open dialog box.

---

2   Assign cell B8 the name Result1.

3   Run the macro. Notice that the dialog box appears with the third option already selected.

4   When the dialog box appears, choose the desired option and click OK. The File Open dialog box will appear.

5   Click Cancel.

Initializing the Dialog Box

The Init/Result column of the definition table doesn't just store the results of button selections, but is also used to initialize a dialog box so that default values are properly set. In this example, the Receivables option was pre-selected because cell CD_DialogChoice1 (K12) was still set from the previous execution of the dialog box. You can override previous values and initialize a dialog box using the SET.VALUE command.

To Modify the Macro to Initialize the Dialog Box

1   Insert a row at cells A8:C8. (You can do this by selecting A7:C7, pressing CTRL + PLUS SIGN, and shifting cells down.)

2   In the now blank cell B8, type **=SET.VALUE(CD_Dialog1Choice,1)**. The modified macro is shown in Figure 3.38.

	A	B	C
6		**Change Dir 1**	
7			
8		=SET.VALUE(CD_Dialog1Choice,1)	*Initialize dialog box*
9	Result1	=DIALOG.BOX(CD_Dialog1)	*Display dialog box*
10		=IF(Result1=FALSE,HALT())	*If Cancelled...*
11		=IF(CD_Dialog1Choice=1)	*If first button...*
12		= SET.NAME("New Dir","C:\Reports")	
13		=ELSE.IF(CD_Dialog1Choice=2)	*If second button...*
14		= SET.NAME("New Dir","C:\Pay")	
15		=ELSE()	*If third button...*
16		= SET.NAME("New Dir","C:\Receive")	
17		=END.IF()	
18		=DIRECTORY (New Dir)	*Change directory*
19		=OPEN?()	*Display file open dialog*
20		=RETURN()	

Figure 3.38   ChangeDir1 macro that initializes dialog box

Understanding the Macro

The line

```
=SET.VALUE(CD_Dialog1Choice,1)
```

sets the value of cell K12 to 1. The lines

```
=DIALOG.BOX(CD_Dialog1)
=If(Result1=FALSE,HALT())
```

display the dialog box, and, if Cancel is selected, halt the macro. The statements

```
=IF(CD_Dialog1Choice=1)
=  SET.NAME("NewDir","C:\Reports")
```

If a name does not already exist, the SET.NAME command will create the name (as well as assign the name a value).

determine that if the first choice was selected, the variable NewDir is assigned the value C:\Reports. The name NewDir didn't exist before we ran the macro, but if you bring up the Define Name dialog box, you will see that NewDir exists and has been given a value. The SET.NAME command, while not absolutely necessary in this example, is very useful for storing settings and values that need to be retrieved later on. The statements

```
=ELSE.IF(CD_Dialog1Choice=2)
=   SET.NAME("NewDir","C:\Pay")
=ELSE()
=   SET.NAME("NewDir","C:\Receive")
=END.IF()
```

set NewDir to the appropriate value based upon the selection made in the dialog box. Finally, the lines

```
=DIRECTORY(NewDir)
=OPEN?()
```

change the working directory and display the File Open dialog box.

Adding List Boxes to the Change Directory Macro

Problem: I have almost two dozen different directories that I need to change to.

Solution: Create a custom dialog box that uses a list box instead of option buttons.

While we could modify the existing dialog box by copying its definition table back into the dialog editor, in this case it makes more sense to fashion a new dialog box from scratch.

Tip   The ability to copy the definition table back into the Dialog Editor can be very useful when you need to make minor modifications to an existing macro.

For this next example we will create a dialog box that looks like the one shown in Figure 3.39.

Notice that this dialog box has a title bar.

Figure 3.39   Change Directory dialog box with list box

To Create a Change Directory Macro that Uses a List Box

1 Activate the Dialog Editor.

2 From the File menu, choose New.

3 From the Item menu, choose List Box.

4 When the List Box Type dialog box appears, choose Standard and click OK.

5 Widen the list box by clicking in the right edge of the scroll box and dragging to the right until the edge is very near the dialog box border.

6 From the Item menu, choose Button.

7 When the Button Type dialog box appears, choose OK as the button type and click OK.

8 With the OK button selected, press the ENTER key to produce a Cancel button.

9 Reposition the OK and Cancel buttons so they look like the example shown in Figure 3.39.

10 Double-click in a blank area of the dialog box. The Dialog Info dialog box will appear.

11 Type **Change Directory** in the Text edit box as shown in Figure 3.40.

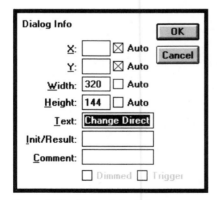

Figure 3.40 Dialog Info dialog box

12 Click OK. Your screen should look similar to the one shown in Figure 3.41.

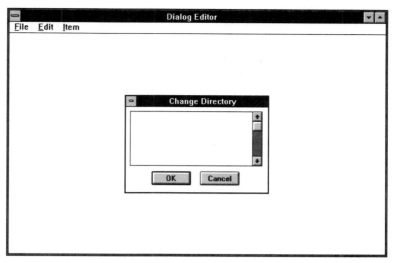

Figure 3.41   Listless list box

Before continuing   Select the dialog box and copy it into cell E22 of DIALOG.XLM. Then assign the name CD_Dialog2 to cells E22:K25.

To Display the New Change Directory Dialog Box

1   Type the following in cells B22:B25.

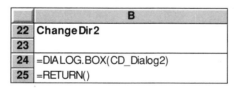

	B
22	Change Dir 2
23	
24	=DIALOG.BOX(CD_Dialog2)
25	=RETURN()

Figure 3.42   ChangeDir2 macro

2   Assign cell B22 the command name ChangeDir2.

3   Run the ChangeDir2 macro to produce a dialog box like the one shown in Figure 3.43.

Figure 3.43   Dialog box presented after running ChangeDir2 macro

4   Click Cancel.

Populating the List Box

At this point we have succeeded in creating a dialog box that has a list box, but we have not yet populated that list box with information to choose nor have we established a method for using that information.

You populate a list box by typing the list you want to appear in the macro sheet, then referring to that list in the applicable row of the dialog box definition table. In this case we should place the reference in the row that contains item number 15, which indicates a list box.

To Populate the Change Directory Macro List Box

1   Type the following entries into the macro sheet in cells M1:N8.

You may want to enter names and paths that are applicable to your computer.

	M	N
1	Reports	C:\Reports
2	Payables	C:\Pay
3	Receivables	C:\Receive
4	Slush Fund	C:\Slush
5	Ransom Notes	C:\Slush\Ransom
6	Proposals	D:\Business\Props
7	Demonstration Files	C:\Misc\Demo
8	Notes	C:\Notes

Figure 3.44   Directory listing (Windows)

1   Type the following entries into the macro sheet in cells M1:N8.

You may want to enter names and paths that are applicable to your computer.

	M	N
1	Reports	WexTech:Reports
2	Payables	WexTech:Payables
3	Receivables	WexTech:Receivables
4	Slush Fund	WexTech:Slush
5	Miscellaneous	WexTech:Misc
6	Ransom Notes	WexTech:Slush:Ransom
7	Proposals	NewDrive:Proposals
8	Demonstration Files	WexTech:Misc:Demos

Figure 3.45   Directory listing (Macintosh)

2   Assign cells M1:M8 the name DirList. Only the items in column M will be used to populate the list box. The entries in column N will be used later.

3   Enter the list reference in the dialog box definition table. In this case type **DirList** in cell J23, as shown in Figure 3.46.

	D	E	F	G	H	I	J	K	L
22	CD_Dialog2				320	132	Change Directory		
23		15	10	6	294	84	DirList		*Choice2*
24		1	58	99	88		OK		
25		2	167	99	88		Cancel		

Figure 3.46

4   Assign cell K23 the name Choice2. Cell K23 will contain the results of the list box selection when the macro is run.

5   Run the ChangeDir2 macro to produce a dialog box like the one shown in Figure 3.47.

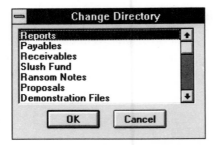

Figure 3.47   Selecting a directory won't do anything. Yet.

From List Box to Pathnames

If we were to follow the methodology of the ChangeDir1 macro, we would modify the ChangeDir2 macro by

- entering a SET.VALUE statement at the beginning of the macro to initialize the dialog box, and

- creating a bevy of IF...ELSE.IF... statements to handle the multiple choice selections.

While a SET.VALUE statement is a good idea, the idea of writing so many IF statements should be repugnant to even the least fastidious programmer. Instead, let's employ the OFFSET function to return the name of the desired directory.

How the OFFSET Function Will Work

Let's say we choose the third item in the list box, Receivables. To return the pathname (which we typed in the column next to DirList), we would employ the following function:

Figure 3.48   Annotated OFFSET statement

The completed macro is shown in Figure 3.49.

	A	B	C
22		**ChangeDir2**	
23			
24		=SET.VALUE(Choice2,1)	*Initialize dialog box*
25		=DIALOG.BOX(CD_Dialog2)	*Display dialog*
26	Result2	=OFFSET(DirList,Choice2-1,1,1,1)	*Choose item one to the right*
27		=DIRECTORY(Result2)	*Change directory*
28		=OPEN?()	*Display file open dialog box*
29		=RETURN()	

Figure 3.49   ChangeDir2 macro code

Dynamic Dialog Boxes

The examples in this section refer to macros in CHDIR.XLM

Problem: I wish the Change Directory dialog box would display the underlying pathname when I click a list box item.

Solution: Redefine the list box as a *trigger* (that is, an item that when selected changes something in the dialog box), so that clicking on different items displays the underlying pathnames.

Open CHDIR.XLM and run the ChangeDirectory macro. A dialog box similar to the one shown in Figure 3.50 will appear on your screen.

Notice that clicking different items will change what appears at the bottom of the dialog box.

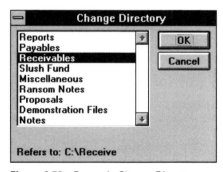

Figure 3.50   Dynamic ChangeDirectory macro at work

Note   Clicking OK will probably produce an error message as the pathnames entered in the macro sheet probably do not exist on your system's disk. You can make the macro work by changing the entries in the second column of DirList.

You can make almost any dialog box item a trigger by adding 100 to the item type number. For example, an option button (12) can become a trigger by redefining its item type number as 112.

In essence, each of the list items now behaves as though it were a button, and our macro redraws a portion of the dialog box based on which "button" was selected. Making the list box a trigger that changes text at the bottom of the dialog box is simply a matter of changing the item type number from 15 to 115 as shown in the dialog box definition table in Figure 3.51.

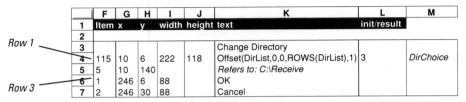

	F	G	H	I	J	K	L	M
1	Item x		y	width	height	text	init/result	
2								
3						Change Directory		
4	115	10	6	222	118	Offset(DirList,0,0,ROWS(DirList),1)	3	DirChoice
5	5	10	140			*Refers to: C:\Receive*		
6	1	246	6	88		OK		
7	2	246	30	88		Cancel		

Row 1 (annotation pointing to Row 4)
Row 3 (annotation pointing to Row 6)

Figure 3.51 Annotated dialog definition table with trigger list box

In this example, clicking a list box item will make the DIALOG.BOX function return a "1" as the list box definition is in row one of the table. Likewise, clicking OK will make the DIALOG.BOX function return a "3" as the OK button definition is in row three of the table. The trigger version of the ChangeDirectory macro is shown in Figure 3.52.

	A	B	C
3		**ChangeDirectory**	
4			
5		=SET.VALUE(DirChoice,1)	*Initialize dialog box*
6	initDialog	=SET.VALUE(DirDescription,"Refers to: "&INDEX(DirList,DirChoice,2))	*Initialize refers to text*
7	dirResponse	=DIALOG.BOX(ChDirDlg)	*Display dialog*
8		=IF(dirResponse=1)	*If a list item is selected...*
9		= GOTO(initDialog)	*Goto initDialog*
10		=ELSE.IF(dirResponse=3)	*If OK is selected*
11		= DIRECTORY(INDEX(DirList,DirChoice,2))	*Change directory*
12		= OPEN?()	*Display file open dialog*
13		=END.IF()	
14		=RETURN()	

Figure 3.52 ChangeDirectory macro, trigger version

Understanding the Macro

The line

```
=SET.VALUE(DirChoice,1)
```

initializes the dialog box so that the first list item is selected when the dialog box first appears. The line

```
=SET.VALUE(DirDescription,"Refers to: "&INDEX(DirList,DirChoice,2))
```

See "INDEX" in the Microsoft Excel Function Reference.

sets the value of DirDescription (cell K5 in the dialog box definition table) so that it reflects the pathname associated with the list item. In this case we use the INDEX function (a close sibling to the OFFSET function) to extract the correct pathname. The line

```
=DIALOG.BOX(ChDirDlg)
```

displays the Change Directory dialog box. The statements

```
=IF(dirResponse=1)
=   GOTO(initDialog)
```

determine that if an item in the list box is clicked (as opposed to clicking OK), the macro should go back to initDialog and redisplay the explanatory text at the bottom of the dialog box. Otherwise, the lines

```
=ELSE.IF(dirResponse=3)
=   DIRECTORY(INDEX(DirList,DirChoice,2))
=   OPEN?()
=END.IF()
```

determine that if the OK button is selected, the macro should change to the directory associated with the selected list box item and display the File Open dialog box.

Note   You will see a slight "hiccup" as Microsoft Excel refreshes the dialog box. Also, you will not be able to select a trigger list box item by double-clicking it.

Multiple-Selection List Boxes

Microsoft Excel will also allow you to select more than one item from a list box. Try running the ChangeDirectoryAndOpen macro, which is also in CHDIR.XLM. The following dialog box will appear.

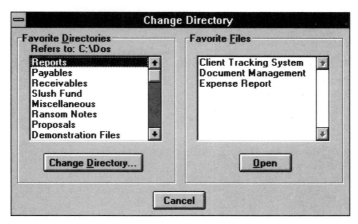

Figure 3.53   ChangeDirectoryAndOpen dialog box

You can make this part of the macro work by changing the entries in the second column of the named area FileList.

Now, select Client Tracking System and ExpenseReport in the Favorite Files list box and click Open. Do not be concerned when Microsoft Excel tells you that it cannot open the desired files and then produces a macro error dialog box—it's very unlikely that your computer contains the files listed in the FileList area of the macro sheet. When this happens, just click OK and halt the macro.

Before we dive into how the macro works, take a look at the Define Name dialog box (by choosing Define Name from the Formula menu) and notice that the name tmpFileList refers to the array value ={1,3}(see Figure 3.54). This value was set when you chose the first and third items in the Favorite Files list box. We'll see how this is used in a moment.

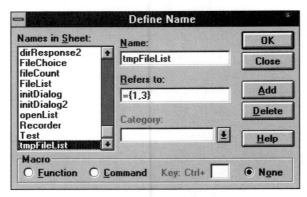

Figure 3.54   tmpFileList refers to an array

The dialog box definition table is depicted in Figure 3.55.

Notice that the numbers of the items selected from the Favorite Files list box are placed in tmpFileList.

	F	G	H	I	J	K	L	M
10	Item	x	y	width	height	text	init/result	
11						Change Directory		
12	115	30	33	222	106	Offset(DirList,0,0,ROWS(DirList),1)	1	DirChoice2
13	15	310	33	222	106	OFFSET(FileList,0,0,ROWS(FileList),1	tmpFileList	FileChoice
14	3	54	145	166		Change &Directory...		
15	3	380	145	88		&Open		
16	5	31	18			Refers to: C:\Dos		
17	2	236	189	88		Cancel		
18	14	289	6	266	175	Favorite &Files		
19	14	10	6	266	175	Favorite &Directories		

Figure 3.55   Dialog box definition of Figure 3.53

The ChangeDirectoryAndOpen macro is shown in Figure 3.56.

	A	B	C
16		**ChangeDirectoryAndOpen**	
17			
18		=SET.VALUE(DirChoice2,1)	*Initialize dialog box*
19		=SET.NAME("tmpFileList")	*Delete the name tmpFileList*
20	initDialog2	=SET.VALUE(DirDescription2,"Refers to: "&INDEX(DirList,DirChoice2,2))	*Initialize refers to text*
21	dirResponse2	=DIALOG.BOX(ChDirOpenDlg)	*Display dialog*
22		=IF(dirResponse2=1)	*If user select an item in the first list box*
23		= GOTO(initDialog2)	*Goto initDialog2*
24		=ELSE.IF(dirResponse2=3)	*If Change Dir button is pressed*
25		= DIRECTORY(INDEX(DirList,DirChoice2,2))	*Change dir*
26		= OPEN?()	*Display file open dialog*
27		=ELSE.IF(dirResponse2=4)	*If Open button is pressed*
28		= IF(NOT(ISNA(COLUMNS(tmpFileList))))	*If at least one file is selected...*
29		= FOR("fileCount",1,COLUMNS(tmpFileList))	*Loop until all selected files are open*
30		= OPEN(INDEX(FileList,INDEX(tmpFileList,1,fileCount),2))	*Open file*
31		= NEXT()	*Increment fileCount counter*
32		= END.IF()	
33		=END.IF()	
34		=RETURN()	

Figure 3.56   ChangeDirectoryAndOpen macro code

Understanding the Macro

The lines

```
=SET.VALUE(DirChoice2,1)
=SET.NAME("tmpFileList")
```

If you don't specify a value or reference when you use SET.NAME, Microsoft Excel deletes the name.

initialize the dialog box and deletes the name tmpFileList, if the name exists. The line

```
=SET.VALUE(DirDescription2,"Refers to: "&INDEX(DirList,DirChoice2,2))
```

sets the value of DirDescription2 (cell K16 in the dialog box definition table) so that it reflects the pathname associated with the list item. The lines

```
=If(dirResponse2=1)
=   GOTO(initDialog2)
```

determine that if an item in the list box is clicked (as opposed to clicking OK), the macro should go back to initDialog2 and redisplay the explanatory text at the bottom of the dialog box. Otherwise, the lines

```
=ELSE.IF(dirResponse2=3)
=   DIRECTORY(INDEX(DirList,DirChoice,2))
=   OPEN?()
=END.IF()
```

determine that if the OK button is selected, the macro should change to the directory associated with the selected list box item and display the File Open dialog box. The line

```
=IF(dirResponse2=4)
```

determines whether the Open button is selected. If this is the case the line

```
=IF(NOT(ISNA(COLUMNS(tmpFileList))))
```

determines whether anything in the Favorite Files list box was selected. Even though tmpFileList is a "memory" variable (that is, it exists only in the Formula Define Name dialog box, and not on the macro sheet itself), the COLUMNS function will act upon it. For example, earlier we saw that tmpFileList had been assigned the array value {1,3}. As far as Microsoft Excel is concerned, these two entries ("1" and "3") mean that tmpFileList takes up two columns. Thus, the line statement we are examining can be interpreted as "if the COLUMNS function doesn't return an #N/A, that is, if at least one item was selected, then execute the next line." The line

```
=FOR("fileCount",1,COLUMNS(tmpFileList))
```

creates a loop and establishes a counter variable called fileCount that starts at "1" and ends with as many items as were selected in the list box. The line

```
=OPEN(INDEX(fileList,INDEX(tmpFileList,1,fileCount),2))
```

merits a detailed explanation. The segment

```
INDEX(tmpFileList,1,fileCount)
```

returns a different number based on the value of fileCount. When fileCount equals 1, this statement returns the first value in tmpFileList, which in our example is 1. When fileCount equals 2, this statement returns the second value in tmpFileList, which in our example equals 3. This result (either 1 or 3) is then passed to the outer INDEX function which extracts the desired file name from the named area FileList. If you're finding this confusing, try running the macro in Single Step mode; or better yet, insert the macro statement =STEP() directly before the OPEN statement so you don't have to plod through the entire macro just to get to the good part.

Custom Commands and Menus

Up to this point we've created several sophisticated macros that we can access using shortcut keys, the Macro Run dialog box and the toolbar. In this next series of exercises we'll examine how we can add a new command to a menu.

It is important here to clarify menu terminology. Consider the illustration shown in Figure 3.57.

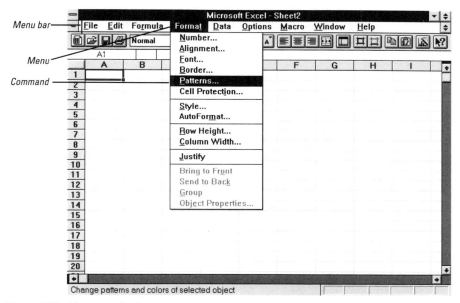

Figure 3.57   Menu terminology

The *menu bar* is the horizontal list of menus along the top of the application window. Microsoft Excel uses six menu bars throughout the worksheet, chart and macro environments, and three additional shortcut menus which change depending on mouse location. Custom applications may use up to 15 additional menu bars at a time.

The *menu* is the drop-down window which appears when you click an item in the menu bar.

The individual items within the drop-down menus are called *commands*. In the next series of exercises we will see how to add a new command to a menu.

Before continuing   Close CHDIR.XLM and open CHDIR2.XLM. CHDIR2.XLM contains a slightly modified version of the Change Directory macro with which we just worked.

The examples in this section refer to macros in CHDIR2.XLM

Creating a Command Table

To create a custom command or menu, you must enter a command table (also called a menu definition table) into the macro sheet. The menu definition provides Microsoft Excel with the text of each command you want to add, the information prompt that appears in the status bar as the command is highlighted and the macro to execute if the item is chosen.

To Create the Command Table for Change Directory

1 Make the entries shown in Figure 3.58 into cells O1:T1.

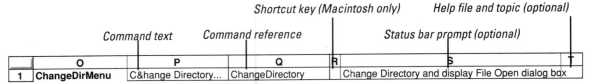

Figure 3.58   Command table annotated

2 Assign cells P1:T1 the name ChangeDirMenu.

Adding Commands to Microsoft Excel Menus

The macro function for adding commands is ADD.COMMAND, the complete syntax of which is as follows:

ADD.COMMAND(*bar_num,menu,command_ref,position*)

The *bar_num* argument refers to the ID number of the menu bar to which the command is added. Each Microsoft Excel built-in menu is assigned a unique ID number, as shown in the table on the following page.

Number	Menu Bar
1	Worksheet and macro sheet (full menus)
2	Chart menu (full menus)
3	Null (displayed when no documents are open or visible)
4	Info
5	Worksheet and macro sheet (short menus)
6	Chart menu (short menus)
7	Cell, toolbar and workbook shortcut menus
8	Object shortcut menu
9	Chart shortcut menu

If the position argument is omitted, Microsoft Excel appends the new command to the bottom of the menu.

The *menu* argument is the name of the menu as it appears on the menu bar, in quotes. The *command_ref* argument is the cell range containing the command definition. The *position* argument specifies the placement of the new command, which can be the text of the command before which your command is to be inserted, or its position number, with the first command in each menu numbered 1 and *separators included* in the count. The value returned by the ADD.COMMAND function is the new command's position number.

For this example, let's say we want to set the command Change Directory... so that it appears before the first menu separator on the File menu (directly below the Links command). We can achieve these results with the following statement:

```
ADD.COMMAND(1,"File",ChangeDirMenu,"-")
```

This will make the command "Change Directory..." appear under the file menu (just before the first separator) whenever you are working with a worksheet or macro sheet. But what happens if you are working on a chart or the null window? Since we have not explicitly added the command to the menu bars associated with these windows, the command will not be available; therefore, when you write macros that add new commands you'll probably want to write several ADD.COMMAND statements to support different window types.

To Add the Change Directory Command to the File Menu

1 With CHDIR2.XLM active, modify the AddNewCommands macro as shown in Figure 3.59.

	B
2	**AddNewCommands**
3	
4	=ADD.COMMAND(1,"File",ChangeDirMenu,"-")
5	=ADD.COMMAND(2,"File",ChangeDirMenu,"-")
6	=ADD.COMMAND(3,"File",ChangeDirMenu,"-")
7	=RETURN()

Figure 3.59   AddNewCommands macro modified

2 Run the AddNewCommands macro. The command Change Directory... will be available under the File menu.

Removing Commands from Menu Bars

Right now, if you were to close CHDIR2.XLM, the Change Directory command would still appear under the File menu. Unless you move CHDIR2.XLM to a new directory, Microsoft Excel would open CHDIR2.XLM and execute the ChangeDirectory macro if its command were selected. To remove a command from a menu, you must explicitly remove it using the DELETE.COMMAND function:

DELETE.COMMAND(*bar_num,menu,command*)

To insure that macros continue to function properly in new versions of Microsoft Excel, use the text form of the menu and command arguments when possible.

where the *bar_num* and *menu* arguments are specified as with the ADD.COMMAND function, and the *command* argument may be the text of the command to delete, or the unique identifying number of a Microsoft Excel built-in command.

To Remove the Change Directory Command from the File Menu

1 With CHDIR2.XLM active, modify the RemoveNewCommands macro as shown in Figure 3.60.

	B
9	**RemoveNewCommands**
10	
11	=DELETE.COMMAND(1,"File","Change Directory...")
12	=DELETE.COMMAND(2,"File","Change Directory...")
13	=DELETE.COMMAND(3,"File","Change Directory...")
14	=RETURN()

Figure 3.60   RemoveNewCommands macro modified

2 Run the RemoveNewCommands macro. The command Change Directory... will no longer be available under the File menu.

Auto Macros: Making it Happen Automatically

We're still working too hard in that we must remember to run one macro to add the Change Directory command and another macro to remove it. We can have Microsoft Excel automatically add the command when we open CHDIR2.XLM, and remove the command when we close CHDIR2.XLM by renaming the macros Auto_Open and Auto_Close.

Auto_Open and Auto_Close

Changes made to the menus from an Add-In do not need to be removed in the Auto_Close macro, because Add-Ins remain open until Microsoft Excel is exited.

In addition to the range names Print_Area, Database, Criteria, and so forth, Microsoft Excel reserves the names *Auto_Open* and *Auto_Close* on each worksheet, macro sheet and Add-In. Each time one of these files is opened by the user, Microsoft Excel searches for the name "Auto_Open" and executes the macro within that area. This is the ideal time to customize the menu and perform any other initialization the macro requires. Likewise, the macro named "Auto_Close" is executed at the time the worksheet, macro sheet or Add-In containing it is closed, providing the opportunity to restore menus and workspace settings the macro may have modified.

To Add Auto_Open and Auto_Close to CHDIR2.XLM

1 Modify the macro sheet so that it looks like the one shown in Figure 3.61.

	B
2	**Auto_Open**
3	
4	=ADD.COMMAND(1,"File",ChangeDirMenu,"-")
5	=ADD.COMMAND(2,"File",ChangeDirMenu,"-")
6	=ADD.COMMAND(3,"File",ChangeDirMenu,"-")
7	=RETURN()
8	
9	**Auto_Close**
10	
11	=DELETE.COMMAND(1,"File","Change Directory...")
12	=DELETE.COMMAND(2,"File","Change Directory...")
13	=DELETE.COMMAND(3,"File","Change Directory...")
14	=RETURN()

Figure 3.61 Add and Remove New Command macros renamed

2 Assign the name Auto_Open to cell B2 and the name Auto_Close to cell B9.

3 Save CHDIR2.XLM.

4 Run the macro Auto_Open. This will add the Change Directory command to the File menu.

5 Close CHDIR2.XLM. This will both close the file and remove the Change Directory command from the File menu.

The next time you open CHDIR2.XLM, the File Change Directory command will appear automatically.

More on Auto Names

Other Auto-Executing Names

Microsoft Excel provides two additional auto-executing names, Auto_Activate and Auto_Deactivate, which are executed when the sheet containing the name is activated or deactivated, respectively.

Defining Multiple Auto-Executing Names

Microsoft Excel allows you to define many auto-executing names of the same type per sheet, by treating the reserved names as prefixes. You may, for example, define the names "Auto_Open1.LoadFiles" and "Auto_Open2.AddMenus" on a single macro sheet. When the user opens the macro sheet, Microsoft Excel runs both Auto_Open macros in alphabetical order.

When Auto-Executing Names Are Not Executed

Users may avoid the execution of automatic macros by holding down the SHIFT key while performing the action that would normally trigger the macro. If, for example, the user wishes to avoid the execution of the Auto_Open macro, he or she may do so by holding down the SHIFT key while opening the file.

Auto-executing macros are only triggered by the user's actions, not by the actions of other macros. An Auto_Close macro, for example, will not run if another macro closes the sheet that contains it. In this case, the macro in control must run the sheet's Auto_Close macro by calling it as a subroutine, or by running it using the RUN command (the macro function equivalent of choosing Run from the Macro menu).

Create Macro and Preview Dialog

One of the most useful aspects of the Microsoft Excel programming language is that you can use the language to build tools that will help you write macros faster. In the exercises that follow we will work with custom tools that allow you to preview dialog boxes and create macros by highlighting cells.

In the examples that follow you will be working with two files. TOOLS.XLM contains the code that will add two new tools to the macro toolbar. TROUBLE.XLM contains a simple macro and a "problem" dialog box.

Before continuing   Open TOOLS.XLM. Microsoft Excel will display the macro toolbar (if it's not already visible) and add two new tools to it. Then open TROUBLE.XLM. Your screen should look like the one shown in Figure 3.62.

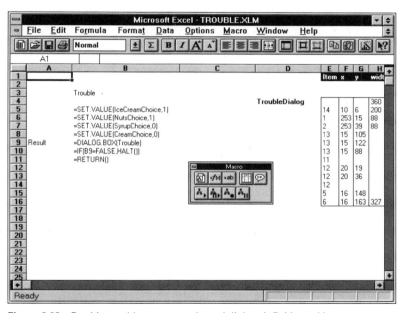

Figure 3.62   Double trouble: macro code and dialog definition table

Working with Trouble

Trouble is (or to be more precise, will be) a macro which displays and acts upon the TroubleDialog dialog box. At this point the Trouble macro has not been named, nor has the name "Result" been applied to cell B9. We can perform both of these tasks—and format the macro—using the custom-built *Create Macro* tool.

To Create and Format a Macro

1 Select the cells that comprise the macro, in this case B3:B11.

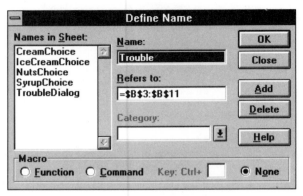

Create Macro tool

2 Click the Create Macro tool in the Macro Toolbar. The Define Name dialog box will appear, as shown in Figure 3.63.

Figure 3.63   Names defined in TROUBLE.XLM

3 Assign the macro the shortcut key CTRL + t (OPTION + COMMAND + t on the Macintosh) and click OK. Your screen should look like the one shown in Figure 3.64.

In addition to creating names, applying names and formatting, the Create Macro macro also automatically applies indention to block IF, WHILE and FOR statements.

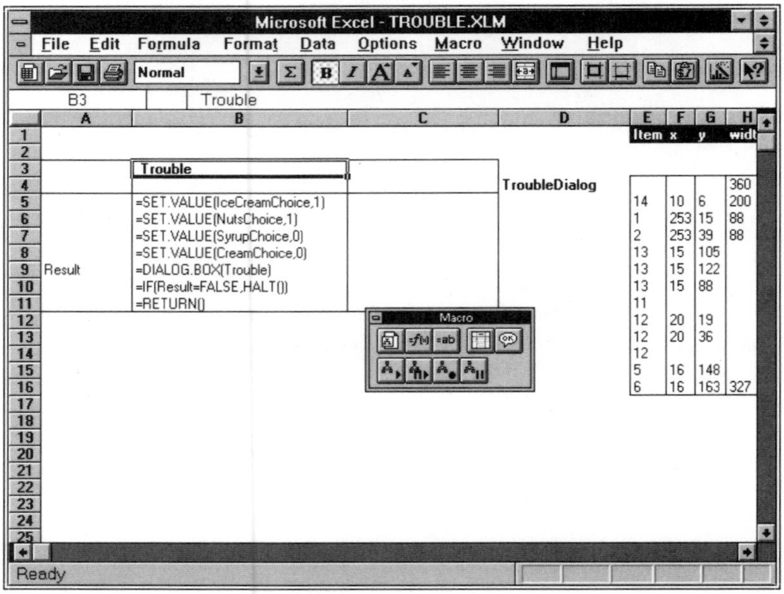

Figure 3.64   Results of Create Macro tool

Some Requirements and Assumptions

- Create Macro assumes you are using a three-column format and that the macro itself is in the middle column.

- You must select the entire macro before clicking the Create Macro tool.

- Create Macro assumes that there is a blank cell below the macro name (in this case cell B4). The blank cell can be useful when you are debugging subroutines and want to force the subroutine into Single Step execution by typing =STEP() in the blank cell.

Previewing a Dialog Box

Having now worked with custom dialog boxes, you can probably appreciate how useful it would be to be able to just view a dialog box without having to run a macro that references that dialog box. The Preview Dialog tool will do just that, as long as the name of the dialog box you want to view has been entered somewhere on the macro sheet.

To Preview a Dialog Box

1   Select the cell that contains the name of the dialog box you want to view, in this case D4.

2   Click the Preview Dialog tool. The following dialog box will appear.

Preview dialog tool

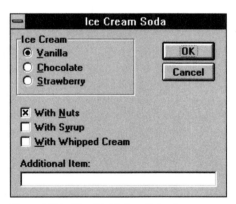

Figure 3.65   TroubleDialog dialog box

3   Click OK.

Before continuing   View the TroubleDialog dialog box again.

Dialog Box Trouble-Shooting

With the TroubleDialog dialog box on the screen, press the TAB key repeatedly until you have cycled through all the options. Notice that the focus skitters about without rhyme or reason.

Unless you specify otherwise, Microsoft Excel will display the elements of a dialog box in the order that the elements were entered when you created the dialog box with the dialog editor. So, unless you remember to always follow an OK button with a Cancel button, you'll end up creating dialog boxes that are "nervous."

Rearranging the Dialog Definition Table

If you examine the dialog box definition table, you will see that some of the items are listed out of order. While you could rearrange the table manually by inserting rows, deleting rows, copying, and so forth, you can rearrange the table more easily using the Data Sort command.

To Rearrange the Dialog Box Definition Table

1   Enter the sort values in cells D5:D16, as shown in Figure 3.66.

	D	E	F	G	H	I	J	K	L
4	Trouble Dialog				360	192			
5	1	14	10	6	200	72	Ice Cream	1	*Ice Cream Choic*
6	11	1	253	15	88		OK	1	
7	12	2	253	39	88		Cancel	1	
8	7	13	15	105			With S&yrup	0	*Syrup Choice*
9	8	13	15	122			&With Whipped Cream	0	*Cream Choice*
10	6	13	15	88			With &Nuts	1	*Nuts Choice*
11	2	11							
12	3	12	20	19			&Vanilla		
13	4	12	20	36			&Chocolate		
14	5	12					&Strawberry		
15	9	5	16	148			Additional Item:		
16	10	6	16	163	327				

Figure 3.66   Out-of-order dialog definition table

2   Select cells D5:L16.

3   From the Data menu, choose Sort.

4   When the Sort dialog box appears, make the sort key $D$5 in ascending order, as shown in Figure 3.67.

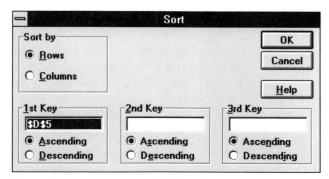

Figure 3.67   Sorting the TroubleDialog definition table

5   Click OK.

The dialog box definition table will now be arranged in a logical fashion (although the borders will look a little strange).

Changing the Focus

There's still one more detail to attend to, and that is the dialog box's initial focus. Unless you specify otherwise, the OK button will have the initial focus. In this example, it would probably make more sense if the edit box under "Additional Item" enjoyed this privilege. You can change the initial focus by entering the row number of the item you want to shift the focus to in the first row of the dialog box's init/result column, as shown in Figure 3.68.

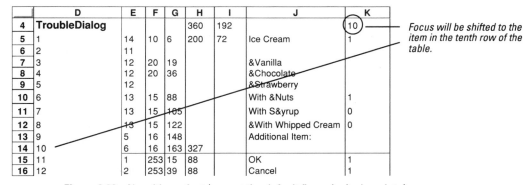

	D	E	F	G	H	I	J	K
4	**TroubleDialog**				360	192		10
5	1	14	10	6	200	72	Ice Cream	1
6	2	11						
7	3	12	20	19			&Vanilla	
8	4	12	20	36			&Chocolate	
9	5	12					&Strawberry	
10	6	13	15	88			With &Nuts	1
11	7	13	15	105			With S&yrup	0
12	8	13	15	122			&With Whipped Cream	0
13	9	5	16	148			Additional Item:	
14	10	6	16	163	327			
15	11	1	253	15	88		OK	1
16	12	2	253	39	88		Cancel	1

Focus will be shifted to the item in the tenth row of the table.

Figure 3.68   Now it's perfect (except the default flavor isn't chocolate)

If you view the dialog box, you will see that the edit box now has the focus.

Some More Useful Tools

Open the file MORETOOL.XLM. This file contains three macros useful to the macro developer. The macro *SideBySide* allows you to choose two windows from a list of windows and arrange these windows side by side. This is particularly useful when you have many files open but just want to work with two of these files. The macro *Comment* is useful for debugging macros in that it allows you to "comment out" sections of program code; that is, it prevents code from executing by removing the equal sign in front of a macro statement and replacing it with two asterisks. The *UnComment* macro does just the opposite: it replaces the two asterisks with an equal sign. You use both macros by first highlighting the section of code you want to change, then running the applicable macro.

SideBySide

The SideBySide macro exploits the Microsoft Excel group editing capability and Window Arrange command to arrange two windows side by side. The macro is shown in Figure 3.69.

	A	B	C
1		SideBySide	
2			
3		=WORKGROUP?()	*Display group edit dialog*
4		=ARRANGE.ALL(1,TRUE)	*Tile only those windows selected*
5		=WORKGROUP(GET.WINDOW(1))	*Activate the first window*
6		=RETURN()	

Figure 3.69   SideBySide macro code

The line

```
=WORKGROUP?()
```

displays the same dialog box as is presented when you choose Group Edit from the Options menu. Assuming you choose two windows to include in the group, the line

```
=ARRANGE.ALL(1,TRUE)
```

tiles horizontally these two windows. The statement

```
=WORKGROUP(GET.WINDOW(1))
```

creates a one window workgroup, effectively cancelling workgroup editing and activating the first window.

Comment

The Comment and UnComment macros both use the FOR.CELL control structure to repeatedly execute a procedure over a range of cells, one cell at a time. The syntax for this function is

FOR.CELL(*ref_name,area_ref,skip_blanks*)

See "FOR.CELL" in the Microsoft Excel Function Reference.

where *ref_name* is the name that Microsoft Excel gives to the cell in the range that is currently being operated on. *Ref_name* refers to a new cell during each loop. *Area_ref* is the range of cells on which you want the loop to operate. If *area_ref* is omitted, the loop operates on the current selection. *Skip_blanks* is a logical value that specifies whether Microsoft Excel should skip blanks. If TRUE, blanks are skipped.

The Comment macro is shown in Figure 3.70.

	A	B	C
8		Comment	
9			
10		=ERROR(FALSE)+ECHO(FALSE)	*Suppress errors and screen redraw*
11		=FOR.CELL("index",SELECTION(),TRUE)	*Loop at first cell until end of selection*
12	aFormula	= GET.FORMULA(Index)	*Evaluate the entry in the current cell*
13		= IF(LEFT(aFormula,1)="=")	*If entry begins with =*
14		= FORMULA("**"&RIGHT(aFormula,LEN(aFormula)-1),Index)	*Substitute ***
15		= END.IF()	
16		=NEXT()	
17		=RETURN()	

Figure 3.70 Comment macro code

The statement

```
=ERROR(FALSE)+ECHO(FALSE)
```

actually combines two different macro commands into one line by separating the commands with a plus sign. ERROR(FALSE) suppresses error messages from being displayed and ECHO(FALSE) turns off screen redrawing. Turning off screen redraw makes the macro faster and less distracting. The statement

```
=FOR.CELL("index",SELECTION(),TRUE)
```

initiates a loop that will operate on the current selection, where "index" is the name assigned to whatever cell the macro is operating on. The statement

```
=GET.FORMULA(index)
```

returns the formula in the current cell as text. The line

```
=IF(LEFT(aFormula,1)="=")
```

employs the LEFT function to determine whether the leftmost charcter in the current cell is an equal sign. If this is true, the statement

```
=FORMULA("**"&RIGHT(aFormula,LEN(aFormula)-1),Index)
```

takes all the characters to the right of the equal sign in the active cell, adds two asterisks to the front of this string, then enters this new string into the active cell. The line

```
=END.IF()
```

closes the If statement and the line

```
=NEXT()
```

activates the next cell in the selection.

FORMULA and GET.FORMULA

The FORMULA and GET.FORMULA functions are used to place formulas into, and extract formulas from, the active cell or reference. The syntax for FORMULA is

FORMULA(*formula_text,reference*)

where *formula_text* can be text, a number, a reference or a formula in the form of text, or a reference to a cell containing any of the above. *Reference* specifies where *formula_text* is to be entered. By specifying a reference, you can enter information into a cell without first selecting the cell.

Note   For more information on FORMULA, GET.FORMULA, LEFT, RIGHT and LEN, see the *Microsoft Excel Function Reference*.

UnComment

The UnComment macro (shown below) works in a manner similar to the Comment macro.

	A	B	C
19		**UnComment**	
20			
21		=ERROR(FALSE)+ECHO(FALSE)	*Suppress errors and screen redraw*
22		=FOR.CELL("Index",SELECTION(),TRUE)	*Loop at first cell until end of selection*
23	aCommForm	= GET.FORMULA(Index)	*Evaluate the entry in the current cell*
24		= IF(LEFT(aCommForm,2)="**")	*If entry begins with* **
25		= FORMULA("="&RIGHT(aCommForm,LEN(aCommForm)-2),Index)	*Substitute "="*
26		= END.IF()	
27		=NEXT()	
28		=RETURN()	

Figure 3.71   UnComment macro code

Assigning Macros to Tools

In Lesson 1 we saw that adding a tool to a toolbar was a fairly easy and straightforward procedure. However, if you will be developing applications that have custom tools, you will need to write a macro that adds tools and removes tools dynamically. That is, when a macro sheet is loaded, a macro should add the applicable tools to the applicable toolbars. When the macro sheet is closed, the tools should be removed.

The macro functions that add tools to toolbars also provide a way to present useful information in the status bar when a tool is clicked. This way we can avoid the less-than-helpful "Blank tool for assigning a macro" message that appears when you add tools without using macros.

Adding tools to a toolbar is very similar to adding command to menus: a toolbar is basically a menu, except the commands you choose from are pictures intead of words. So, just as you would create a command table to add new a command to a menu, you create a toolbar definition table to add new tools to a toolbar. Figure 3.72 shows the toolbar definition table that adds a SideBySide tool to the Macro toolbar.

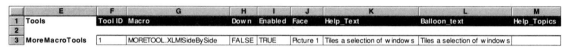

	E	F	G	H	I	J	K	L	M
1	Tools	Tool ID	Macro	Down	Enabled	Face	Help_Text	Balloon_text	Help_Topics
2									
3	MoreMacroTools	1	MORETOOL.XLM!SideBySide	FALSE	TRUE	Picture 1	Tiles a selection of windows	Tiles a selection of windows	

Figure 3.72   Toolbar definition table

Tool_ID can be a zero, which indicates a gap (much like a "-" indicates a separator on a menu), a tool number associated with a built-in tool, or a number between 200 and 231, which is the range of numbers reserved for custom tools. If you are going to be using your own tool face (either by drawing your own or using one of the custom faces that come with Microsoft Excel), you can use a Tool_ID for one of the built-in tool faces. In this case, since we will be using a custom tool face (as indicated by "Picture 1" in cell J3, the fact that we're using a Tool_ID of "1"—which represents the File Open tool—won't matter. In other words, if you're going to use a custom tool face you can repeatedly use a Tool_ID of "1" and everything will work fine.

Note   For a listing of tool faces and the associated Tool_IDs, see "Standard Toolbar Tools" in the *Microsoft Excel User's Guide 2*.

Macro contains the name of the macro you want to run when the tool is clicked. In this example the name of the macro sheet has been included so that Microsoft Excel will load the macro sheet if the tool is clicked but the macro sheet is closed.

Down is either TRUE or FALSE and determines whether or not the tool appears "pushed in" on the toolbar. If Down is TRUE, the tool appears pushed in.

Enabled determines whether the tool can be used. If *enabled* is TRUE, the tool is enabled; if FALSE, it is disabled.

Face specifies a tool face associated with the tool. In our example we have entered a reference to the picture we want to appear as the tool face. Figure 3.73 shows the tool face that was copied into cell N3 of the macro sheet. When this image was copied, Microsoft Excel assigned it the name Picture 1.

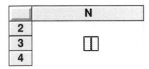

Figure 3.73   Picture 1

Help_text is the text that appears in the status bar when you click on the tool.

Balloon_text is the balloon help text associated with the tool. *Balloon_text* is available only in Microsoft Excel for the Macintosh using system software version 7.0 or later.

Help_topics is a reference to a topic in a Help file.

ADD.TOOL

You add a tool (as described by the toolbar definition table) using the ADD.TOOL command. The syntax for ADD.TOOL is

ADD.TOOL(*bar_id,position,tool_ref*)

Bar_id is either a number from 1 to 9 specifying one of the built-in toolbars, or the name of a built-in or custom toolbar. *Position* specifies the position within the toolbar. If position is omitted, the tool is added to the end of the toolbar. *Tool_ref* is either a Tool_ID specifying a built-in tool or a reference to the toolbar definition table.

To Add a Tool

1   Enter the macro shown in Figure 3.74.

B
30 AddSideBySideTool
31
32 =ADD.TOOL("Macro",,MoreMacroTools)
33 =RETURN()

Figure 3.74   AddSideBySideTool macro

2   Select cells B30:B33.

3   Click the Create Macro tool.

4   When the Define Name dialog box appears, click OK to assign the name AddSideBySideTool to cell B30.

5   Run the AddSideBySideTool macro. The Side by Side tool will be added at the end of the Macro toolbar.

How Do We Remove the Tool?

You use the DELETE.TOOL command to remove a tool from the toolbar, but to use this tool you need to know the name of the toolbar you want to change and the position number of the tool you want to remove. Unfortunately, the ADD.TOOL command does not return the position number when you add a new tool. To remove the Side by Side tool, we will need to use the COLUMNS and GET.TOOLBAR functions to determine the number of the last tool on the toolbar (the Side by Side tool). The syntax of GET.TOOLBAR is

See "GET.TOOLBAR"
in the Microsoft
Excel Function
Rreference.

GET.TOOLBAR(*type_num*,*bar_id*)

Type_num determines the type of information to return. A type_num of "1" returns a horizontal array of all tool IDs on the toolbar, ordered by position, including gaps. Thus

```
GET.TOOLBAR(1,"Macro")
```

will return an array with all the tool IDs in the Macro toolbar, so

```
COLUMNS(GET.TOOLBAR(1,"Macro"))
```

will return the number of items in the array, giving us the total number of tools. Thus if this nested function returns a value of "9," we know the tool we want to remove is tool "9" because the Side by Side tool is the last tool in the toolbar.

The macro that removes the Side by Side tool is shown in Figure 3.75.

	A	B	C
35		**DeleteSideBySideTool**	
36			
37	*macroToolCount*	=COLUMNS(GET.TOOLBAR(1,"Macro"))	*how many tools are on the Macro toolbar*
38		=DELETE.TOOL("Macro",macroToolCount)	*delete the last one*
39		=RETURN()	

Figure 3.75   DeleteSideBySideTool macro code

Before continuing   Type the macro shown in Figure 3.75 into your macro sheet and use the Create Macro ool to assign the names DeleteSideBySideTool to cell B35 and macroToolCount to cell B37.

Adding and Removing the Tool Automatically

The only thing we need to do is add Auto_Open and Auto_Close macros so that MORETOOL.XLM will add the Side by Side tool when the macro sheet is opened and remove the Side by Side tool when the macro sheet is closed.

To Add Auto_Open and Auto_Close Macros

1 Select cells A1:C10.

2 From the Edit menu, shoose Insert.

3 When the Insert dialog box appears, choose Shift Cells Down and click OK.

4 Enter the macros shown in Figure 3.76 and assign the name Auto_Open to cell B1 and the name Auto_Close to cell B6.

	A	B	C
1		**Auto_Open**	
2			
3		=AddSideBySideTool()	*Add the Side by Side tool to Macro toolbar*
4		=RETURN()	
5			
6		**Auto_Close**	
7			
8		=DeleteSideBySideTool()	*Remove Side By Side tool from Macro toolbar*
9		=RETURN()	

Figure 3.76   Auto_Open and Auto_Close macros

Lesson Summary

In this lesson we saw how to get information from the user with input boxes and custom dialog boxes, and how to write macros that act upon this information. We used the SET.VALUE function to initialize dialog boxes, and worked with dynamic and multi-selection dialog boxes. We also examined techniques for dealing with problematic dialog boxes and worked with several tools for creating macros and previewing dialog boxes.

We also examined how to add and remove menu commands, add and remove tools using macro statements and how to use Auto_Open and Auto_Close macros.

Preview of the Next Lesson

In the next lesson, you will create a collection of macros that replace the built-in data sort command with an enhanced, friendlier version.

Improving the Data Sort Command

In this section we will expand upon the skills learned in the previous section to build more comprehensive (and therefore more complex) macros. In working through this series of related exercises you will both extend and enhance the native sorting capabilities of Microsoft Excel, as well as learn many of the skills needed to develop a custom application.

As we mentioned in the introduction, you must be comfortable with Microsoft Excel as an end-user before you can develop macros and custom applications. Since this chapter deals with improving and extending the sorting features of Microsoft Excel, you should make sure you are comfortable with sorting before tackling these exercises.

This lesson explains how to do the following:

- Determine whether a named area exists on the worksheet
- Use the OFFSET function to select just the rows in a database
- Create a Custom Sort dialog box
- Make dynamic drop-down list boxes
- Replace the built-in Sort command with the custom Sort command

Note   At this point you should be comfortable with the basics of entering macro statements into a macro sheet, naming macros, running macros, and so on. We will therefore be less explicit about the steps needed to perform these basic functions.

Improving Basic Sorting

Problem: Even though I have used the Set Database command to define a Database area on my worksheet, I still have to highlight all of the records in the database to sort them.

Solution: Replace the built-in command with a macro that sorts the records of the Database area if the name "Database" is defined on the sheet.

Open the file SMALBASE.XLS. Using the Formula Define Name command, notice that the range called DATABASE refers to cells $A$4:$G$8. However, when you sort the database, you should only select the rows of data records without columns headings, that is $A$5:$G$8, as shown in Figure 4.1.

LastName	FirstName	Company	Address	City	State	Zip
Weber	Jon	World Wide Importers	555 Fifth Avenue	New York	NY	10019
Miller	Barbara	West Coast Sales	322 Bryant Avenue	Menlo Park	CA	90543
Keefe	John	Keefe & Associates	1010 Main Street	Fairbanks	AK	70123
Eltron	Louise	Parnell Aerospace	500 Wallace Lane	Princeton	OH	33123

"Database" refers to these cells...

LastName	FirstName	Company	Address	City	State	Zip
Weber	Jon	World Wide Importers	555 Fifth Avenue	New York	NY	10019
Miller	Barbara	West Coast Sales	322 Bryant Avenue	Menlo Park	CA	90543
Keefe	John	Keefe & Associates	1010 Main Street	Fairbanks	AK	70123
Eltron	Louise	Parnell Aerospace	500 Wallace Lane	Princeton	OH	33123

...but when you sort, you should select these cells.

Figure 4.1   Database area vs. Sort area

How a Smarter Data Sort Should Work

The completed solution, as well as the intermediary steps, can be found in SMRTSORT.XLM.

When you choose Data Sort, Microsoft Excel should first determine whether or not the area Database has been defined on the active worksheet. If it's not defined, Microsoft Excel should display the standard Sort dialog box. If the area *is* defined, Microsoft Excel should select only the records from the Database and *then* display the Sort dialog box. So, our plan of attack will be as shown in Figure 4.2.

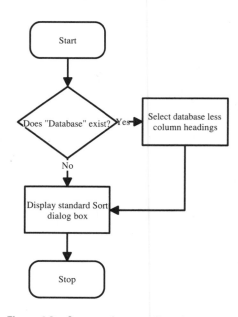

Figure 4.2   Smarter data sort flowchart

Before continuing   Create a new macro sheet and enter the SmartDataSort macro shown in Figure 4.3.

	SmartDataSort	
NameIndex	=MATCH("Database",NAMES(),0)	returns #NA if name not in list
	=IF(ISNUMBER(NameIndex))	Database defined on worksheet
	= SELECT(OFFSET(!Database,1,0,ROWS(!Database)-1,))	first data row through last data row
	=END.IF()	
	=SORT?()	bring up Excel's sort dialog
	=RETURN()	

Figure 4.3   SmartDataSort macro

How the Macro Works

We can see if the name "Database" exists on the active sheet by calling the NAMES function to obtain a list of the names defined on the sheet and using the MATCH function to search for "Database" within that list. The function

```
=MATCH("Database",NAMES(),0)
```

combines these two functions into one macro formula. The third argument to the MATCH function specifies which of several kinds of matches we are interested in, with a zero meaning an exact match. If there is a match, the result will be the number of the matching item; if not, MATCH returns #NA.

We want one of two things to happen, depending on the value returned by MATCH. If it is #NA, then there is no Database, so we should call up the standard sort dialog box. If the result is a number (meaning "Database" exists), we select the records of the database first.

Selecting the Data Records

If we've determined that the Database exists, we can find the cells we want to sort using the OFFSET function. We know that the database records are in the second through the last rows of the Database range. In this case, the cell range we are interested in calculating begins one row and zero columns from the top of the Database, has one row fewer than the Database area itself, and has the same number of columns as the Database. This translates to the function

```
OFFSET(!Database,1,0,ROWS(!Database)-1,)
```

Since we have omitted the last argument to OFFSET, the resulting range will have the same width as Database.

where the starting reference argument !Database means "the Database range on the active sheet." Because what we want to do is select this range, we enter the whole thing as an argument to the SELECT function, resulting in the formula

```
=SELECT(OFFSET(!Database,1,0,ROWS(!Database)-1,))
```

Sorting the Selection

At this point, the cells to be sorted have been selected, either by the macro, or by the user if no Database range exists. All that remains is to call SORT?, the macro command that calls up the Microsoft Excel sort dialog box.

Fielding Error Conditions

Problem: If I select a noncontiguous range on a worksheet that has no Database defined, I get a macro error message in addition to the normal message warning me about the multiple selection.

Solution: Before displaying the Data Sort dialog box, determine if the current cell selection is noncontiguous and if so, display an error message to the user instead.

Modify the SmartDataSort macro so it looks like the one shown in Figure 4.4.

	SmartDataSort	
		checks for multiple selection error
NameIndex	=MATCH("Database",NAMES(),0)	*returns #NA if name not in list*
	=IF(ISNUMBER(NameIndex))	*Database defined on worksheet*
	= SELECT(OFFSET(!Database,1,0,ROWS(!Database)-1,))	*first record row through last data row*
	=END.IF()	
	=IF(AREAS(SELECTION())=1)	*Cell selection is contiguous*
	= SORT?()	*bring up Excel's sort dialog*
	=ELSE()	
	= ALERT("Cannot do that command on a multiple selection.",3)	*Display the same message Excel does.*
	=END.IF()	
	=RETURN()	

Figure 4.4   SmartDataSort macro that tests for noncontiguous selection

How the Macro Works

We determine if the current selection can be sorted with the statement

```
=IF(AREAS(SELECTION())=1)
```

We used the AREAS function in the PrintSelection macro on page 39.

If only one area is selected, then we sort it as before. Otherwise, we use the ALERT function to display the same message Microsoft Excel does in this circumstance.

Sorting Other Ranges

Problem: If a Database is defined on my worksheet, the SmartDataSort doesn't allow me to sort anything but the records in the Database. I'm thinking of renaming this macro "StupidDataSort."

Solution: Change SmartDataSort so that it gives you a choice of sorting your current selection or the Database if you run the macro with a group of cells selected.

Ideally, macro customization should enhance the product, not limit its usefulness. In this case, we want the Data Sort command to work more intelligently with the Database defined on the sheet without sacrificing the flexibility of the built-in version. Here, then, is our revised plan of attack:

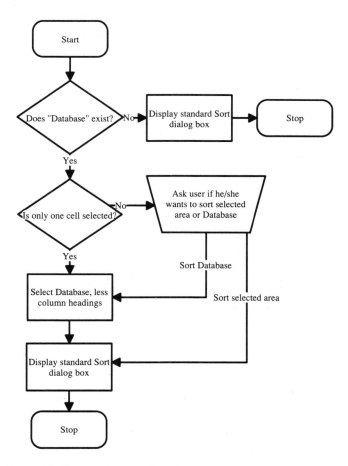

Figure 4.5 Smarter data sort flowchart

Before continuing   Modify the SmartDataSort macro so that it looks like the one shown in Figure 4.6.

	SmartDataSort	
		lets user sort selection if Database exists
NameIndex	=MATCH("Database",NAMES(),0)	*returns #NA if name not in list*
	=IF(ISNUMBER(NameIndex))	*Database defined on worksheet*
SelectionSize	= IF(AREAS(SELECTION())>1,2,ROWS(SELECTION())*COLUMNS(SELECTION()))	
	= IF(SelectionSize=1)	*just a single cell selected*
	= SELECT(OFFSET(!Database,1,0,ROWS(!Database)-1,))	*only highlighting one cell; use Database*
	= ELSE()	*ask if user wants to sort database*
UseDatabase	= ALERT("Sort Database records?",1)	
	= IF(UseDatabase)	
	= SELECT(OFFSET(!Database,1,0,ROWS(!Database)-1,))	*select Database*
	= END.IF()	
	= END.IF()	
	=END.IF()	
	=IF(AREAS(SELECTION())=1)	*Cell selection is contiguous*
	= SORT?()	*bring up Excel's sort dialog*
	=ELSE()	
	= ALERT("Cannot do that command on a multiple selection.",3)	*Display the same message Excel does.*
	=END.IF()	
	=RETURN()	

Figure 4.6   SmartDataSort macro that permits other sorts

Because the change to this version is designed to allow users who have set the Database to sort some other range, all of the new code is contained between the IF function that checks for the existence of the Database and its END.IF companion.

Letting the User Decide

First, we determine the total number of cells selected by multiplying the number of rows in the current selection by the number of columns in the current selection. If the user selected a single cell, the macro selects the data records as before. Otherwise, the user must have selected an area of cells and may want to sort it instead of the Database. To get the user's choice we call the function

```
=ALERT("Sort Database records?",1)
```

in the cell named UseDatabase, which in Microsoft Excel for Windows displays the dialog box shown in Figure 4.7...

Figure 4.7   SmartDataSort Alert (Windows)

... and in Microsoft Excel for the Macintosh, displays the dialog box shown in Figure 4.8.

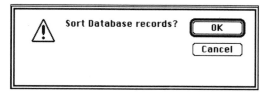

Figure 4.8   SmartDataSort Alert (Macintosh)

This function returns TRUE if the user clicks the OK button, so we can use this as the condition for another IF function. In this case, if the user clicks OK, we select the Database records. Clicking Cancel allows the user to sort the selected range.

Shouldn't We Use a Dialog Box Instead of an Alert Box?

Yes. We're being lazy and breaking standard interface guidelines a little here by using the OK and Cancel buttons of the ALERT dialog as though they were Yes and No buttons. If the user clicks Cancel, the macro will not halt as might be expected; it will assume that the user wants to sort the highlighted range and bring up the Sort dialog box (from which the Cancel button behaves normally). Our macro's user interface would be more intuitive if we allowed the user to select from a custom dialog box like the one shown in Figure 4.9:

Figure 4.9   SmartDataSort alternative to Alert box

We'll stick with the ALERT function for now, but you should find this dialog box simple enough to create yourself using the techniques discussed in the previous lesson.

Making the Sort Dialog Friendlier

Problem: The standard Sort Dialog box is bewildering. I understand sorting by fields, not by cell addresses.

Solution: If SmartDataSort is sorting the records from the Database range, display the field names in a scrolling list and translate the user's field choices into the proper SORT arguments.

Our mission here involves two separate challenges:

- Creating a smart dialog box that displays the field names from the database.
- Using the responses entered into the dialog box to create a corresponding SORT command.

Designing the Smart Sort Dialog

Because we want to duplicate the capabilities of the standard Sort dialog box, we will need to provide the capability of selecting up to three field names from the database as key fields, and of choosing the direction of the sort on each of those keys, as in the dialog boxes shown in Figures 4.10 and 4.11.

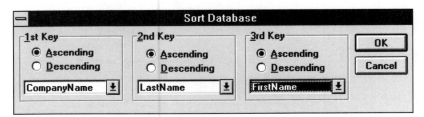

Figure 4.10 Custom Sort dialog box (Windows)

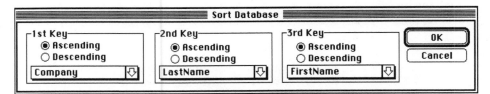

Figure 4.11 Custom Sort dialog box (Macintosh)

On your own, use the Dialog Editor to create the applicable dialog box shown above. If you run into problems, see "Dialog Box Trouble Shooting" on page 116.

Making a Dynamic Drop-down List Box

The challenge now is in displaying the list of field names from the Database of the active sheet. As with many of the macros in this book, the OFFSET function does the hard work for us.

Listing the Database Fields

All three of the drop-down list boxes in the dialog box in Figure 4.10 should point to a list that contains the field names from the Database. If this were simply a static list, we would create it on the macro sheet, name it and enter the name into the Text column for each drop-down list box in the dialog range, as shown in Figure 4.12:

SmartSortDialog

					Sort Database		1
1	568	10	88		OK		
2	568	38	88		Cancel	**Static list on sheet**	
14	10	6	173	84	&1st Key		
11							1
12	29	22			&Ascending		
12					&Descending		
21	16	63	160	54	**FieldList**		1
14	198	6	173	84	&2nd Key		
11							1
12	220	26			&Ascending		
12					&Descending		
21	205	63	160	54	**FieldList**		#N/A
14	385	6	173	84	&3rd Key		
11							1
12	404	26			&Ascending		
12					&Descending		
21	392	63	160	54	**FieldList**		#N/A

Figure 4.12   First try at SmartSort dialog box definition table

However, we want to build a dialog box that works with any database, that is, one that populates the list box with any database's field names. The OFFSET function can return an array, so it seems logical that one could replace each of the FieldList entries with an OFFSET formula describing the first row of the Database, as follows:

```
=OFFSET(!Database,0,0,1,COLUMNS(!Database))
```

If you try this, though, the drop-down list boxes in the dialog box will be empty. The reason: entries in the Text column have to be text. Fortunately, Microsoft Excel gives special treatment to formulas that return arrays and have been entered into the Text column as text, that is, without the equal sign. The dialog definition shown in Figure 4.13 will display the field names from the Database of the active sheet:

SmartSortDialog						Sort Database		1
	1	568	10	88		OK		
	2	568	38	88		Cancel	Array-returning formula entered as text	
	14	10	6	173	84	&1st Key		
	11							1
	12	29	22			&Ascending		
	12					&Descending		
	21	16	63	160	54	OFFSET(!Database,0,0,1,COLUMNS(!Database))		1
	14	198	6	173	84	&2nd Key		
	11							1
	12	220	26			&Ascending		
	12					&Descending		
	21	205	63	160	54	OFFSET(!Database,0,0,1,COLUMNS(!Database))		#N/A
	14	385	6	173	84	&3rd Key		
	11							1
	12	404	26			&Ascending		
	12					&Descending		
	21	392	63	160	54	OFFSET(!Database,0,0,1,COLUMNS(!Database))		#N/A

Figure 4.13   A more flexible SmartSort dialog box definition table

If you examine the OFFSET formulas in this definition, you may notice that we are explicitly calculating the value of the fourth argument (number of columns) that would be the default value if we omitted the argument altogether, as shown below:

```
=OFFSET(!Database,0,0,1,)
```

If the formula is entered as text in the Text column of a dialog definition (as is the case here), you must specify the number of columns (and number of rows) yourself.

Using the Dialog

We're now ready to tackle translating the SmartSortDialog responses into valid SORT arguments. We'll be using the Init/Result values in SmartSortDialog's definition area for the three sets of option buttons and all three drop-down list boxes, so let's name them. Figure 4.14 shows the completed dialog definition area with labels to the right of each named Init/Result cell.

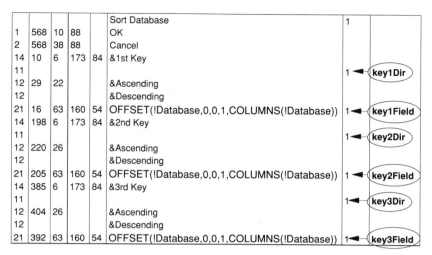

1	568	10	88		Sort Database	1	
1	568	10	88		OK		
2	568	38	88		Cancel		
14	10	6	173	84	&1st Key		
11						1	key1Dir
12	29	22			&Ascending		
12					&Descending		
21	16	63	160	54	OFFSET(!Database,0,0,1,COLUMNS(!Database))	1	key1Field
14	198	6	173	84	&2nd Key		
11						1	key2Dir
12	220	26			&Ascending		
12					&Descending		
21	205	63	160	54	OFFSET(!Database,0,0,1,COLUMNS(!Database))	1	key2Field
14	385	6	173	84	&3rd Key		
11						1	key3Dir
12	404	26			&Ascending		
12					&Descending		
21	392	63	160	54	OFFSET(!Database,0,0,1,COLUMNS(!Database))	1	key3Field

Figure 4.14   SmartSort dialog box definition table with named cells

Using the SORT Function

Let's take a moment to examine the SORT function, and how it relates to the standard dialog box. The complete syntax of the SORT function is:

SORT(*sort_by,key1,order1*,*key2,order2,key3,order3*)

which bears a close correspondence to the SORT dialog box:

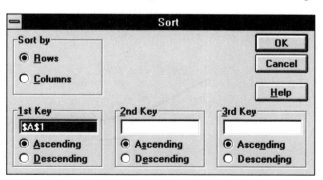

Figure 4.15   Sort dialog box

When we are sorting records from the Database area of the sheet, we will only be interested in sorting the rows of the database, not columns, so we can assume that the *sort_by* argument will always be 1.

For each of the key fields, we will need to translate the user's choice of field names to a corresponding cell address. If, for example, the user has chosen the second field in the list as the first sort key, our *key_1* argument should be the address of some cell in the second column of the database. Looks like a job for OFFSET.

The field names will be listed in the drop-down list boxes in the order in which they appear in the Database. The item chosen by the user will be returned as a number in the Init/Result column of the dialog definition for each drop-down list box, with the item numbers starting at 1. We can subtract one from this number and use the result as the second argument to the OFFSET function. The following formula would therefore return the address of the cell containing the field name chosen by the user as the primary sort key:

```
=OFFSET(!Database,0,key1Field-1,1,1)
```

and the complete function to sort the database on that field in the order specified by the user would be

```
=SORT(1,OFFSET(!Database,0,key1Field-1,1,1),key1Dir)
```

Handling the Optional Sort Arguments

So far, the translation of custom sort options to real sort options has been a fairly straightforward one. The tricky part is in handling the second and third sort keys and directions, which may or may not be specified by the user. If the user chooses not to use the optional arguments, then the SORT function we call should omit them. Unfortunately, because there is no way in which to calculate an *omitted* argument, the only way we can handle this is with the following strategy:

- If the user has chosen only one field to sort by, call the SORT function with only three arguments.

- If the user selected two fields to sort by, call the SORT function with five arguments.

- Otherwise, call the SORT function with all arguments.

We can initialize the second and third drop-down list boxes in SmartSortDialog with #NA values to cause Microsoft Excel to display no selected item. If the user makes no selection from these boxes, they will still contain this #NA error value. So we can check the contents of the key2Field and key3Field cells to determine which SORT function to run, as shown in Figure 4.16 in the SortDataRecords subroutine.

	SortDataRecords
sortResponse	=SET.VALUE(key1Field,1) =SET.VALUE(key2Field,NA()) =SET.VALUE(key3Field,NA()) =SET.VALUE(key1Dir,1) =SET.VALUE(key2Dir,1) =SET.VALUE(key3Dir,1) =DIALOG.BOX(SmartSortDialog) =IF(sortResponse<>FALSE) = SELECT(OFFSET(!Database,1,0,ROWS(!Database)-1,)) = IF(ISNA(key2Field)) = SORT(1,OFFSET(!Database,0,key1Field-1,1,1),key1Dir) = ELSE.IF(ISNA(key3Field)) = SORT(1,OFFSET(!Database,0,key1Field-1,1,1),key1Dir,OFFSET(!Database,0,key2Field-1,1,1),key2Dir) = ELSE() = SORT(1,OFFSET(!Database,0,key1Field-1,1,1),key1Dir,OFFSET(!Database,0,key2Field-1,1,1),key2Dir,OFFSET(!Database,0,key3Field-1,1,1),key3Dir) = END.IF() =END.IF() =RETURN()

Figure 4.16 SortDataRecords subroutine

Notice we have packaged the whole routine as a subroutine, which removes the detail of sorting the records of the sheet's Database from the more general-purpose SmartDataSort. Likewise, it makes sense to isolate the part of our original code which sorts the current selection (after insuring that it is contiguous) in another subroutine, as shown in Figure 4.17.

	SortSelection	
	=IF(AREAS(SELECTION())=1) = SORT?() =ELSE() = ALERT("Cannot do that command on a multiple selection.",3) =END.IF() =RETURN()	*Cell selection is contiguous* *bring up Excel's sort dialog* *Display the same message Excel does.*

Figure 4.17 SortSelection subroutine

These changes leave our final version of SmartDataSort clear and uncluttered, as shown in Figure 4.18.

	SmartDataSort	
NameIndex	=MATCH("Database",NAMES(),0) =IF(ISNUMBER(NameIndex))	returns #NA if name not in list Database defined on worksheet
SelectionSize	= IF(AREAS(SELECTION())>1,2,ROWS(SELECTION())*COLUMNS(SELECTION()))	
	= IF(SelectionSize=1)	just a single cell selected
	= SortDataRecords()	only highlighting one cell; use Database
	= ELSE()	let user choose database or selection
UseDatabase	= ALERT("Sort Database records?",1)	
	= IF(UseDatabase<>FALSE)	
	= SortDataRecords()	
	= ELSE()	
	= SortSelection()	
	= END.IF()	
	= END.IF()	
	=ELSE()	no Database – sort current selection
	= SortSelection()	
	=END.IF()	
	=RETURN()	

Figure 4.18   SmartDataSort macro code

There's Still Something Missing

What limits the usefulness of SmartDataSort and the other routines we have developed in this chapter is that users have to choose the extended versions, and *know they are there to choose*. If we want to truly extend the functionality of the built-in Data Sort command, for example, we must direct Microsoft Excel to run our SmartDataSort instead of the built-in command when the user selects Sort from the Data menu.

Let's replace the built-in Data Sort command with our custom version.

Replacing the Built-in Sort Command

Figure 4.19 shows the command table for the SmartDataSort macro.

SmartSortMenu	&Sort...	SmartDataSort	Sort selected cells or Database

Figure 4.19   SmartSortMenu command table

In the previous lesson we looked at adding commands and removing commands. In this example we want add a new version of "Sort..." and remove the built-in of Sort. The macro that accomplishes this is shown in Figure 4.20.

	Auto_Open
sortCommand	=ADD.COMMAND(1,"Data",SmartSortMenu,"Sort...") =DELETE.COMMAND(1,"Data",sortCommand+1) =RETURN()

Figure 4.20   In with the new, out with the old

The line

```
=ADD.COMMAND(1,"Data",SmartSortMenu,"Sort...")
```

inserts the new Sort command defined in the area named SmartSortMenu onto the Data menu located on the worksheet and macro sheet menu bars. By specifying "Sort..." as the position, we instruct Microsoft Excel to place the new command just before the built-in Sort command. The ADD.COMMAND function also returns the position number of the new command. We take advantage of this position number with the statement

```
=DELETE.COMMAND(1,"DATA",sortCommand+1)
```

which removes the built-in command by adding one to the value in the cell named sortCommand and specifying that as the argument of the command to delete.

A Preview of Things to Come: Adding Menus to Menu Bars

While we will cover adding new menus and menus bars in detail in Lesson Six, here's a quick preview of how you go about adding new menus.

Adding a complete menu is a relatively simple extension of the ADD.COMMAND and DELETE.COMMAND discussed in Lesson Three. The macro function for adding menus is ADD.MENU, the complete syntax of which is as follows:

ADD.MENU(*bar_num,command_ref,position*)

If you must specify the position as a number, be aware that the Restore menu occupies menu position 1 when Microsoft Excel windows are maximized.

The optional *position* argument is treated like that of the ADD.COMMAND function. In this case the argument may be the name of an existing menu on the bar specified by bar_num, or it may be the position at which the new menu is to be inserted, with the menus numbered left to right starting with the first menu on the bar at number 1. If this argument is omitted, the new menu is inserted after the last menu of standard menu bars, or appended to the right end of custom menu bars.

In Figure 4.21, the name CustomMenu has been assigned to the menu definition for a menu named "Custom." Notice that the only difference between this menu definition and a multiple command definition is the menu name in the first cell of the range. Because no macro is associated with menu names, the remainder of this row is empty.

Microsoft Excel Macros Step by Step

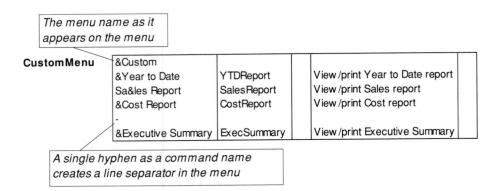

Figure 4.21   Menu definition sample

The code shown in Figure 4.22 adds this menu to the worksheet menu bar. By omitting the optional position argument, we instruct Microsoft Excel to append the new menu after the last menu and just before the Help menu.

```
=ADD.MENU(1,CustomMenu)
=RETURN()
```

Figure 4.22   Add CustomMenu to worksheet menu bar

Lesson Summary

In this session we tackled the more comprehensive problem of improving the sorting capabilities in Microsoft Excel. We used the MATCH and NAMES functions to determine whether the named area "Database" exists on the current worksheet. We used the OFFSET function to select only the rows of the database. Finally, we created a custom sort dialog box with dynamic drop-down menus that show field names instead of cell references, and replaced the built-in sort command with this enhanced version.

Preview of the Next Lesson

In the next lesson you will learn how to install and use the Client Tracking System sample application.

A Sample Application

In the preceding lessons, we have developed several useful extensions to Microsoft Excel user and macro environments. Throughout the lessons that follow, we will create macros in the context of building a custom application. The complete code to this application, a Client Tracking System, is on the accompanying disk.

In this lesson, we'll examine how the Client Tracking System works by actually installing and using it. As you will see, a thorough discussion of each component would be impractical for a book of this sort. We will instead concentrate in the following lessons on those portions that best illustrate the challenges you are likely to encounter in other Microsoft Excel development projects.

The Client Tracking System

The Client Tracking application manages client lists, generates invoices, and tracks invoices using several reports generated with the Microsoft Excel Crosstab utility. The system consists of the following modules:

- Client mail list with customized data entry forms and simplified access to the sorting, searching and extraction capabilities of Microsoft Excel.

- Invoice generator which pulls address information from the client database.

- Tracking System database for storage and analysis of invoice information, including crosstabs and graphics.

 - Communication between Word for Windows and Microsoft Excel to retrieve client addresses for correspondence.

Components of the Client Tracking System

FINISHED is a directory within TRACKING.

The Client Tracking System can be found in the TRACKING and FINISHED directories and is composed of the following files:

- TRACKING.XLA
- TRACKING.XLS
- MAILLIST.XLS
- INVOICE.XLS
- YTD.XLS
- CATEGORY.XLS
- OUTSTAND.XLS
- EXEC.XLA
- EXEC.XLS
- LETTER.DOT (Word for Windows template)

Where to Place the Client Tracking System Files

All files in the TRACKING and FINISHED directories except for LETTER.DOT should be placed together in a single directory of your choosing. The LETTER.DOT template should be copied to the directory that contains your other Word for Windows templates.

Loading the Client Tracking System

You can load the Client Tracking System by starting Microsoft Excel and opening the file TRACKING.XLA. This Add-In opens the following supporting files when it is loaded:

File Name	Description
MAILLIST.XLS	Worksheet on which the Client Mail List is stored
TRACKING.XLS	Worksheet on which invoice data are stored and from which reports are generated
INVOICE.XLS	A hidden worksheet from which invoices are printed and on which unprinted invoices are temporarily stored
YTD.XLS	Year-to-date report of data from the tracking database summarized by month
CATEGORY.XLS	Quarterly breakdown of tracking data summarized by category of items invoiced
OUTSTAND.XLS	Report of invoices in the tracking database that have not been paid

Windows users may want to add an icon to the Program Manager that opens this file automatically when double-clicked.

Working with the Client Tracking System's Menus

The commands for the Client List, Invoice generator and Analysis modules of the Client Tracking System are all available from a single Tracking menu that is appended to the Microsoft Excel menu bar when the TRACKING.XLA Add-In is loaded. The choice of commands available from this menu changes depending on which file is active, so that the commands that are applicable to the current worksheet appear first on the menu. If, for example, MAILLIST.XLS is the active worksheet, the commands for maintaining the Client list are listed first.

To avoid cluttering the rest of the menu with commands for the other modules, a single command for each of the other modules appears below the commands relevant to the current worksheet. If, for example, MAILLIST.XLS is *not* the active worksheet, the commands for maintaining the Client list are available from a single Client List command. When you choose this command, the commands that would appear first on the Tracking menu with MAILLIST.XLS active appear as pushbuttons in a dialog box. The commands for the Invoice module are always accessed in this way, because there is no worksheet for this module with which the user interacts.

This design results in three different versions of the Tracking menu—one that appears when MAILLIST.XLS is active, another that appears when TRACKING.XLS is active, and a third that appears when neither of these sheets is active.

The Client Mail List

Central to the Client Tracking application is the Client Mail List, stored on a Microsoft Excel worksheet. You enter and edit client records with a custom data form. When the Client Mail List is the active worksheet, a custom menu with options for sorting, selecting, extracting and exporting client data appears. This menu also includes options for accessing the other modules of the Client Tracking System.

The Client Mail List database contains the following fields:

Field Name	Description
LastName	
FirstName	
Title	Personal title such as Mr., Ms. and so forth
Position	Name of Client's position within company
CompanyName	
Address1	First line of Client's address
Address2	Second line of Client's address
City	
State	
Zip	
Phone	
Fax	
Category	Reference for grouping entries, such as PROSPECT, PERSONAL, FORMER, and so forth
ID	Unique client ID number to facilitate relationship between this and other databases

The Client ID provides the link between the Client Mail List, invoicing and tracking modules of the system, to avoid storing redundant client data. The diagram in Figure 5.1 illustrates the use of the Client ID field.

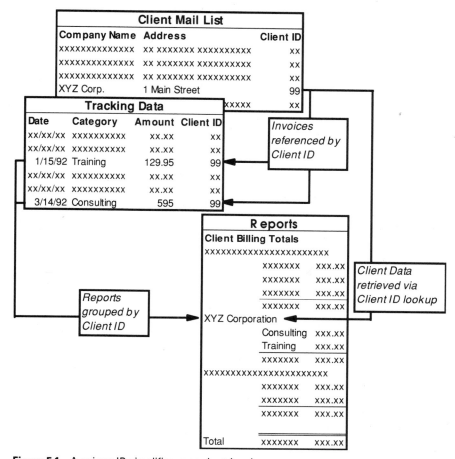

Figure 5.1   A unique ID simplifies record retrieval

Adding and Editing Client Records

The easiest way to add new records to the database is to use the custom entry form that is accessed by choosing Add from the Tracking menu. For this next example, let's suppose we want to add the name Peter McIntyre to the database.

To Add Client Records

 1 From the Tracking menu, choose Add Client. A dialog box like the one shown in Figure 5.2 will appear.

 1 From the Tracking menu, choose Add/Edit/Delete. A dialog box like the one shown in Figure 5.2 will appear.

*Macintosh users will
need to click New if
the entry form is not
empty. In the
Windows version we
are using a
SEND.KEYS
statement to force a
new record. The
SEND.KEYS
command is not
available in
Microsoft Excel for
the Macintosh.*

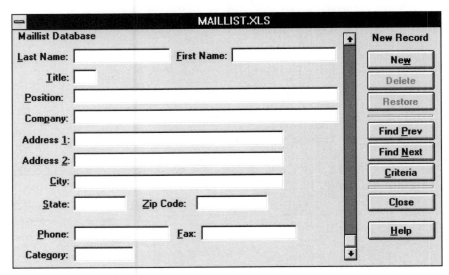

Figure 5.2   Sample entry form for Client Mail List

2   Type **McIntyre** and press the TAB key to move to the next field. Do *not* press the
ENTER key; pressing ENTER will add the incomplete record to the database.

3   Type **Peter** and press the TAB key.

4   Continue to fill in the entry form as shown in Figure 5.3.

*Notice the Zip Code
entry. The entry form
has trouble with
leading zeros, so if
your zip codes start
with a zero, begin the
zip code with an
apostrophe to force
Microsoft Excel to
accept the zip code
as literal text.*

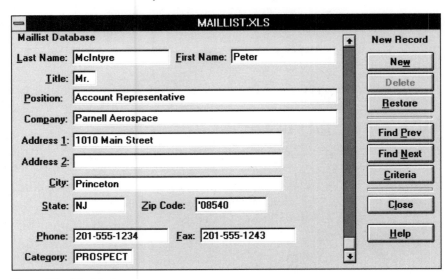

Figure 5.3   Filled-in form

5   When you have finished, either choose the New button or press the ENTER key.
The record will be inserted into the database and a blank entry form will appear.

After you have completed the form for your last record, choose the Close button to enter it into the database and dismiss the data form. If you forget and choose the New button instead, you can dismiss the data form without entering a new record by pressing the ESC key.

To Edit Records

1 From the Tracking menu, choose Edit/Delete (Add/Edit/Delete on the Macintosh). A dialog box like the one shown in Figure 5.4 will appear.

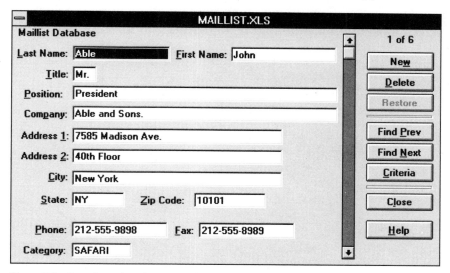

Figure 5.4   Data form that represents information already in the database

2 Use the scroll arrows to move to the record you want to edit.

3 Use the TAB key to move to the field you want to edit.

4 Edit the field as needed.

5 Scroll to the next record you need to edit, or choose the Close button.

To Delete Records

1 From the Tracking menu, choose Edit/Delete (Add/Edit/Delete on the Macintosh).

2 When the entry form appears, scroll to the record you want to delete.

3 Choose the Delete button. The dialog box shown in Figure 5.5 will appear:

Microsoft Excel Macros Step by Step

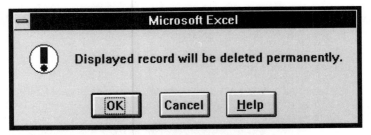

Figure 5.5 No kidding. You cannot undo a record deletion.

4 Choose the OK button.

5 Scroll to the next record you want to delete or edit, or choose the Close button.

Saving Your Work

The Client Tracking System does not automatically save MAILLIST.XLS when you make changes, so you should save the sheet after every significant change.

Sorting

The Tracking menu contains a command for sorting the database on up to three different fields.

For the next example, let's suppose you want to sort the database by last name in ascending order.

To Sort on One Key

1 From the Tracking menu, choose Sort. The dialog box shown in Figure 5.6 will appear:

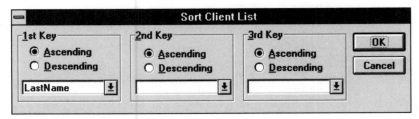

Figure 5.6 The custom Sort dialog box

2 By default, the system is set up to sort the database by last name in ascending order, so choose the OK button.

Sorting on Multiple Keys

From time to time you may find it necessary to sort on more than one key. If, for example, there were four clients with the last name "Smith" in your database, you would probably want Adam Smith to come before Zelda Smith. In this case you would specify LastName as the first key and FirstName as the second key, sorting both fields in Ascending order.

For this next example, let's suppose you want to organize the client records by State, with multiple records for each state sorted by CompanyName, and with multiple records for each company sorted by LastName.

To Sort on Multiple Keys

1 From the Tracking menu, choose Sort.

2 In the 1st key field box, select State.

3 Complete the dialog as shown in Figure 5.7.

Figure 5.7   Completed Sort dialog box

4 Click OK.

Finding Records

The Client Tracking System makes it very easy to find specific records based on simple criteria. For the next example, let's suppose we want to find all clients in New York State.

To Find Records

1 From the Tracking menu, choose Find. The dialog box shown in Figure 5.8 will appear:

Figure 5.8   Find Clients Records dialog box

2   In the field box, select the field you want to search, in this case State, as shown in Figure 5.9.

Figure 5.9   Completed dialog box

3   In the operator box, select =.

4   Type **NY** in the text box.

5   Choose the OK button.

Microsoft Excel will highlight the first record that matches your criteria and will remain in *Find Mode*, in which you can move to the other records that match by pressing the DOWN ARROW and UP ARROW keys, or by clicking the scroll arrows.

Note   To cancel Find Mode, press ESC.

Extracting Records

The Client Tracking System's Extract feature works just like Find except that it will copy all records that match your criteria to a separate Extract range on the sheet instead of just highlighting the records.

For the next example, let's suppose you want to extract a list of clients in New York State.

To Extract Records

1   From the Tracking menu, select Extract.

2   Enter your selection criteria into the Extract Client Records dialog box. In this case, select State from the field box, = from the operator box, and type **NY** in the edit box.

3   Choose the OK button. Microsoft Excel will copy the records that match your criteria to the Extract range.

Microsoft Excel Owns Everything Beneath the Extract Range

As a general word of caution, don't place anything useful underneath the field names in the extract range as Microsoft Excel erases *everything* underneath the field names just prior to extracting records.

Exporting Records for Mail Merge

Although Word for Windows can merge information from a Microsoft Excel worksheet, the Client Tracking System exports records to a text file because Word for Windows can assimilate text files more easily, and because you may want to exchange Client List data with other applications that are more likely to read text files.

The *Export to Text File* command allows you to export:

- The entire database

- The records that you most recently extracted

- Whatever records are currently highlighted

For this next example, let's suppose you want to export all records to a text file.

To Export Records to a Text File

1 From the Tracking menu, choose Export to Text File. The dialog box shown in Figure 5.10 will appear.

Figure 5.10   Export dialog box

 2 Choose the source of the data you want to export, in this case, Entire Database. A dialog box similar to the one shown in Figure 5.11 will appear:

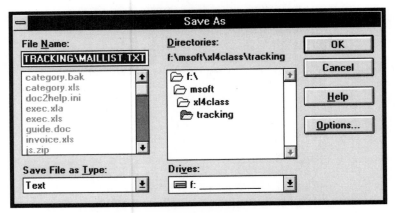

Figure 5.11   Save As dialog box (Windows)

 2   Choose the source of the data you want to export, in this case, Entire Database. A dialog box similar to the one shown in Figure 5.12 will appear:

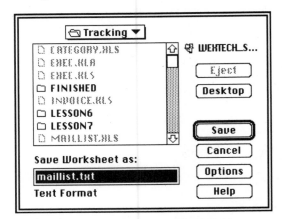

Figure 5.12   Save As dialog box (Macintosh)

3   The Client Tracking Sytem proposes the name MAILLIST.TXT for the new text file. If you want, you can enter a different name and directory.

4   Choose the OK button.

Writing Invoices

The Invoicing module consists of three commands for writing, printing and reprinting invoices. These commands are available from all three versions of the Tracking menu through a single Invoice command. When you choose this command, the dialog box shown in Figure 5.13 appears.

Figure 5.13   Invoice Options dialog box

The button labeled Print Invoice is available when there are invoices that have been written but not printed. At the time invoices are printed, the invoice information is transferred to the database in TRACKING.XLS, from which invoices may be reprinted (the Analysis module generates reports from this data, as well). The Reprint Invoice button on the Invoice Options dialog box is available when the Tracking database contains at least one record.

To Write Invoices

1   From the Tracking menu, choose Invoice.

2   From the Invoice Options dialog box which appears, choose the Write Invoice button. A dialog box similar to the one shown in Figure 5.14 will appear.

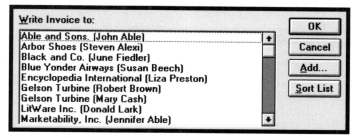

Figure 5.14   Write Invoice dialog box

3   Select the name of the client or clients that you wish to invoice. Selecting more than one client will produce multiple invoices with the same line items.

4   Choose the OK button. The Line Item dialog box will appear (see Figure 5.15).

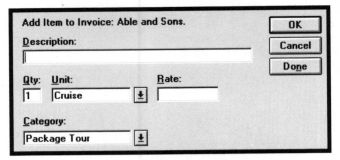

Figure 5.15

5   Type a description for the product and the quantity of products sold.

6   Type the name of the item or select one from the units box.

7   Type the item's category or select one from the category box.

8   Each of the units has a default price associated with it. If you want to override the default price or if you typed in a unit that is not listed, type the price in the Rate box.

9   Choose the OK button to enter this line item into the invoice and to display the Line Item dialog box for another entry.
– or –
Choose the Done button to enter this as the last line item in the invoice. The dialog box shown in Figure 5.16 will appear:

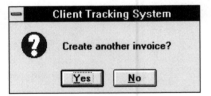

Figure 5.16   After the Done button

Choose the Yes button to repeat steps 3-9 for another invoice.
– or –
Choose the No button to end writing invoices. The dialog box shown in Figure 5.17 will appear:

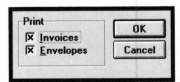

Figure 5.17   After the No button

10 Select Invoices to print all unprinted invoices and to transfer each invoice's line items to the Tracking database. Select Envelopes to print envelopes for the invoices. Choose the OK button.

– or –

Choose the Cancel button to defer printing until later.

Reprinting Invoices

All of the information that the invoicing module needs to reproduce an invoice is stored in the Tracking database after the invoice is printed (to produce a report listing the invoice numbers, Client names and invoice dates of all outstanding invoices, see "Producing Reports" later in this lesson).

To Reprint an Invoice

1 From the Tracking menu, choose Invoice.

2 From the Invoice Options dialog box, choose Write Invoice. A dialog box similar to the one shown in Figure 5.18 will appear:

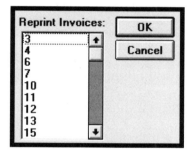

Figure 5.18 Reprint Invoices dialog box

3 Select the number(s) of the invoice(s) you want to reprint, and choose the OK button.

The selected invoices will be reprinted with their original invoice numbers but with the current date.

Producing Reports

The Client Tracking System includes the following custom reports:

Report Name	Description
Year-to-Date	Monthly totals of all invoice data in TRACKING.XLS
Category Breakdown	Quarterly totals of all invoice data broken down by item categories
Outstanding Invoices	List including invoice number, date sent, client name and invoice total for all invoices that have not been paid

To Produce the Reports (Method One)

1 Switch to TRACKING.XLS. From the Tracking menu, choose the report you want to produce. The report will be recalculated from the data in TRACKING.XLS, and will be displayed on your screen.

2 Close the report by clicking the Close Report button that is on the report worksheet.

To Produce the Reports (Method Two)

1 From the Tracking menu, choose Analysis. The dialog box shown in Figure 5.19 will appear:

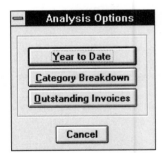

Figure 5.19   Analysis Options dialog box

2 Choose the report you want to produce.

3 Close the report by clicking the Close Report button that is on the report worksheet.

Using the Letter Template (Windows Only)

When the macros in the Letter template attempt to retrieve an address from the Client Mail List, they first look for a setting in the WIN.INI file to determine the location of the file MAILLIST.XLS. Before you use the Letter template for the first time, you need to create this setting.

To Tell the Letter Template Where the Client List Is

1   Switch to Word for Windows. From the Tools menu, choose Options.

2   In the Options dialog box, select Win.ini from the Category box. The area to the right of the Category box will change to resemble Figure 5.20.

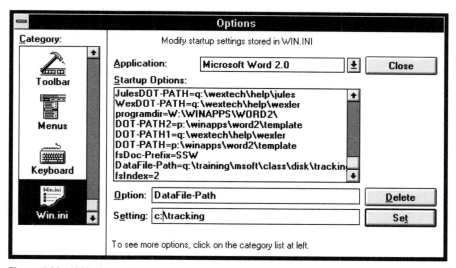

Figure 5.20   WIN.INI options

3   In the Option box, type **DataFile-Path**.

4   In the Setting box, type the directory into which you placed the Client Tracking System's worksheet and Add-In files.

5   Choose the Set button.

6   Choose the Close button.

Addressing Letters Automatically

For the next series of examples we will go through the steps needed to create a new letter and address it from the information stored in the Client Mail List.

Keep the Client Tracking System Open

The LETTER.DOT template is a modified version of the LETBLOCK.DOT template that ships with Word for Windows 2.0. The modification ties the template into the Client Tracking System so that you can address letters by choosing client names from the Client Mail List. If the Client Tracking System is closed, the letter template will open it but things will move a lot faster if you keep the Client Tracking System open.

To Create a New Letter

1   From the File menu, choose New.

2   In the Use Template box, type Letter or choose it from the template box. Choose the OK button. The dialog box shown in Figure 5.21 will appear.

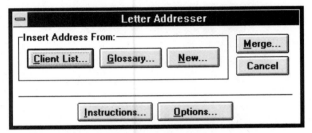

Figure 5.21   Letter Addresser dialog box

3   Word for Windows can retrieve an address from the Client Tracking System, or from a glossary entry contained within the template, or you can insert a new address. Choose the Client List button. The dialog box shown in Figure 5.22 will appear:

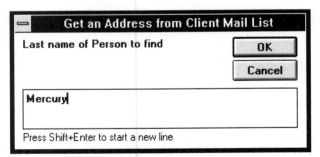

Figure 5.22   Get Address dialog box

4   Type the last name of the person to whom you want to send the letter. (For this example, we'll type **Mercury**.) Click OK.

5   If there is more than one "Mercury" in the database, you will be prompted to choose from a dialog box listing each matching record's full name and company name; otherwise, Word for Windows will insert the address.

> **Note**   For more information on using the LETTER template, consult the instructions for the LETBLOCK template in the *Microsoft Word User's Guide*.

Using the EIS Front Panel

The Analysis portion of the Client Tracking System is available as a separate Executive Information System (EIS) with dedicated menus and a main screen with macro buttons. In this version of the Client Tracking System, the EIS module does not recalculate reports dynamically, as does the analysis module of the larger Client Tracking System.

Loading the EIS Module

> **Before continuing**   Make sure you have exited the Client Tracking System before opening EXEC.XLA.

You can load the EIS module by starting Microsoft Excel and opening the file EXEC.XLA. This Add-In opens the following supporting files when it is loaded:

File Name	Description
EXEC.XLS	Main screen of the system, with major commands available through macro buttons
YTD.XLS	Year-to-date report of data from the tracking database summarized by month
CATEGORY.XLS	Quarterly breakdown of tracking data summarized by category of items invoiced
OUTSTAND.XLS	Report of invoices in the tracking database that have not been paid

Windows users may want to add an icon to the Program Manager that opens this file automatically when double-clicked.

Using the EIS Panel

At the time EXEC.XLA is loaded, it creates a custom File menu with a single Exit command. All of the remaining commands may be accessed through the system's main screen, which is shown in Figure 5.23.

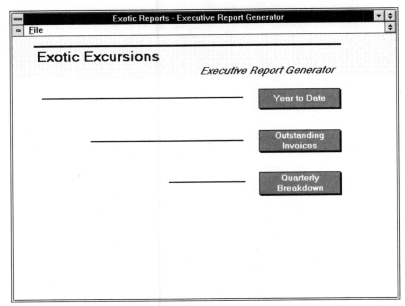

Figure 5.23   Microsoft Excel masquerading as "Executive Report Generator"

Each of the support documents of the system is assigned a custom window title, as is the Microsoft Excel application window. The ability to make Microsoft Excel look less like a spreadsheet program and more like a standalone application is an appealing feature for many users.

To Access the Reports

1   From the Executive Report Generator worksheet, click the name of the desired report. The report worksheet will be unhidden.

2   Close the report by clicking the Close Report button that is on the report worksheet.

To Exit the EIS

▶   From the File menu, choose Exit. All of the supporting files will be closed, the Microsoft Excel application title will be restored to its default, and menus, toolbars and other workspace settings will be restored to their states at the time the Add-In was loaded.

Customizing the Client Mail List: Adding Fields

Adding a new field to the database involves changing the Database range, the Criteria range, the Extract range, and the entry form. For the next example, let's suppose we want to add a field to handle Federal ID numbers.

Reserved Fields

To maintain compatibility with the Invoicing and Tracking modules as well as the LETTER.DOT template, the first 12 fields of the database must remain unchanged. Likewise, the Client ID field must remain in the last column of the database. The best location for new data fields is therefore between the Category and ID fields.

To Add a New Field to the Database Range

1   Adjust your screen so that you can see the last field of the database, in this case column O.

2   Select column O.

3   From the Edit menu, choose Insert to insert a new column.

4   In cell O1, type **FederalID** and press ENTER.

To Add a New Field to the Criteria and Extract Ranges

1   Adjust your screen so that column AE is visible.

2   Select column AE.

3   From the Edit menu choose Insert.

4   Copy cell O1 (the cell that has the new field name) to cells AE1 and AE6.

Updating the Custom Entry Form

The Client Tracking System uses a custom entry form to facilitate data entry. Like the Database and Extract ranges, the entry form must be adjusted to accommodate the new field.

To Update the Custom Data Form

1   Using the Go to command, select the area named Data_Form.

2   Copy the selected cells onto the Clipboard.

3   Run the Microsoft Excel Dialog Editor.

4   Paste the dialog box into the Dialog Editor.

5   Add a Text Item to act as a label for the new field.

6   Add an Edit Box for the new field.

7   Position the new items after the Category field.

8 Double-click the new edit box to display the Edit Text Info dialog box.

9 In the Init/Result box, type **FederalID**. Choose the OK button. This will associate the new edit box with the new field of the database.

10 Copy the dialog box onto the Clipboard and paste it into MAILLIST.XLS, overwriting the previous data form.

11 Using the Define Name command, assign the name Data_Form to the new dialog definition.

Customizing the Invoicing Module

Most features of the invoice module are generic, except for the design of the invoice itself and the default values that appear in the dialog box used to gather line item entries.

Customizing the Invoice

The invoice is printed from an area called Invoice_Area of the file INVOICE.XLS, a hidden worksheet that is opened during the execution of the TRACKING.XLA Auto_Open macro. When the invoice is printed, the macro calls the VIEW.SHOW function from the View Manager Add-In that ships with Microsoft Excel. This function resets the print settings and column widths to those defined in the view named Invoices. Likewise, the Envelopes view contains the settings for printing envelopes. To alter the layout of either invoices or envelopes, simply redefine the appropriate view.

Note   For more information on using the View Manager Add-In, see "Creating Different Views of a Worksheet" in Book 1 of the *Microsoft Excel User's Guide*.

Altering the Invoice Area

You can easily customize the appearance of the invoice itself by replacing Exotic Excursions' address at the bottom of the invoice area with another or with a graphic, such as a company logo. You might also change the title of the invoice or the general formatting such as fonts, borders and shading.

Line Items

Each of the invoice's two-line item descriptions is calculated in a pair of string formulas within the body of the invoice. The first line of the description contains the product description, as entered in the Description box in the Line Item dialog box. The second line of the description contains the quantity, unit and price expressed in English, for example, "3 Australian Outback Adventures at $4,000 each."

The formulas for the first invoice item description are shown in Figure 5.24.

```
=LineItem1 Description
=IF(LineItem1 ID,LineItem1 Qty&" "&LineItem1 Unit&IF(LineItem1 Qty>1,"s","")&" at $"&LineItem1 Rate&" each","")
```

Figure 5.24 Invoice line item formulas

Understanding the Line Item Formulas

The names LineItem1, Qty, Description, Unit and Rate point to areas within the range Extract.Detail, into which each invoice's line items are placed just prior to printing the invoice. Extract.Detail is shown in Figure 5.25.

	A	B	C	D	E	F	G	H
4		ID	Invoice #	Description	Category	Qty	Unit	Rate
5	LineItem1	103	7	Bahama Bash	Package Tour	1	Cruise	3,500.00
6	LineItem2							
7	LineItem3							
8	LineItem4							
9	LineItem5							
10	LineItem7							
11	LineItem7							

Figure 5.25 Extract.Detail: invoice items to be printed

This range contains seven rows, the maximum number of items per invoice. Because the line item detail is calculated from formulas that are in fixed locations within the invoice page, these formulas must produce a description for each line item that was used, and blank lines for the unused ones. If, for example, the invoice contains two line items, the third through seventh line item descriptions within the invoice should be blank.

The formulas shown in Figure 5.24 produce blank lines for unused line items in different ways. The first formula

```
=LineItem1 Description
```

points to the intersection of the row within Extract.Detail labeled LineItem1 and the column labeled Description. This returns the description text for the first line item or a zero if it is blank (realistically, only the second through seventh rows would ever be blank, but we've chosen to calculate all seven descriptions in the same way). To hide zero values, we've formatted each of the cells containing simple references such as these with the custom format "General;;".

The second of the line item description formulas is more complicated because it concatenates the values from three different fields of Extract.Detail with constant text. A custom format won't handle blank fields here, because the constant text precludes the possibility of the formula resulting in zero. What we do in this case is evaluate the ID field of Extract.Detail within an IF function. If this field is not zero, then the concatenated string will be the result; otherwise the result is an empty string.

The portion of the formula that combines the fields into an English phrase,

```
LineItem1 Qty&" "&LineItem1 Unit&IF(LineItem1 Qty>1,"s","")&" at
$"&LineItem1 Rate&" each"
```

looks daunting, but is mostly straightforward concatenation. The only complication is in the part that pluralizes the Unit when the quantity is greater than one:

```
LineItem1 Unit&IF(LineItem1 Qty>1,"s","")
```

Changing the Line Item Formulas

A business such as a law firm which bills in time units might prefer the second line of each description to be calculated as follows:

```
Lease Negotiation
16 Hours at $160 per Hour
```

Figure 5.26   A variation on the invoice format

This can be accomplished with the following formula:

```
=LineItem1 Description
=IF(LineItem1 ID,LineItem1 Qty&" "&LineItem1 Unit&IF(LineItem1 Qty>1,"s","")&" at $"&LineItem1 Rate&" per "&LineItem1 Unit,"")
```

Figure 5.27   Quantity at rate per unit

Saving Changes to the Invoice Sheet

INVOICE.XLS is not meant for display and should be protected from inadvertent changes by the user. When you have completed changes to the sheet, be sure to save it in a hidden state. A macro which simplifies saving hidden files is shown on page 50.

Customizing the Line Item Dialog

The lists of default categories and units and the prices for each default unit are stored in tables on TRACKING.XLA. You can easily change these defaults by replacing the contents of these tables with new values, and you can lengthen or shorten the lists by redefining the ranges on this sheet.

Default Categories

The list of categories displayed in the line item dialog are in the range categoryList on the TRACKING.XLA add-in.

To Customize Invoice Categories

1 Redefine the range categoryList on TRACKING.XLA so that it contains enough rows to accommodate the desired categories.

2 Enter the categories into the cells of the categoryList range.

3 Save TRACKING.XLA.

Default Units

The list of default units for each invoice item is defined in the first column of the range unitTable on TRACKING.XLA. The second column of the unitTable range contains the default prices for the units in the first column.

To Customize Line Item Units

1 Redefine the range unitTable on TRACKING.XLA so that it contains enough rows to accommodate the desired units.

2 Enter the names of the units into the first column of the unitTable range. To take advantage of the default line description calculations, enter the units as singular nouns.

3 Enter the default price of each unit beside it in column two.

4 Save TRACKING.XLA.

Customizing Reports

All three of the reports in the Client Tracking System use the Crosstab utility to extract data and calculate totals from the Database area of TRACKING.XLS. When these reports are displayed, a subroutine called RecalculateReport on TRACKING.XLA uses information on the report worksheets to recalculate and reformat the report with new data. Part of this information was placed onto the report worksheet by the Crosstab utility; we placed the remainder there afterwards. You can customize the reports by following the guidelines described in this section.

The Crosstab_Range Area

When you create a crosstab, the Crosstab utility defines the name Crosstab_Range to include the entire output area, from the title at the top to the grand total at the bottom. Both the RecalculateReport subroutine on TRACKING.XLA and the Crosstab utility use this named area to locate the output of the report and the headings, titles, grand totals, and so forth, within it. Any changes you make to the report worksheets must keep the Crosstab_Range intact.

Changing Report Labels

The Crosstab utility places several CROSSTAB formulas within the Crosstab_Range and uses these formulas both in displaying the final results and in recalculating them. The CROSSTAB formula takes a variable number of arguments, depending on the location of the formula within the Crosstab_Range. The first argument is always the text that should appear at the location of the formula, which acts as a label for the data.

To change these labels and guarantee that these changes do not prohibit recalculation of the report, do not overwrite the CROSSTAB formulas; change the formulas' first arguments instead.The RecalculateReport routine preserves changes that you make to the CROSSTAB formula in the upper left corner of the Crosstab_Range, which acts as the crosstab's title, as well as the formulas that appear at the column headings within the crosstab.

Understanding the Report Criteria

When the Crosstab utility creates a crosstab on a new worksheet, it defines a Database range on the sheet which is linked to the Database range of the crosstab's source data and a Criteria range linked to the source sheet's Criteria range. When it recalculates the crosstab, the Crosstab utility refers to these ranges, and includes the current records in the source Database that match its current Criteria. To recalculate a custom report with the Crosstab utility, we must ensure that the criteria used to create it is also used to recalculate it. To calculate the Outstanding Invoices report, for example, the Criteria on TRACKING.XLA must describe all records within the Tracking database that have no entries in the Date Paid field.

The values that should be entered within each report's Criteria range are defined as horizontal memory arrays named xtabCriteria on the report worksheets. These values are transferred to the report's Criteria range by the RecalculateReport subroutine before recalculating the crosstab. You should not need to alter the definition of the report's criteria unless you want to change the nature of the report itself.

AutoFormat Style

Each of the reports is formatted using the FORMAT.AUTO command, which is the equivalent of choosing AutoFormat from the Microsoft Excel Format menu. This command formats the selected cells in one of a number of styles, which is identified by its number within the Table Format list of the AutoFormat dialog box.

The name AutoFormat on each report worksheet is defined as the number of the Table Format used on the report. If you format the report with a different style and want to preserve this format when the report is rebuilt, enter the number of the new style as the definition of the AutoFormat name on the report worksheet.

Recalculating vs. Rebuilding the Crosstab

The RecalculateReport macro recomputes the values in the crosstab by calling the CROSSTAB.RECALC function, which takes a single argument specifying whether the table should be completely rebuilt or just recomputed in its current location with its current format. This distinction is important for reports that vary in size with each recalculation, such as the Outstanding Invoices report.

The RecalculateReport subroutine determines which argument to pass CROSSTAB.RECALC by evaluating the name xtabRecalc on the report worksheet. If this name equals TRUE, the crosstab is rebuilt; a FALSE definition recalculates the crosstab in place.

Why Not Always Rebuild the Crosstab?

We don't rebuild the Year-to-Date and Quarterly Breakdown by Category crosstabs so that the report always shows the entire year at a glance. If, for example, these reports were rebuilt in March, with only three months of data in the Tracking database, the Year-to-Date report would only contain rows for January, February and March, while the Quarterly Breakdown would contain only the first quarter. In the case of the Year-to-Date report, using a static report layout is purely a matter of aesthetic preference. The Quarterly Breakdown by Category would be much more difficult to manage if it were rebuilt each time it is recalculated, however, because it has embedded within it a chart whose data series are linked to the Crosstab table.

Saving Changes to the Reports

After changing any of the report worksheets, hide the sheet and save it in its hidden state.

Customizing the EIS Panel

Main Screen

The main panel of the EIS module is the sheet EXEC.XLS, which contains the macro buttons for accessing each of the reports. You can easily change the company name or add a logo to customize this screen for another company.

Reports

The EIS system displays the same report worksheets that the Client Tracking System's Analysis module displays. See "Customizing Reports" on page 165 for more information on customizing the report worksheets.

Application and Window Titles

The EXEC.XLA Add-In changes the titles of each of the worksheet windows displayed by the EIS system as well as the title within of the program window.

To Customize the Application Title

1 Open EXEC.XLA for editing (by holding down the SHIFT key while opening it).

2 Go to the macro named Auto_Open.

3 Find the cell that contains the following formula:

```
=APP.TITLE("Exotic Reports")
```

4 Enter the title you want to display in the program window as the argument to the APP.TITLE function.

To Customize the EIS Panel Title

1 Open EXEC.XLA for editing (by holding down the SHIFT key while opening it).

2 Go to the cell named eisWindow.

3 Enter the title you want to display for the EIS panel into the cell.

To Customize the Report Titles

1 Open EXEC.XLA for editing (by holding down the SHIFT key while opening it).

2 Go to the cell that contains the report worksheet's custom title, as shown in the table below:

Report Type	Name of the Cell to Go to
Year-to-Date	ytdWindow
Quarterly Breakdown	categoryWindow
Outstanding Invoices	outstandingWindow

3 Enter the title you want to display for the report into the cell.

To Save Changes to the Custom Titles

Save EXEC.XLA. To see the changes, close EXEC.XLA and open it in the normal mode (without holding down the SHIFT key).

Lesson Summary

In this lesson, we introduced our custom application, the Client Tracking System, as it would appear to the user. We edited and searched the Client Mail List, exported Mail List data as text for use in a word processing application, and wrote and printed invoices. We showed two ways to access the report-generating macros. Windows users changed a setting in their WIN.INI file to accommodate our custom Letter template that, as we saw, fills in addresses from the Client Mail List. We added a field to the mailing list, considered some changes we might want to make to the invoice set-up and reviewed the report-generation process, which uses the Crosstab

utility. Finally, we showed how to customize the appearance of the Executive
Information System main panel.

Preview of the Next Lesson

In the next two chapters, we will build several essential components of the Client
Tracking System, and in doing so we'll encounter many of the challenges which
recur in project after project, including:

- Using Custom Forms for Data Entry
- Entering and Validating Data with Custom Dialog Boxes
- Providing Commands from Custom Menus
- Changing Menus Dynamically
- Co-existing with the Standard Microsoft Excel Environment
- Making Microsoft Excel Look Less Like Microsoft Excel

Developing Applications: Part I

The Client Tracking System is a big application with hundreds of lines of code. In developing it ourselves, we started in small steps, creating each of the modules separately and integrating them later. For this introduction to application development, we'll take the same approach and develop a subset of the Client Mail List module that stands on its own.

This lesson explains how to do the following:

- Set up the Client Mail List database

- Devise and display a custom data form for entering records into the Client Mail List

- Create a custom menu with commands for maintaining the Client Mail List

- Open the Client Mail List and install the custom menu with an Auto_Open macro

- Exit the Client Mail List module, closing all of its files and removing the custom menu, with an Auto_Close macro

---

How We Will Proceed

We won't be developing the macros in this application in the order in which they will eventually run. We'll start with the core of the system—the commands the user will run from the menu. Then we'll turn back to the macros that set everything up when the application loads. We'll finish with the macros that close the system.

Before continuing   Open TRACKING.XLA from the LESSON6 directory.

What's in the Add-In Already

We assume you know how to create macros, name them and organize your macro sheet with labels, comments and borders, so we've done much of this for you in TRACKING.XLA and in the version of TRACKING.XLA you will work with in Lesson 7. Many of the macros that you will create already exist on the Add-In as sketches, with comments that describe the macro in the place of the formulas you will enter. You may want, as you progress through these lessons, to use the comments as hints for writing the macros yourself, and to check your work against the results in the lessons.

You'll find also that several of the macros on these Add-Ins are complete. For the most part, you would gain little beyond review by creating these macros yourself, but some of them venture into more advanced territory. We encourage you to examine all of the code and the comments in the complete Client Tracking System after you have finished the lessons in this book.

Developing the Client Mail List

The heart of the Client Tracking System is the Client Mail List module, a group of macros on TRACKING.XLA that manipulate the Client data stored on the worksheet MAILLIST.XLS. We'll begin by creating the Client database and a custom data form for entering and editing the records within it.

The Client Mail List database contains the following fields:

Field Name	Description
LastName	
FirstName	
Title	Personal title such as Mr., Ms., etc.
Position	Name of Client's Position within Company
CompanyName	
Address1	First line of Client's address
Address2	Second line of Client's address
City	
State	
Zip	
Phone	
Fax	
Category	Reference for grouping entries, such as PROSPECT, PERSONAL, FORMER, etc.
ID	Unique client ID number to facilitate relationship between this and other databases

To Create the Client Database

1 Create a new worksheet.

2 Type the field names in the table above into cells B1:O1 of the worksheet.

3 Define cells B1:O2 as the Database area by selecting them and choosing Set Database from the Data menu.

4 Save the worksheet in the LESSON6 directory as MAILLIST.XLS.

A Custom Data Form for the Client Mail List

If you choose the Form command from the Data menu, you will see that the default form is not practical for a database with so many fields. We can remedy this fairly quickly by customizing the form. Since a custom data form is simply a dialog box, you can create it using the Microsoft Excel Dialog Editor, with one important limitation—you can only use static text and edit boxes in the form. The Data Form command won't accept anything fancier.

If you want to use other elements such as scrolling lists, option buttons or custom push buttons, you must use the DIALOG.BOX function instead of the DATA.FORM command, and update the database yourself with custom macros, a subject we'll explore in the next lesson. For the Client Mail List, the DATA.FORM command will suffice.

The general procedure for creating a custom data form is as follows:

1   Create a dialog box using the Microsoft Excel Dialog Editor with edit boxes for each field and static text as field prompts.

2   Select the dialog and copy it onto the Clipboard.

3   Paste the dialog definition into the worksheet that contains the Database.

4   Associate the edit boxes in the form with the fields in the Database by entering each field name into the init/result column of its corresponding edit box.

5   Assign the name Data_Form to the definition. When you choose Form from the Data menu and Microsoft Excel finds this name on the sheet, it uses the form defined there to display the records instead of the default form.

The form we will use for the Client Mail List is shown in Figures 5.2 and 5.3 in the previous lesson.

The Custom Data Form for the Client Mail List

In cells Q1:W30 of MAILLIST.XLS, enter the following dialog definition:

	Q	R	S	T	U	V	W
1							
2	5	9	2			Maillist Database	
3	5	7	25			&Last Name:	
4	6	101	22	161			LastName
5	5	273	25			&First Name:	
6	6	366	22	176			FirstName
7	5	56	50			&Title:	
8	6	101	47	40			Title
9	5	19	72			&Position:	
10	6	101	69	441			Position
11	5	19	96			Com&pany:	
12	6	101	93	441			Company
13	5	15	121			Address &1:	
14	6	101	118	350			Address1
15	5	15	146			Address &2:	
16	6	101	143	350			Address2
17	5	62	170			&City:	
18	6	101	168	350			City
19	5	50	196			&State:	
20	6	101	193	87			State
21	5	216	196			&Zip Code:	
22	6	305	193	120			Zip
23	5	39	231			&Phone:	
24	6	101	228				Phone
25	5	273	231			&Fax:	
26	6	313	228				Fax
27	5	20	255			Cate&gory:	
28	6	101	252	100			Category
29	5	228	254			&ID Number:	
30	6	315	252	60			ID

Figure 6.1   The custom data form definition table

Assign the name Data_Form to cells Q1:W30.

A Macro For Entering New Client Names

It's not difficult to choose the Form command from the Data menu, but the Client Mail List will be easier to use if we write a custom macro that activates the MAILLIST.XLS worksheet for the user and then displays the custom form.

Go to the area named AddToMailList on TRACKING.XLA. Figure 6.2 shows the pseudo-code that has been placed there for guidance.

AddToMailList
Activate the sheet containing the Client Mail List Show the Data Form =RETURN()

Figure 6.2   AddToMailList macro pseudo-code

Replace the pseudo-code with the completed macro instructions shown in Figure 6.3:

AddToMailList
=ACTIVATE("maillist.xls") =DATA.FORM() =RETURN()

Figure 6.3   AddToMailList macro code

Forcing the Data Form to Display a New Record (Windows Only)

The SEND.KEYS function is not available on Microsoft Excel for the Macintosh.

The DATA.FORM command always displays the first record of the Database. To create a new record, the user must choose New from the form. In Microsoft Excel for Windows, we can do this for the user by simulating from the macro the keystroke equivalent of choosing New. The function we use to generate keystrokes is SEND.KEYS, which uses the syntax

SEND.KEYS(*key_text*,*wait_logical*)

For a list of keystrokes and their string equivalents, see "ON.KEY" in the Microsoft Excel Function Reference.

where key_text is the string representation of the keystrokes you want to generate, and wait_logical is a TRUE or FALSE value that indicates whether Microsoft Excel should wait for the keys to be processed before continuing with the macro. You would enter a TRUE value here if you were sending the keystrokes to some other application upon whose action the remainder of the macro depended.

In this case, we want to simulate choosing the data form's New button by sending the keystroke combination ALT + w to the data form, as in the following:

```
=SEND.KEYS("%w",FALSE)
```

It would seem that the logical time to call this function is right after we display the form, as shown in Figure 6.4:

=ACTIVATE("maillist.xls") =DATA.FORM() =SEND.KEYS("%w",FALSE) =RETURN()	*WRONG!!!*

Figure 6.4   This won't work

What Microsoft Excel would actually do with this macro is send the keystrokes after the user closes the data form. It may seem counter-intuitive, but you need to send keys to a dialog box just before you display it, as shown in Figure 6.5:

AddToMailList
=ACTIVATE("maillist.xls") =SEND.KEYS("%w",FALSE) =DATA.FORM() =RETURN()

Figure 6.5   Send keystrokes before displaying the data form

Before continuing   Modify AddToMailList so that it looks like the one shown in Figure 6.5.

Avoiding Constant Values in Macros

AddToMailList is the first of several macros that activate MAILLIST.XLS. If we decide later to rename MAILLIST.XLS, we'll need to replace every reference to it in TRACKING.XLA with the new name. We can avoid this nuisance by storing the name in a cell on the Add-In. Every macro that accesses the worksheet will refer to that cell and *not* to the worksheet by name. There are a few other such values that we'll refer to throughout the Add-In, some calculated rather than constant, so we'll enclose all of these variables in a subroutine called Global and run Global when we open the Add-In.

To create the Global subroutine, go to the area named Global on TRACKING.XLA. The following pseudo-code has been placed there for guidance:

	Global
mailSheet *thisMacroSheet* *thisPath*	the file name of the Client Mail List this macro's file name the directory containing this macro =RETURN()

Figure 6.6   Global macro pseudo-code

Replace the pseudo-code with the completed macro instructions shown in Figure 6.7.

	Global
mailSheet *thisMacroSheet* *thisPath*	maillist.xls =GET.CELL(32,A1) =GET.DOCUMENT(2,thisMacroSheet) =RETURN()

Figure 6.7   Global macro code

Other Values in the Global Subroutine

Referring to the Client Mail List through the mailSheet cell protects us as long as we never change the name of the file without entering the new name in mailSheet. Keeping the Add-In informed of its own name is a little simpler, because we can have Microsoft Excel calculate it with the GET.CELL function. You use GET.CELL to determine a cell's attributes such as its formatting, location or contents. The syntax of GET.CELL is

GET.CELL(*type_num,*reference*)

where type_num is a number that specifies the information you want about the cell in the reference argument. If you omit the reference argument, Microsoft Excel returns information about the active cell. The formula

```
=GET.CELL(32,A1)
```

in the cell named thisMacroSheet returns the name of the file that contains cell A1, a reference to the Add-In's own top left cell. We specify a cell in the Add-In because we want to know *its* name. Then, in the formula

```
=GET.DOCUMENT(2,thisMacroSheet)
```

we determine the directory where the Add-In is saved so we can locate MAILLIST.XLS when we need to open it. This depends on a minor restriction in our application's design: that all files the Add-In needs must be in its directory. If we needed to access a large number of files, we could organize them into subdirectories below the one containing the Add-In. Either way, the macro will know exactly how to find the files we need and still allow the user to move the application to a convenient location.

Calculating and Using the Global Values

Run the Global subroutine to calculate the cells within it. To calculate its values automatically at the time TRACKING.XLA is loaded, we'll call the Global subroutine from the Auto_Open macro, which we'll create later in this lesson. For now, so that you can experiment with the AddToMailList macro, change the constant argument "maillist.xls" within the AddToMailList macro to a reference to the cell mailSheet, as in Figures 6.8 and 6.9.

AddToMailList
=ACTIVATE(mailSheet)
=SEND.KEYS("%w ",FALSE)
=DATA.FORM()
=RETURN(TRUE)

Figure 6.8   Activating a sheet through a cell reference (Windows)

```
AddToMailList

=ACTIVATE(mailSheet)
=DATA.FORM()
=RETURN(TRUE)
```

Figure 6.9   Activating a sheet through a cell reference (Macintosh)

A Better Way to Activate the Client Mail List

We can now activate the Client Mail List, whatever its file name may be, but the macros in Figures 6.8 and 6.9 could still produce an error if the user has closed the sheet. To protect ourselves from this, we should modify the AddToMailList macro so that it activates the list if it is open, or opens it if it is not. We'll need to do this from every macro that accesses the Client Mail List, so we'll create a subroutine for it.

Go to the area named ActivateOrOpen on TRACKING.XLA The following pseudo-code has been placed there for guidance:

```
ActivateOrOpen

=ARGUMENT("aWorksheet")
If the worksheet is not open already
   Open it from the directory where this Add-In is saved
END.IF
Activate the worksheet
=RETURN()
```

Figure 6.10   ActivateOrOpen macro pseudo-code

Replace the pseudo-code with the completed macro instructions shown in Figures 6.11 and 6.12.

```
ActivateOrOpen

=ARGUMENT("aWorksheet")
=IF(FileNotOpen(aWorksheet))
=   OPEN(thisPath&"\"&aWorksheet)
=END.IF()
=ACTIVATE(aWorksheet)
=RETURN()
```

Figure 6.11   ActivateOrOpen macro code (Windows)

```
ActivateOrOpen

=ARGUMENT("aWorksheet")
=IF(FileNotOpen(aWorksheet))
=   OPEN(thisPath&":"&aWorksheet)
=END.IF()
=ACTIVATE(aWorksheet)
=RETURN()
```

Figure 6.12 ActivateOrOpen macro code (Macintosh)

Understanding ActivateOrOpen

First, we prepare ActivateOrOpen to receive an argument containing the name of the
worksheet to activate. This may seem unnecessary since the Client Mail List is the
only worksheet we ever activate in this application, but ActivateOrOpen is a
substitute for the ACTIVATE command, so we give it the same syntax. Thus, the
subroutine is more valuable for future applications.

In the formula

```
=IF(FileNotOpen(aWorksheet))
```

we determine if the sheet is open by calling the macro function FileNotOpen, which
returns TRUE if the file is not open, FALSE otherwise. FileNotOpen is shown in
Figure 6.13.

```
FileNotOpen

=ARGUMENT("aFileToOpen")
=RETURN(ISNA(DOCUMENTS(1,aFileToOpen)))
```

Figure 6.13 FileNotOpen function

We use the DOCUMENTS function to search for the name in the list of open
documents. The DOCUMENTS function uses the syntax

DOCUMENTS(*type_num,match_text*)

returning the names of all open documents or some subset of them as a horizontal
array. You specify the type of documents to include in the array with the type_num
argument; the type_num 1 indicates all open documents except Add-Ins. You specify
the names of files to include with the match_text argument, which can include
wildcard characters, such as "*.xls". If there is no match, DOCUMENTS returns
#NA.

In the formula

```
=RETURN(ISNA(DOCUMENTS(1,aFileToOpen)))
```

we ask Microsoft Excel to give us the names of all open files (except Add-Ins) that
exactly match the name in the argument aFileToOpen. The result will either be the
file name, if it's open, or #NA, if it's not, so we convert this to a logical value by

enclosing the whole thing in the ISNA function, which is itself the argument to RETURN.

If FileNotOpen returns TRUE, ActivateOrOpen opens the file (in Windows) with the command

```
=OPEN(thisPath&"\"&aWorksheet)
```

or, on the Macintosh,

```
=OPEN(thisPath&":"&aWorksheet)
```

The OPEN command, which is the function equivalent of choosing Open from the File menu, uses the syntax

OPEN(*file_text*,*update_links,read_only,format,prot_pwd, write_res_pwd,ignore_rorec,file_origin*)

This lengthy argument list corresponds to the various options that appear in the File Open dialog box, but the file_text argument is the only one we need in this case. This argument can be a full path to the file, a path relative to the current directory, or the file name alone. In case the user changes the current directory, we specify the complete path of the file using the value of thisPath in the Global macro as the file's directory.

We complete ActivateOrOpen by activating the file, even if we just opened it. We can't assume the file will be active after we open it, because it may have been saved hidden, and Microsoft Excel does not activate hidden sheets when it opens them.

Before continuing   Substitute the custom ActivateOrOpen subroutine for the ACTIVATE command in the AddToMailList macro, as shown in Figures 6.14 and 6.15.

AddToMailList
=ActivateOrOpen(mailSheet)
=SEND.KEYS("%w",FALSE)
=DATA.FORM()
=RETURN()

Figure 6.14   ACTIVATE replaced with ActivateOrOpen (Windows)

AddToMailList
=ActivateOrOpen(mailSheet)
=DATA.FORM()
=RETURN(TRUE)

Figure 6.15   ACTIVATE replaced with ActivateOrOpen (Macintosh)

Adding Custom Menus to the Client Mail List

We've designed the Client Mail List to be used within the Microsoft Excel standard environment, rather than as a standalone application. To make its commands easily accessible, yet unobtrusive, we'll place them all in a single menu that we append to the standard worksheet menu bar.

Go to the area named MaillistMenu on TRACKING.XLA and enter the menu definition shown in Figures 6.16 or 6.17.

MaillistMenu

Trac&king				
&Add Name...	AddToMailList		Add records to the database	
&Edit / Delete...	EditMailList		Edit or delete existing database records	
-				
&Sort...	SortMailList		Sort the database	
-				
E&xit Client Tracking	QuitMe		Exit the Client Tracking Application	

Figure 6.16 Tracking menu definition (Windows)

MaillistMenu

Trac&king				
&Add/ Edit / Delete...	AddToMailList		Add, edit or delete Client records	
-				
&Sort...	SortMailList		Sort the database	
-				
E&xit Client Tracking	QuitMe		Exit the Client Tracking Application	

Figure 6.17 Tracking menu definition (Macintosh)

Create a macro to add the menu defined in MaillistMenu to the worksheet menu bar by entering the code shown in Figure 6.18 in the area named InstallTrackMenu.

InstallTrackMenu
=ADD.MENU(1,MaillistMenu)
=RETURN()

Figure 6.18 InstallTrackMenu macro code

You'll recall from our discussion of custom menus in Lesson 4 that the menu bar Microsoft Excel displays when worksheets or macro sheets are active is identified by the bar ID 1, so the formula

```
=ADD.MENU(1,MaillistMenu)
```

adds the menu defined in the area MaillistMenu to this menu bar. By not specifying a position for the menu, we append it to the end of the bar (but before the Help menu in Microsoft Excel for Windows).

Before continuing Run InstallTrackMenu.

Where We Are So Far

We've set up a Client Mail List database, created a friendly custom data form and added a custom menu to the standard worksheet menu bar. Experiment with the commands on the Tracking menu. The Edit/Delete command in the Windows version runs a macro named EditMaillist, which, like the AddToMaillist macro we created earlier in this lesson, uses the DATA.FORM command. The only difference between these two macros is that EditMaillist does not use SEND.KEYS to create a new record.

The Sort command runs the macro SortMaillist, a slight variation of the SortDatabase macro we created in Lesson 4. The final command on the Tracking menu, Exit Client Tracking, doesn't do anything yet, because the macro it runs, QuitMe, is incomplete. We'll delve into the art of the graceful exit later in this lesson. For now, let's work on our entrance.

The Auto_Open Macro

Go to the area named Auto_Open on TRACKING.XLA and enter the following code in the space provided:

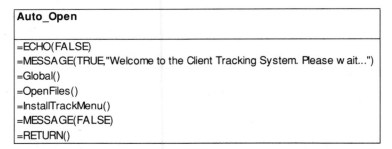

```
Auto_Open

=ECHO(FALSE)
=MESSAGE(TRUE,"Welcome to the Client Tracking System. Please wait...")
=Global()
=OpenFiles()
=InstallTrackMenu()
=MESSAGE(FALSE)
=RETURN()
```

Figure 6.19   Auto_Open macro code

We begin by turning off screen updates so that the screen doesn't flash while we set things up. It could take a few seconds for us to open files, create the menu and so on, so we display a message in the status bar with the formula

```
=MESSAGE(TRUE,"Welcome to the Client Tracking System. Please wait...")
```

Then we run the Global subroutine to update the variables within it, and call the subroutine OpenFiles, shown in Figures 6.20 and 6.21, to open the Client Mail List.

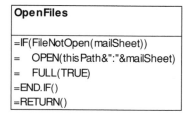

```
OpenFiles

=IF(FileNotOpen(mailSheet))
=   OPEN(thisPath&"\"&mailSheet,0)
=   FULL(TRUE)
=END.IF()
=RETURN()
```

Figure 6.20   OpenFiles macro code (Windows)

```
OpenFiles

=IF(FileNotOpen(mailSheet))
=   OPEN(thisPath&":"&mailSheet)
=   FULL(TRUE)
=END.IF()
=RETURN()
```

Figure 6.21   OpenFiles macro code (Macintosh)

OpenFiles calls the FileNotOpen function we developed earlier before attempting to open the Client Mail List, because we don't want to open it if the user already did. If we did try to reopen it, the message shown in Figure 6.22 would be displayed:

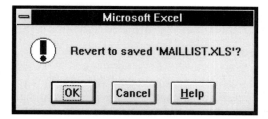

Figure 6.22   An Alert box we don't want the user to see

After we open the Client Mail List, we maximize the sheet with the formula

=FULL(TRUE)

Before continuing   Go to the area named OpenFiles and enter the macro shown in Figure 6.20 or 6.21.

We complete the Auto_Open macro by calling the InstallTrackMenu subroutine to attach the Tracking menu to the worksheet menu bar, and by restoring standard messages to the status bar.

Exiting the Application

The user could exit the Client Tracking System by either exiting Microsoft Excel itself or by choosing Exit Client Tracking from the Tracking menu. In the latter case, we should remove the Tracking menu and close any files we opened. To be polite, we should also in this case free up the memory used by the Add-In by closing TRACKING.XLA.

Most of this work belongs in an Auto_Close macro, while the rest should happen within the QuitMe macro that runs when the user chooses Exit Client Tracking (we'll create the QuitMe macro later in this lesson). The Auto_Close macro is the place for closing files, removing custom menus and restoring any other settings within Microsoft Excel that it would be rude of us to leave behind. This is more for our own convenience than out of consideration for the user, because, during development, we'll open and close the Add-In ourselves and will want it to clean up after itself when we close it.

Go to the area named Auto_Close, and enter the following macro into the space provided:

Auto_Close
=ECHO(FALSE)
=DELETE.MENU(1,"Tracking")
=CloseFiles()
=RETURN()

Figure 6.23   Auto_Close macro code

This macro is structured like a reversal of the Auto_Open macro. After turning off screen updates, we delete the custom Tracking menu from the worksheet menu bar, and then close the files we opened by calling the subroutine CloseFiles, shown in Figure 6.24:

CloseFiles
=ActivateAndClose(mailSheet,TRUE)
=RETURN()

Figure 6.24   CloseFiles macro code

CloseFiles, in turn, calls the subroutine ActivateAndClose, shown in Figure 6.25, to activate the Client Mail List if it is open, and close it, saving the changes.

	ActivateAndClose
tryToActivate	=ARGUMENT("aWindow Name") =ARGUMENT("fileSaveFlag") =ERROR(FALSE) =ACTIVATE(aWindow Name) =IF(ISERROR(tryToActivate)) = RETURN() =ELSE() = FILE.CLOSE(fileSaveFlag) =END.IF() =RETURN()

Figure 6.25 ActivateAndClose macro code

ActivateAndClose is another subroutine that we've designed with an eye toward future applications. Some of the supporting worksheets used by an application will be maintained by macros alone, while others, like the Client Mail List, will be modified by both the user and macros. ActivateAndClose accepts, along with an argument specifying the name of the window to activate, a logical argument called fileSaveFlag. We use this argument to control whether or not changes are saved as the file is closed.

The command we use to close the file, FILE.CLOSE, is the equivalent of choosing Close from the File menu. FILE.CLOSE uses the syntax

FILE.CLOSE(*save_logical*)

where a TRUE save_logical argument saves the file before closing and a FALSE argument closes without saving. If you omit this argument and there are unsaved changes on the sheet, Microsoft Excel displays a dialog box similar to the following:

Figure 6.26 Save changes dialog box

We want to save any changes the user may have made to the Client Mail List, so in this case we call ActivateAndClose with the fileSaveFlag set to TRUE. The complete Client Tracking System closes some files without saving them because any necessary changes will have been saved earlier by the macros that access them.

Two Routes to the Same Result

As with ActivateOrOpen, we have ActivateAndClose determine if the file in question is open before acting on it, but we go about it in a different way. Instead of calling the FileNotOpen function to search for the file in the list of open documents, we suppress standard error messages and then try to activate the file. If it is not open, the ACTIVATE function will return an error, but won't interrupt the macro. We'll know from this result whether we should continue and close the file or not.

This method of checking for the open file is neither better nor worse than the one we used in ActivateOrOpen—you might prefer using the FileNotOpen function if you just want to see if a file is open without activating it, while the alternative we've used in ActivateAndClose may be a bit more efficient if you want to activate the file anyway.

Before continuing   Enter the CloseFiles and ActivateAndClose subroutines as shown in Figures 6.24 and 6.25 into the space provided on TRACKING.XLA.

Exiting the Application from the Menu

We now have an Auto_Close macro that removes all traces of the Client Mail List if we close TRACKING.XLA, or Microsoft Excel does as it exits. We still need to provide a method for the user to exit the application and explicitly close TRACKING.XLA without exiting Microsoft Excel.

Go to the area named QuitMe on TRACKING.XLA. The following pseudo-code has been placed there for your guidance:

QuitMe
Remove the Tracking menu and close files we opened
Activate this Add-In sheet
Close it
=RETURN()

Figure 6.27   QuitMe macro pseudo-code

Enter the completed QuitMe macro as shown in Figure 6.28:

QuitMe
=Auto_Close()
=ACTIVATE(thisMacroSheet)
=FILE.CLOSE()
=RETURN()

Figure 6.28   QuitMe macro code

Remember that the Auto_Close macro won't be called when the QuitMe macro closes the Add-In. If we close the file from a macro, we need to run the Auto_Close macro ourselves. So the QuitMe command calls the Auto_Close macro as a subroutine, and then closes the Add-In by activating it (using the name in the Global subroutine variable thisMacroSheet) and closing it with the FILE.CLOSE command.

Lesson Summary

In this lesson, we created some of the building blocks of our Client Tracking System application. We set up the Client Mail List database, created a custom data form called by the DATA.FORM command and used the SEND.KEYS command (in Windows) to force the data form to display a new record. We established a set of constants in a macro called Global to be used throughout the application. Custom Auto_Open and Auto_Close macros were developed to open the files and set up the menu used by our application and to close those files and remove the menu when the user exits our application.

Preview of the Next Lesson

In the next lesson, we'll look at the techniques you can use to add a professional polish to custom applications in Microsoft Excel.

Developing Applications: Part II

We're now ready to exploit the skills learned in the previous six lessons to create a complete, sophisticated application using Microsoft Excel. While we won't be able to cover everything one needs to know to become a Microsoft Excel demi-god, we will examine many of the most important—and thorny—issues in developing custom applications.

This lesson explains how to do the following:

- Use custom dialog boxes instead of the Data Form for database entry
- Create dynamic menus that change when the active worksheet changes
- Create an application that looks like a standalone application as opposed to a spreadsheet

---

Before continuing   Copy the files from the TRACKING directory into the LESSON7 directory. Then, while holding down the SHIFT key (so the file can be edited), open TRACKING.XLA from the LESSON7 directory.

Data Entry with Custom Dialog Boxes

The Data Form command provides a simple mechanism for entering data into a database, but lacks many of the features of dedicated database management environments, including the ability to

- initialize forms with default data
- simplify data entry forms with such features as list boxes, option buttons and check boxes
- validate data before entering it into the database

With custom dialog boxes and macros that manipulate the database directly, you can build these features into your applications, making them both more reliable and easier to use than would be possible with the Data Form command.

The general scheme for entering new data records from a macro is shown in Figure 7.1.

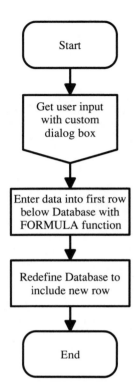

Figure 7.1 Flowchart for entering new data records

Writing Invoices

The Invoicing module of the Client Tracking System uses this scheme to gather line item information from the user and save it in a temporary database prior to printing. Before we tackle the custom data entry macro, let's take a look at how the whole Invoicing module works.

We want the user to be able to write several invoices at a time, each of which might consist of one or more line items, so we store all unprinted invoices in a database on the hidden worksheet INVOICE.XLS. This sheet also contains the areas from which invoices and envelopes are printed.

The Invoice database includes the following fields:

Field Name	Description
ID	ID from Client Mail List
Invoice #	Unique serial number for invoice
Description	Text description of line item
Category	Category of line item, for analysis
Qty	Quantity of units in line item
Unit	Name of unit in line item
Rate	Cost of unit

The value for the ID field is calculated by a function macro in the TRACKING.XLA Add-In. The user chooses the name of the client for each invoice from the dialog box shown in Figure 7.2.

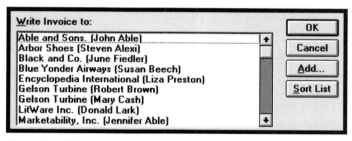

Figure 7.2   Write Invoice dialog box

This dialog box lists Client names from the Client Mail List on MAILLIST.XLS, in the order in which they are stored. When the user selects a name from the list, Microsoft Excel enters the number of the selected item within the table that defines the dialog box as the result of the list box. If, for example, the user were to select Arbor Shoes from the dialog box shown in Figure 7.2, the result of the list box would be 2 because Arbor Shoes is the second item in the list.

By adding 1 to this number, we can use it as the row argument to the INDEX function to access the Client's record in the Database area on MAILLIST.XLS. We have to add 1, remember, to skip the row that contains the field names. If, for example, we named the list box result selectedClient, the formula

```
=INDEX(MAILLIST.XLS!,selectedClient+1,1)
```

would return the contents of the LastName field for that Client.

We use this technique in a number of subroutines in TRACKING.XLA, including the function macro named ClientIDFromIndex, shown in Figure 7.3. This function uses the value passed to it as its clientIndex argument to look up the value in the ID field, the last field of the Client Mail List database. Notice that ClientIDFromIndex assumes that the clientIndex argument has already been converted to a number that skips the first row of the database.

ClientIDFromIndex	
=ARGUMENT("clientIndex") =RETURN(INDEX(clientDatabase,clientIndex,COLUMNS(clientDatabase)))	*ID is always in last column*

Figure 7.3   ClientIDFromIndex macro

The value for the Invoice # field is retrieved from a cell named NextInvoiceNumber on the INVOICE.XLS worksheet. The custom data entry macro increments this number after each invoice is written.

The values for the remaining fields of the Invoice database are transferred directly from the user's input in the Line Item dialog box, shown in Figure 7.4.

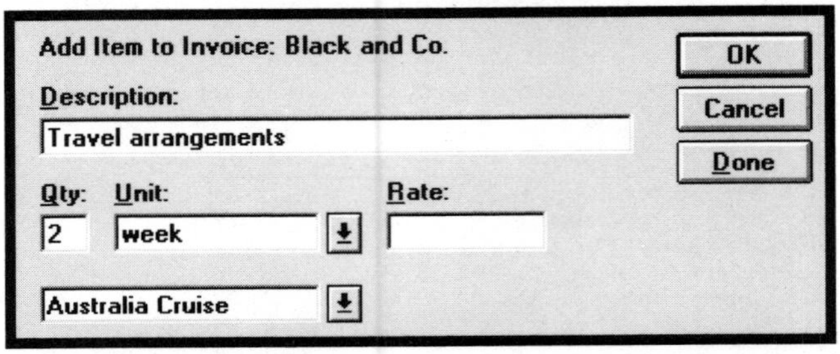

Figure 7.4   Line Item dialog box

After writing invoices, the user can print all unprinted invoices immediately, or defer printing them until later (this version of the Client Tracking System doesn't allow the user to choose which unprinted invoices to print). After the user prints the invoices, all of the information needed for reprinting them or for generating consolidated reports is saved in the Tracking database. The Invoice database is then emptied for the next round.

The WriteInvoices Macro

Figure 7.5 shows the structure of the WriteInvoices macro, which is executed when the user chooses Write Invoices from the Invoice Options dialog box.

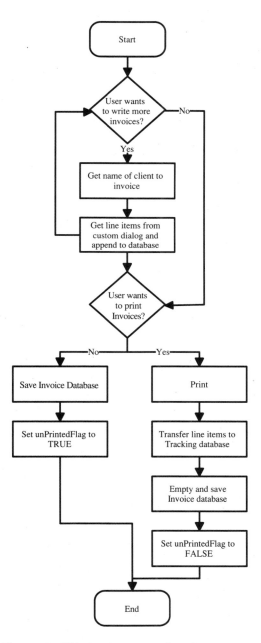

Figure 7.5   WriteInvoices macro flowchart

The unPrintedFlag set at the end of the macro is used to determine whether to make the Print Command available from the Invoice Options dialog box.

Building the Data Entry Macro

The function macro GetClient in TRACKING.XLA displays the dialog box shown in Figure 7.2, and returns the row argument number to use with the INDEX function to access the selected Client's record. If the user cancels, GetClient returns zero.

To gather line item information for each invoice and store it in the Invoice database, WriteInvoices calls the macro function GetLineItems, passing it the number returned by GetClient. GetLineItems uses this number to determine both the Client's company name, which it displays in the Line Item dialog box, and the Client's ID, which it places into each line item's record in the Invoice database. To determine the Client's company name, GetLineItems calls the function macro ClientNameFromIndex.

The user may cancel an invoice in progress, so GetLineItems returns TRUE to WriteInvoices if the user completes the invoice, or FALSE if the user cancels. The design of the GetLineItems macro is shown in Figure 7.6.

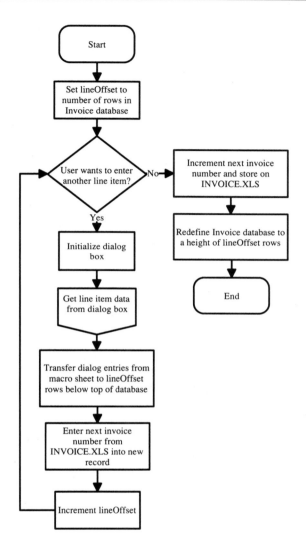

Figure 7.6   GetLineItems macro flowchart

The GetLineItems Macro

Go to the area named GetLineItems on TRACKING.XLA. The formulas and pseudo-code shown in Figure 7.7 have been placed there for guidance.

	GetLineItems
	=ARGUMENT("clientToInvoice")
	Set prompt line in LineItemDialog to say "Add Item to Invoice: [Client's name]"
startingSize	How many rows in the Invoice Database?
	Set lineOffset cell to number to use in OFFSET to find first row below database
moreItems	=TRUE
enterLine	=TRUE
	WHILE(user wants to enter more line items)
	Initialize the LineItemDialog with quantity of 1, 1st item in each list selected
lineItemResponse	Display the LineItemDialog
	IF user cancelled
	RETURN(FALSE)
	ELSE()
	IF user clicked Done button
	Last entry for this invoice; don't show dialog box anymore
	IF user clicked Done without entering anything
	Don't put dialog box values into database (previous entry was the last one)
	END.IF()
	END.IF()
	IF Init/ Result values in LineItemDialog should be transferred to database
	IF entries are not valid, say so and have user try again
clientID	what goes into the ID field for this invoice's line items?
nextInvNumber	what's the next invoice number to use?
	what Description did user input?
	what product category did user select or type?
	what quantity did the user input?
	what unit did the user select or type?
rate	what is the product's rate?
	transfer everything from clientId to rate into next row of Invoice database
lineOffset	lineOffset+1
	END.IF()
	END.IF()
	NEXT()
	make INVOICE.XLS active, so we can:
	redefine the Database to include the new entries
	Increment NextInvoiceNumber on INVOICE.XLS
	=RETURN(TRUE)

Figure 7.7 GetLineItems macro pseudo-code

Replace the pseudo-code with the completed GetLineItems macro, as shown in Figure 7.8.

	GetLineItems
	=ARGUMENT("clientToInvoice")
	=SET.VALUE(lineClientPrompt,"Add Item to Invoice: "&ClientNameFromIndex(clientToInvoice))
startingSize	=ROWS(invDatabase)
	=SET.VALUE(lineOffset,startingSize)
moreItems	=TRUE
enterLine	=TRUE
	=WHILE(moreItems)
	= InitializeLineItemDialog()
lineItemResponse	= DIALOG.BOX(LineItemDialog)
	= IF(lineItemResponse=FALSE)
	= RETURN(FALSE)
	= ELSE()
	= IF(lineItemResponse=15)
	= SET.VALUE(moreItems,FALSE)
	= IF(AND(DialogUnchanged(),lineOffset>startingSize))
	= SET.VALUE(enterLine,FALSE)
	= END.IF()
	= END.IF()
	= IF(enterLine)
	= IF(NOT(IsValidLineItem()),GOTO(lineItemResponse))
clientID	= ClientIDFromIndex(clientToInvoice)
nextInvNumber	= INDIRECT(invSheet&"!NextInvoiceNumber")
	= lineDescription
	= lineCategory
	= lineQty
	= lineUnit
rate	= IF(lineRate>0,lineRate,IF(ISNA(lineUnitNum),0,INDEX(UnitTable,lineUnitNum,2)))
	= FORMULA.ARRAY(TRANSPOSE(clientID:rate),OFFSET(invDatabase,lineOffset,0,1))
lineOffset	= lineOffset+1
	= END.IF()
	= END.IF()
	=NEXT()
	=ACTIVATE(invSheet)
	=DEFINE.NAME("Database",OFFSET(!Database,0,0,lineOffset,))
	=FORMULA(nextInvNumber+1,!NextInvoiceNumber)
	=RETURN(TRUE)

Figure 7.8 GetLineItems macro code

Understanding the Macro

The formula

```
=ARGUMENT("clientToInvoice")
```

prepares GetLineItems for an argument containing the row index within the MAILLIST.XLS database of the Client to be invoiced.

The formula

```
=SET.VALUE(lineClientPrompt,"Add Item to Invoice: "&
ClientNameFromIndex(clientToInvoice))
```

initializes the prompt within the Line Item dialog to a string consisting of the text "Add Item to Invoice: " concatenated with the Client's company name.

The LineItemDialog definition is shown in Figure 7.9.

Dialog Name	item	x	y	width	height	text	init/ result	<--name labels
LineItemDialog							2	
	5	16	28			&Description:		
	6	16	44	384				lineDescription
	5	16	72			&Qty:		
	8	16	88	32			1	lineQty
	5	64	72			&Unit:		
	6	64	88	160	18			lineUnit
	22	64	106	160	108	UnitList	1	lineUnitNum
	5	240	72			&Rate:		
	8	240	88	104				lineRate
	5	16	120			&Category:		
	6	16	138	208	18			lineCategory
	22	16	138	208	48	CategoryList	1	lineCategoryList
	1	428	8	88		OK		
	2	428	32	88		Cancel		
	3	428	56			Do&ne		
	5	16	6			Add Item to Invoice: Black & Co.		

Figure 7.9 Line Item dialog box definition

Note   The dialog box definition table coordinates will be different if you are running Microsoft Excel for the Macintosh.

The formula

```
=ROWS(invDatabase)
```

in the cell named startingSize calculates the number of rows in the the area named invDatabase, which is defined as the Database area of INVOICE.XLS. We'll need to refer to this value later, to determine how many items the user added to the current invoice. The formula

```
=SET.VALUE(lineOffset,startingSize)
```

sets the value of the cell named lineOffset to the value in startingSize. If you examine lineOffset, you will see that it contains the formula

```
=lineOffset+1
```

Two interesting things are at work here. Previously, we have used the SET.VALUE function to place constant text or numbers into cells of the macro sheet, as if we had typed the values into the cells ourselves. Every cell in a macro sheet has two layers, however—the formula layer and the value layer. The SET.VALUE function acts on the value layer only, leaving the formula layer unchanged. In GetLineItems, the *formula* in lineOffset adds 1 to the *value* of lineOffset, thereby incrementing itself.

Besides taking advantage of this use of SET.VALUE, the formula in lineOffset is a circular reference. Because Microsoft Excel calculates macro sheets one cell at a time instead of dynamically, circular references such as these present no problem.

The next two formulas

| *moreItems* | =TRUE |
| *enterLine* | =TRUE |

Figure 7.10   GetLIneItems macro code initializing flags

initialize cells that GetLineItems uses as flags. The first, in the cell labeled moreItems, is used in the loop that prompts for new line item records. Each time the user clicks OK from the Line Items dialog box, the macro saves the new line item in the Invoice database and prompts the user to enter the next one. This continues until the user clicks either the Done or Cancel button, in which case the macro sets the moreItems flag to FALSE with the code

```
=SET.VALUE(moreItems,FALSE)
```

When this happens, the condition set forth in the code

```
=WHILE(moreItems)
```

is no longer true so the loop terminates. The second flag value, enterLine, is used in conjunction with the Done button, which we'll detail shortly.

Now we come to the WHILE loop that displays the Line Item dialog box, validates the user's input and enters the validated data into the next row below the database, continuously, until the user clicks Done or Cancel. The formula

```
=InitializeLineItemDialog()
```

calls the subroutine in Figure 7.11 to clear the Description and Rate boxes in the Line Item dialog box, enter a 1 into the Quantity box, and select the first item in the Category and Unit lists.

```
InitializeLineItemDialog

=SET.VALUE(lineDescription,"")
=SET.VALUE(lineQty,1)
=SET.VALUE(lineUnit,"")
=SET.VALUE(lineUnitNum,1)
=SET.VALUE(lineRate,"")
=SET.VALUE(lineCategory,"")
=SET.VALUE(lineCategoryList,1)
=RETURN()
```

Figure 7.11   InitializeLineItemDialog subroutine

The formula in the cell named lineItemResponse within GetLineItems displays the dialog box, and will contain a result of FALSE if the user chooses the Cancel button, 13 if the user chooses the OK button, or 15 if the user chooses the Done button. If the user chooses either the OK or Done buttons, the macro evaluates the data the user entered into the dialog box and transfers it to the Invoice database if it is valid. Otherwise, if the user chooses the Cancel button, GetLineItems stops prompting for line items and returns FALSE to WriteInvoices, indicating that the current invoice was not completed.

Processing the Entry

Handling the Done button is a bit tricky. Some users will enter data into the dialog box and choose Done to indicate that it is the last line item for the invoice. Other users will be a little less efficient, choosing OK to enter the line item and then choosing Done the *next* time the dialog box is displayed. When a user does this, he or she wants the previous line item to be the last one for the invoice. We allow for this with the code shown in Figure 7.12.

```
=     IF(lineItemResponse=15)
=         SET.VALUE(moreItems,FALSE)
=         IF(AND(DialogUnchanged(),lineOffset>startingSize))
=             SET.VALUE(enterLine,FALSE)
=         END.IF()
=     END.IF()
```

Figure 7.12   GetLineItems macro code handling the Done button

We determine if the user wants to add this entry to the invoice by comparing the results in the LineItemDialog to their initial values. The function macro DialogUnchanged, shown in Figure 7.13, returns TRUE if the dialog box is still in its initial state, or FALSE otherwise.

DialogUnchanged	
=IF(lineDescription=0)	*no description entered*
= IF(lineQty=1)	*default Quantity value*
= IF(NOT(ISNA(lineUnitNum)))	*no unit typed in*
= IF(lineRate=0)	*no rate typed in*
= IF(NOT(ISNA(lineCategoryList)))	*no category typed in*
= IF(lineUnitNum=1)	*default unit still chosen*
= IF(lineCategoryList=1)	*first category still*
= RETURN(TRUE)	*yes! This is how we initialized it.*
= END.IF()	
= END.IF()	
= END.IF()	
= END.IF()	
= END.IF()	
= END.IF()	
=END.IF()	
=RETURN(FALSE)	*not the initial values*

Figure 7.13   DialogUnchanged function

If the user has changed the contents of the dialog box, we assume the user means to enter this as the last line item. We assume the same thing if this is the *first* line item for the invoice, which we determine by comparing lineOffset to its initial value saved in the cell startingSize.

If we conclude that the user means for us to ignore the current entry, we do so by setting the value of enterLine to FALSE. The remaining code within the WHILE loop, shown in Figure 7.14, treats the results of the dialog box as an entry to be placed into the database only if enterLine is TRUE.

	=	IF(enterLine)
	=	IF(NOT(IsValidLineItem()),GOTO(lineItemResponse))
clientID	=	ClientIDFromIndex(clientToInvoice)
nextInvNumber	=	INDIRECT(invSheet&"!NextInvoiceNumber")
	=	lineDescription
	=	lineCategory
	=	lineQty
	=	lineUnit
rate	=	IF(lineRate>0,lineRate,IF(ISNA(lineUnitNum),0,INDEX(UnitTable,lineUnitNum,2)))
	=	FORMULA.ARRAY(TRANSPOSE(clientID:rate),OFFSET(invDatabase,lineOffset,0,1))
lineOffset	=	lineOffset+1
	=	END.IF()

Figure 7.14   GetLineItems macro code transferring dialog box entries into Database

Validating the Line Item

The code

```
=IF(NOT(IsValidLineItem()),GO TO(lineItemResponse))
```

displays the dialog box again (without initializing it first) if the function macro IsValidLineItem, shown in Figure 7.15, returns FALSE.

	IsValidLineItem
validLineItem	=FALSE
	=IF(lineDescription=0)
	= ALERT("Please enter a description for the line item.")
	=ELSE.IF(AND(ISNA(lineUnitNum),lineRate=0))
	= ALERT("Please enter a rate for "&lineUnit&".")
	=ELSE()
	= SET.VALUE(validLineItem,TRUE)
	=END.IF()
	=RETURN(validLineItem)

Figure 7.15   IsValidLineItem function

Here we define an invalid line item as one missing either a description or a rate. Because we have a list of default units with associated rates, the user could legitimately leave the Rate box empty. We judge lineRate, the Rate box's result, as invalid only if it is empty *and* the user typed a unit instead of selecting a default. We determine which kind of unit the user entered within the formula

```
=ELSE.IF(AND(ISNA(lineUnitNum),lineRate=0))
```

The cell named lineUnitNum contains the result of the Unit list box. If the user selected from the Unit list (or typed in a unit that matches one in the list), lineUnitNum will contain the number of the selected item. Otherwise, lineUnitNum will contain the value #NA.

Entering the New Record

Our technique for transferring valid entries to the database is a little fancy, but quicker than the alternatives. Rather than using the FORMULA command to enter the values into the database individually, we assemble them into a contiguous range and transfer them in one step to the database as an array formula. To do this, we use the FORMULA.ARRAY command, the equivalent of entering an array formula into a cell or range of cells.

The syntax of FORMULA.ARRAY is

FORMULA.ARRAY(*formula_text,reference***)**

where, as with the FORMULA function, formula_text is the text of the formula you want to enter and reference is the cell range into which you want to enter it. Let's examine the formula_text and reference arguments we use individually.

The formula_text argument

```
TRANSPOSE(clientID:rate)
```

refers to the range of cells beginning with the one named clientID through the one named rate. These cells calculate each of the values for the new record, in the same order as the fields of the database. They're arranged in the macro vertically, of course, because that's the way Microsoft Excel calculates cells in a macro sheet. We need to enter the values into the database horizontally, so we use the TRANSPOSE function to transpose our vertical array into a horizontal one. The syntax of TRANSPOSE is

TRANSPOSE(*array*)

where array can either be the result of some other function that returns an array, such as DOCUMENTS, or, as in this case, a cell range that Microsoft Excel converts into an array from a reference.

Returning to our reference argument to the FORMULA.ARRAY command,

```
OFFSET(invDatabase,lineOffset,0,1)
```

we use the OFFSET function to calculate the reference of the new record in the database. The initial value of lineOffset is the number of rows in the Invoice database, so when we use it as the row_offset argument to the OFFSET function, it points to the first row below the database. The remaining arguments cause OFFSET to return a reference that is the size of one complete record, starting in the first column of the database. After the array has been entered and the lineOffset cell has incremented itself, this OFFSET calculation will return a reference to a similar range, one row below the previous one.

Because the formula_text argument to FORMULA.ARRAY is itself an array, we must enter the FORMULA.ARRAY formula in the macro *as an array formula* (using CTRL+SHIFT+ENTER in Microsoft Excel for Windows or COMMAND+ENTER in Microsoft Excel for the Macintosh). We would not need to do this if we were using FORMULA.ARRAY to enter a single formula into an array of cells.

Tip   Because Microsoft Excel displays no indicator that a formula has been entered as an array except in the Formula Bar when that cell is active, it is useful to shade cells containing array formulas to distinguish them visually from regular formulas.

Redefining the Database

After the last line item for the invoice is transferred to the database, GetLineItems finishes by redefining the Database area of INVOICE.XLS to include all of the new entries and incrementing the NextInvoiceNumber cell. This code is shown in Figure 7.16.

```
=ACTIVATE(invSheet)
=DEFINE.NAME("Database",OFFSET(!Database,0,0,lineOffset,))
=FORMULA(nextInvNumber+1,!NextInvoiceNumber)
=RETURN(TRUE)
```

Figure 7.16 GetLineItems macro redefining the Database

Note that we must activate INVOICE.XLS before redefining its Database range, because the DEFINE.NAME command, which is the equivalent of choosing Define Name from the Formula menu, only acts on the active sheet.

What Did We Just Do, and What's Next?

With GetLineItems complete, we've accomplished the first of our three goals for this lesson—managing data entry through macros so that we can use the full range of features in a custom dialog box. Was it worth all this hard work? We think so. Besides the immediate goal of providing an elegant interface for our users, we've accomplished something more important—we now know how to enter values or formulas from just about anywhere to just about anywhere. This is what Microsoft Excel macros are all about.

That was the steak. For some sizzle, let's look at the subject of dynamic menus.

Dynamic Menus

Microsoft Excel changes its menu structure as you activate different types of windows, so that the commands you are most likely to use are within convenient reach. You can create dynamic menus such as these in custom applications by defining event-triggered macros that are associated with window activation. To create such an event trigger, you use the ON.WINDOW function, which is similar to the ON.TIME function we looked at on page 48. The syntax of the ON.WINDOW function is as follows:

ON.WINDOW(*window_text,macro_text*)

where window_text is the name of the window which, when activated by the user, will trigger the execution of the macro specified in macro_text. Omitting the window_text argument associates a macro with the activation of all windows not specified in other ON.WINDOW functions, as in the following:

```
=ON.WINDOW(,"DefaultMacro")
```

Calling ON.WINDOW with the macro_text argument omitted removes the trigger for the specified window.

Handling the Client Tracking System's Menus

The Client Tracking System has a number of commands that are particular to either the Client List or Analysis modules. When MAILLIST.XLS is the active sheet, we want the commands for maintaining the Client List to appear at the top of the custom Tracking menu, but when TRACKING.XLS is active, we want the custom report commands to appear first. On the other hand, we don't want to force the user to activate a particular worksheet in order to access the commands associated with it.

To meet both of these challenges and to keep the number of commands on the Tracking menu to a minimum, we'll use three different versions of the Tracking menu, and trigger the installation of each onto the active menu bar using ON.WINDOW. The menus and their associated windows are shown in the following table.

Window Name	Windows Menu	Macintosh Menu
MAILLIST.XLS	**Tracking** Add Name... Edit / Delete... Sort... Find... Extract... Export for Mail Merge... Invoice... Analysis... Exit Client Tracking	**Tracking** Add / Edit / Delete... Sort... Find... Extract... Export for Mail Merge... Invoice... Analysis... Exit Client Tracking
TRACKING.XLS	**Tracking** Year to Date Category Breakdown Outstanding Invoices Reprint Invoice... Client List... Invoice... Exit Client Tracking	**Tracking** Year to Date Category Breakdown Outstanding Invoices Reprint Invoice... Client List... Invoice... Exit Client Tracking
All other windows	**Tracking** Client List... Invoice... Analysis... Exit Client Tracking	**Tracking** Client List... Invoice... Analysis... Exit Client Tracking

The Invoice, Analysis and Client List commands will each display the commands associated with that module arranged as pushbuttons in a dialog box. These "submenu" dialog boxes are shown in the table on the following page.

Choosing This Command	Produces This Dialog Box (Windows)	Produces This Dialog Box (Macintosh)

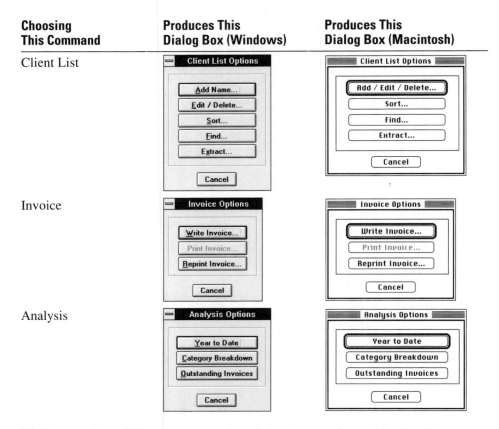

We'll create three different macros to install the three versions of the Tracking menu, and associate each with a window during the execution of the Auto_Open macro on TRACKING.XLA.

Replacing One Tracking Menu with Another

When the user activates a window, we want to replace the current version of the Tracking menu with the version appropriate for the window. We'll be using the ADD.MENU command to install the menu onto the active menu bar, but we must first delete the Tracking menu that is there; Microsoft Excel provides no single function for replacing menus. To delete the menu, we'll use the DELETE.MENU command, which uses the syntax

DELETE.MENU(*bar_num,menu*)

You can specify the menu to delete either as a position number (with menus numbered from left to right on the menu bar, starting with 1), or its name as text. In this case, as in most, it is much simpler to use the text form of the menu argument, as in

```
=DELETE.MENU(1,"Tracking")
```

which would delete the Tracking menu from the worksheet menu bar.

How to Avoid Deleting Non-Existent Menus

Trying to delete the Tracking menu from a bar on which it has not been installed will cause a macro error. We can protect ourselves from this by calling the GET.BAR function, with which we can determine various information about the current or other menu bars. There are two forms of GET.BAR, each with different syntax. The form

GET.BAR()

returns the ID number of the current menu bar. The second form

GET.BAR(*bar_num,menu,command*)

returns the position and text of menus and commands. As with the other functions for controlling custom menus, the menu and command arguments may be specified as either a position number or text. With GET.BAR, the type of the menu and command arguments determines the type of the result.

Determining a Menu Command's Position

If we wanted to locate the Invoice command on the current Tracking menu, we would do so by specifying the command argument as text, as in the following:

```
=GET.BAR(GET.BAR(),"Tracking","Invoice...")
```

Here we use GET.BAR with no arguments to return the ID number of the current menu bar, and then use that as the menu_bar argument to the other form of GET.BAR. In this case, since the menu and command arguments are text, GET.BAR would return the position number of the Invoice command or #NA if the command did not exist.

Determining a Menu Command's Text

To determine the text of a menu command, we specify a position number for the command argument. The following would return the text "Contents" when any Microsoft Excel built-in menu bar is active:

```
=GET.BAR(GET.BAR(),"Help",1)
```

Determining the Existence of a Menu

By specifying a command argument of 0, we direct our inquiry to the menu itself. The following would return the position number of the Tracking menu on the current menu bar or #NA if it were not present:

```
=GET.BAR(GET.BAR(),"Tracking",0)
```

Removing the Tracking Menu

Now that we know how to determine whether a menu exists, we're ready to create a subroutine that will remove the Tracking menu from the current bar. This subroutine, which we'll call RemoveTrackMenu, will be called each time one of our ON.WINDOW macros is triggered.

Go to the area named RemoveTrackMenu on TRACKING.XLA. The following pseudo-code has been placed into the RemoveTrackMenu macro for guidance:

RemoveTrackMenu
If the tracking menu is installed on the current bar   Delete the tracking menu from the current bar END.IF() =RETURN()

Figure 7.17   RemoveTrackMenu macro pseudo-code

Replace the pseudo-code with the completed macro instructions, as shown in Figure 7.18:

RemoveTrackMenu
=IF(NOT(ISNA(GET.BAR(GET.BAR(),"Tracking",0)))) =   DELETE.MENU(GET.BAR(),"Tracking") =END.IF() =RETURN()

Figure 7.18   RemoveTrackMenu macro code

Creating the Tracking Menus

The Tracking menus are defined in the tables shown in Figures 7.19, 7.20 and 7.21. Enter these into TRACKING.XLA in cells T5:X38. The names MailListMenu, AnalysisMenu and GenericMenu have already been defined for you.

	S	T	U	V	W	X
5	MaillistMenu	Trac&king				
6		&Add Name...	AddToMailList		Add records to the database	
7		&Edit / Delete...	EditMailList		Edit or delete existing database records	
8		-				
9		&Sort...	SortMailList		Sort the database	
10		-				
11		&Find...	FindClient		Query the database	
12		Ex&tract...	ExtractRecords		Extract selected records	
13		-				
14		Ex&port for Mail Merge...	ExportAsText		Export from database to a text file	
15		-				
16		&Invoice...	AccessInvoicing		Write/Print invoices	
17		A&nalysis...	AccessAnalysis		View reports	
18		-				
19		E&xit Client Tracking	QuitMe		Exit the Client Tracking Application	

Figure 7.19   MailListMenu command table (Windows)

	S	T	U	V	W	X
5	MaillistMenu	Trac&king				
6		&Add / /Edit / Delete...	AddToMailList		Add , edit or delete Client records	
7		-				
8		&Sort...	SortMailList		Sort the database	
9		-				
10		&Find...	FindClient		Query the database	
11		Ex&tract...	ExtractRecords		Extract selected records	
12		-				
13		Ex&port for Mail Merge...	ExportAsText		Export from database to a text file	
14		-				
15		&Invoice...	AccessInvoicing		Write/Print invoices	
16		A&nalysis...	AccessAnalysis		View reports	
17		-				
18		E&xit Client Tracking	QuitMe		Exit the Client Tracking Application	

Figure 7.20   MailListMenu command table (Macintosh)

	S	T	U	V	W	X
21	**AnalysisMenu**	Trac&king				
22		&Year to Date	YTDReport			
23		&Category Breakdow n	CategoryReport			
24		&Outstanding Invoices	UnpaidReport			
25		-				
26		&Reprint Invoice...	ReprintInvoices			
27		-				
28		&Client List...	AccessMailList		View / Edit Client List	
29		&Invoice...	AccessInvoicing		Write/Print invoices	
30		-				
31		E&xit Client Tracking	QuitMe		Exit the Client Tracking Application	
32						
33	**GenericMenu**	Trac&king				
34		&Client List...	AccessMailList		View / Edit Client List	
35		&Invoice...	AccessInvoicing		Write/Print invoices	
36		A&nalysis...	AccessAnalysis		View Reports	
37		-				
38		E&xit Client Tracking	QuitMe		Exit the Client Tracking Application	

Figure 7.21   AnalysisMenu and GenericMenu command tables (Windows and Macintosh)

Creating the Menu Installer Macros

All three of our trigger macros will perform essentially the same tasks, the only difference being the menu definition reference that these macros will pass as the argument to ADD.MENU. For this reason, we'll define a generic subroutine called InstallTrackingMenu, which will accept the menu definition area as its argument, remove the current Tracking menu and install the new one.

We'll only install the Tracking menu onto the standard menu for worksheets and macro sheets. This limitation will make it easier for us to clean up after ourselves when the user chooses to exit the Client Tracking System—if we never attach the Tracking menu to any other menu bar, we avoid closing the application with the Tracking menu still visible somewhere.

Go to the area named InstallTrackingMenu on TRACKING.XLA. The following pseudo-code has been placed there for guidance:

InstallTrackingMenu

argument for menu definition range: "menuRange"
if current menu bar is built-in bar for w orksheets
  turn off screen redraw
  Remove the current Tracking menu
  append menu defined in menuRange to current bar
END.IF()
=RETURN()

Figure 7.22   InstallTrackingMenu macro pseudo-code

Replace the pseudo-code with the completed macro instructions, as shown in Figure 7.23:

```
InstallTrackingMenu

=ARGUMENT("menuRange",8)
=IF(GET.BAR()=1)
=   ECHO(FALSE)
=   RemoveTrackMenu()
=   ADD.MENU(1,menuRange)
=END.IF()
=RETURN()
```

Figure 7.23   InstallTrackingMenu macro code

Notice that we need to specify a type_num of 8 as the second argument to the ARGUMENT function, indicating that we will be passing a reference argument to the subroutine. The InstallTracking Menu subroutine must be called with the appropriate argument each time the active window changes. When the Client Mail List is activated, we will install the Tracking menu for the Client Mail List module with the macro InstallMailMenu, shown in Figure 7.24:

```
InstallMailMenu

=InstallTrackingMenu(MaillistMenu)
=RETURN()
```

Figure 7.24   InstallMailMenu macro code

Type the macro in Figure 7.24 into the area named InstallMailMenu. Type the appropriate code (with different arguments) in the areas named InstallAnalysisMenu and InstallGenericMenu, as shown in Figure 7.25:

```
InstallAnalysisMenu

=InstallTrackingMenu(AnalysisMenu)
=RETURN()
```

```
InstallGenericMenu

=InstallTrackingMenu(GenericMenu)
=RETURN()
```

Figure 7.25   InstallAnalysisMenu and InstallGenericMenu macro code

To experiment with the menus, run each of the installer macros.

Installing the Tracking Menus Dynamically

Now we're ready to have Microsoft Excel run the installer macros for us. We'll want to create the ON.WINDOW triggers as the Client Tracking System is loaded, and we'll want to clear these triggers when the user closes the system. We'll handle both of these through a single custom function called from the Auto_Open and Auto_Close macros on TRACKING.XLA. This function, named InstallWindowHandlers, will accept a single argument called true_false. If the true_false argument is TRUE, we'll create the ON.WINDOW triggers for MAILLIST.XLS, TRACKING.XLS and all other windows; if the argument is FALSE, we'll clear the triggers.

Go to the area named InstallWindowHandlers on TRACKING.XLA. The following pseudo-code has been placed there for guidance:

InstallWindowHandlers
function ARGUMENT: TRUE=create trigger; FALSE=remove trigger attach (or detach) MailListMenu to activation of MAILLIST.XLS attach (or detach) AnalysisMenu to activation of TRACKING.XLS attach (or detach) TrackingMenu to activation of other windows =RETURN()

Figure 7.26   InstallWindowHandlers macro pseudo-code

Replace the pseudo-code with the completed macro instructions, as shown in Figure 7.27.

InstallWindowHandlers
=ARGUMENT("true_false") =ON.WINDOW(mailSheet,IF(true_false,"InstallMailMenu","")) =ON.WINDOW(trackingSheet,IF(true_false,"InstallAnalysisMenu","")) =ON.WINDOW(,IF(true_false,"InstallGenericMenu","")) =RETURN()

Figure 7.27   InstallWindowHandlers macro code

Go to the area named Auto_Open on TRACKING.XLA. You will see within the body of the macro a call to InstallWindowHandlers which has been commented out:

```
**InstallWindowHandlers(TRUE)
```

using the Comment macro discussed in Lesson 3. Restore the commented formula to an actual call to the InstallWindowHandlers subroutine by either replacing the two asterisks that precede the subroutine name with an equal sign or by running the Uncomment macro with the commented cell selected.

To experiment with the dynamic menus, run the portion of Auto_Open which calls InstallWindowHandlers.

And Now, the Complications

With the exception of ON.TIME, Microsoft Excel only triggers its event macros in response to user action. If the user opens a macro sheet that contains an Auto_Open macro, Microsoft Excel runs that macro. If there is an ON.WINDOW macro triggered by the activation of that window, Microsoft Excel then runs that. But if a macro opens the same sheet under the same circumstances, Microsoft Excel will not run either of these automatic macros.

We must address this behavior in the Client Tracking System to guarantee that the proper form of the Tracking menu is always displayed, because some of the macros will change the active window. As you will see, we handle this in two ways, one quite straightforward and the other, well, not so. Let's look at the simpler solution first, and then discuss why the more complicated one is necessary.

The Simple Workaround

In many of our macros, we can anticipate exactly which automatic macros we need to run ourselves, because we know what file will be active when the macro returns. An example of this is the OpenFiles subroutine, shown in Figures 7.28 and 7.29, which we call from the Auto_Open macro to open the files used by the various modules of the Client Tracking System.

OpenFiles
=IF(FileNotOpen(trackingSheet),OPEN(thisPath&"\"&trackingSheet,0))
=IF(FileNotOpen(ytdSheet),OPEN(thisPath&"\"&ytdSheet,0))
=IF(FileNotOpen(outstandingSheet),OPEN(thisPath&"\"&outstandingSheet,0))
=IF(FileNotOpen(categorySheet),OPEN(thisPath&"\"&categorySheet,0))
=IF(FileNotOpen(invSheet),OPEN(thisPath&"\"&invSheet,0))
=IF(FileNotOpen(mailSheet))
=   OPEN(thisPath&"\"&mailSheet,0)
=   FULL(TRUE)
=END.IF()
=RETURN()

Figure 7.28   OpenFiles subroutine (Windows)

```
OpenFiles

=IF(FileNotOpen(trackingSheet),OPEN(thisPath&":"&trackingSheet,0))
=IF(FileNotOpen(ytdSheet),OPEN(thisPath&":"&ytdSheet,0))
=IF(FileNotOpen(outstandingSheet),OPEN(thisPath&":"&outstandingSheet,0))
=IF(FileNotOpen(categorySheet),OPEN(thisPath&":"&categorySheet,0))
=IF(FileNotOpen(invSheet),OPEN(thisPath&":"&invSheet,0))
=IF(FileNotOpen(mailSheet))
=   OPEN(thisPath&":"&mailSheet,0)
=   FULL(TRUE)
=END.IF()
=RETURN()
```

Figure 7.29   OpenFiles subroutine (Macintosh)

OpenFiles opens the file MAILLIST.XLS last because we want the Client Mail List to be the active window when the Client Tracking System first loads. Therefore, we need to include in Auto_Open a call to the InstallMailMenu subroutine.

Go to the area named Auto_Open on TRACKING.XLA. You will see, just after the call to InstallWindowHandlers, a call to InstallMailMenu which has been commented out. Replace the comment with an actual call to the InstallMailMenu subroutine.

Other Uses for the Simple Workaround

After the system is loaded, several of the macros that are executed from menu commands or push buttons on the submenu dialogs change which window is active and leave it changed. In these cases, we must install the proper menu for the window ourselves. An example of this is in the macro called AccessMaillist, shown in Figure 7.30, which is executed from the Client List command on the generic and analysis versions of the Tracking menu.

	AccessMailList
mailListChoice	=DIALOG.BOX(mailListOptions)
	=IF(mailListChoice)
	= ECHO(FALSE)
	= SET.NAME("currentWindow",GET.WINDOW(1))
	= ActivateOrOpen(mailSheet)
actionCompleted	= CHOOSE(mailListChoice,AddToMailList(),EditMailList(),SortMailList(),FindClient(),ExtractRecords())
	= IF(actionCompleted)
	= InstallMailMenu()
	= ELSE()
	= ACTIVATE(currentWindow)
	= END.IF()
	=END.IF()
	=RETURN()

Figure 7.30   AccessMailList macro code

If the user carries out any of the commands listed in the Client List Options dialog box, AccessMailList switches to MAILLIST.XLS and attempts to perform the action by running the appropriate macro. Each of these macros returns TRUE if the user completes the chosen command (that is, never chooses Cancel from any of the dialog boxes the macro displays). This value becomes the result of the formula in the cell named actionCompleted. When this cell is TRUE, AccessMailList leaves MAILLIST.XLS as the active window, on the assumption that the user may want to further examine or modify the Client List. In this case, because the macro changed the active window, it ensures that the proper menu is displayed by running InstallMailMenu.

Anticipating the Unknown

Now we come to the situation which we cannot so easily anticipate. Each of the reports displayed from either the analysis form of the Tracking menu or the Analysis Options dialog box contains a macro button on the worksheet that hides the report by running the macro HideThisReport. When the macro hides the report, whatever window is behind the report window becomes active, and HideThisReport needs to install the proper menu for the window. Unfortunately, there's no way to *calculate* what macro to run.

We could use the GET.WINDOW function to get the name of the active window, compare that to window names we know about, and then run the appropriate macro, as in the following:

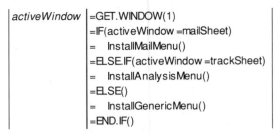

Figure 7.31   Possible method of determining which macro to run

but this method is less open-ended than we would like, because we would have to change this macro if we added new modules (with new window names and associated menus) to the Client Tracking System. We may never do this, but just in case, we'd prefer to make the Client Tracking System easily extensible, without too many obscure details to remember.

The system that we have devised to solve this problem saves the reference of the macro that installed the previous menu, so that we can run it after we hide the report. In order to do this, we need to save the references of two macros—the one that installed the current menu, and the one that installed the previous menu. This means that we need to modify InstallMailMenu, InstallAnalysisMenu and InstallTrackingMenu so that they update these two references.

Saving the Names of the Menu Installer Macros

We'll save the references of the current and previous trigger macros by calling a custom subroutine, called SaveMenuMacro, which will maintain the names prevMenuMacro and curMenuMacro. The code for this subroutine is shown in Figure 7.32.

SaveMenuMacro	
=ARGUMENT("new Handler",8)	reference of the menu installer that is in effect
=SET.NAME("prevMenuMacro",curMenuMacro)	save the previous menu installer reference
=SET.NAME("curMenuMacro",new Handler)	save the current menu installer
=RETURN()	

Figure 7.32   SaveMenuMacro subroutine

The formula

```
=SET.NAME("prevMenuMacro",curMenuMacro)
```

assigns the definition of curMenuMacro to the name prevMenuMacro, and the formula

```
=SET.NAME("curMenuMacro",newHandler)
```

then redefines curMenuMacro as the reference in the newHandler argument. We'll be calling SaveMenuMacro with the appropriate newHandler argument from

InstallMailMenu, InstallAnalysisMenu and InstallGenericMenu, but before we modify those macros let's think about how SaveMenuMacro will work.

The first time we'll call SaveMenuMacro is when the Auto_Open macro calls InstallMailMenu. At this point, the names prevMenuMacro and curMenuMacro either won't exist (depending upon the state of the Add-In when we last saved it) or won't be meaningful. When SaveMenuMacro returns from this first call, the name prevMenuMacro will still be meaningless, but the name curMenuMacro will contain the correct reference to the InstallMailMenu macro.

The next time SaveMenuMacro will be called will be in response to some action by the user, either by activating a window or choosing one of the commands from the Tracking menu that activates a window. In the first case, Microsoft Excel will run the window's trigger macro automatically. In the latter case, we will run the appropriate macro ourselves as a subroutine, as discussed previously in this lesson. After SaveMenuMacro returns the second time (and every time thereafter when the user exits the Client Tracking System), both curMenuMacro and prevMenuMacro will be correctly defined.

The only time the prevMenuMacro could possibly contain the wrong reference, then, is just after the Client Tracking System has loaded. This will probably never cause a problem, but, just to be safe, we initialize the name prevMenuMacro in Auto_Open before calling InstallMailMenu, with the formula

```
=SaveMenuMacro(InstallGenericMenu)
```

Changing the Menu Installer Macros

With a mechanism in place for saving the macro references, we need to call SaveMenuMacro from our three menu intaller macros, as shown in Figure 7.33, the modified InstallMailMenu macro:

InstallMailMenu
=SaveMenuMacro(InstallMailMenu) =InstallTrackingMenu(MaillistMenu) =RETURN()

Figure 7.33 InstallMailMenu macro code that updates the curMenuMacro name

Modify InstallMailMenu as shown, and modify InstallAnalysisMenu and InstallGenericMenu with the appropriate argument in the SetMenuMacro call.

Running the Previous Menu Installer Macro

We run the macro whose reference is saved in the prevMenuMacro name by simply calling it as a subroutine from HideThisReport, as follows:

SAVE.AS(,0) is discussed on page 225.

HideThisReport	
=SET.NAME("currentWindow ",GET.WINDOW(1))	
=ECHO(FALSE)	
=HIDE()+ACTIVATE(currentWindow)	*hide it*
=SAVE.AS(,0)	*make sure it's not dirty*
=prevMenuMacro()	*run previous window's ON.WINDOW macro*
=RETURN()	

Figure 7.34   HideThisReport macro code

Go to the area named HideThisReport on TRACKING.XLA. You will see a call to prevMenuMacro which has been commented out. Replace the comment with an actual call to prevMenuMacro, save the Add-In, and then run the Auto_Open macro to experiment with the dynamic menus.

Are We There Yet?

As we discovered with fully customized data entry, some elements of a sophisticated user interface require a lot of hard work. Our third and final goal in this lesson is to make our application look more like a standalone program.

Disguising Microsoft Excel

Some people distrust custom applications that reveal their spreadsheet origins, or merely prefer that the development environments of their dedicated systems remain anonymous. At the same time, users of Microsoft Excel appreciate the myriad ways they can customize it for their own use and don't welcome unexpected changes to their environments. In the remainder of this lesson, we will examine the techniques you can use in your custom applications to satisfy users in both categories.

Changing Window Settings

If you run the EIS module as described in Lesson 5, you will see that we have changed a number of settings on the EIS module's main worksheet window, EXEC.XLS, to make it look less like a spreadsheet. The most obvious of these changes, of course, is that we've turned off its gridlines. We've also hidden the window's system menu in Microsoft Excel for Windows and its Close box in Microsoft Excel for the Macintosh by protecting the window.

You can make changes such as these to the windows that you show to users without affecting any changes they may have made to their own environments, because these settings live with the documents, not Microsoft Excel itself. And because the settings are saved with the file, you can generally make the changes at development time rather than runtime.

Of course, there's always an exception, in this case, the protected window. We want the main window maximized, but this is a setting that is not saved with the document, and which we cannot change at runtime with the window protected. To maximize a protected window, therefore, we unprotect it first and protect it again afterwards, as in the following:

```
=PROTECT.DOCUMENT(,FALSE,)
=FULL(TRUE)
=PROTECT.DOCUMENT(,TRUE,)
```

Figure 7.35   Code for maximizing a protected window

The PROTECT.DOCUMENT command, which uses the syntax

PROTECT.DOCUMENT(*contents,windows,password,objects*)

is a little different from other Microsoft Excel commands in its handling of omitted arguments. With the WORKSPACE command, for instance, you can leave a setting as it is by omitting its argument. With PROTECT.DOCUMENT, however, you turn off all protection by turning off just the contents, windows, or objects settings. So if we want to unprotect the document temporarily and protect it again with the former settings intact, we need to determine those settings using the GET.DOCUMENT function before we unprotect it, and then use the return values of those functions when we protect the document. An example of this technique is shown in Figure 7.36.

```
protectCells   =GET.DOCUMENT(7)                                    are cells protected?
protectObjects =GET.DOCUMENT(44)                                   are objects protected?
               =PROTECT.DOCUMENT(,FALSE,)                          unprotect the document
               ...Do stuff
               =PROTECT.DOCUMENT(protectCells,TRUE,,protectObjects)
```

Figure 7.36   More considerate code for changing protected windows

Changing Workspace Settings

Microsoft Excel saves workspace settings, such as the display of the formula bar, status bar, scrollbars and toolbars, as it exits, so if we want to change any of these settings temporarily, we must first save the current settings and restore them before Microsoft Excel terminates.

In the EIS module, we hide the toolbars, scrollbars, status bar and formula bar in a subroutine named ChangeWorkspace, which is called from the EXEC.XLA Add-In's Auto_Open macro. First, though, we determine the current status of those settings in the subroutine SaveStatus.

Go to the area named SaveStatus on EXEC.XLA. The following pseudo-code has been placed there for guidance:

	Save Status
scrollStatus statusStatus formulaStatus	is scrollbar on? is status bar on? is formula bar on? save horizontal array of all visible toolbars =RETURN()

Figure 7.37   SaveStatus macro pseudo-code

Replace the pseudo-code with the completed macro instructions, as shown in Figure 7.38.

	Save Status
scrollStatus statusStatus formulaStatus	=GET.WORKSPACE(5) =GET.WORKSPACE(6) =GET.WORKSPACE(7) =SET.NAME("toolbarStatus",GET.TOOLBAR(9)) =RETURN()

Figure 7.38   SaveStatus macro code

The GET.WORKSPACE function tells us the current settings for the scrollbars, status bar and formula bar with the calls GET.WORKSPACE(5), GET.WORKSPACE(6) and GET.WORKSPACE(7), respectively. We can determine which toolbars are visible using GET.TOOLBAR(9), which returns the ID numbers of all visible toolbars as a horizontal array. The values returned by the calls to GET.WORKSPACE can be recalled later through simple references to the cells containing the formulas, but we need to store the array returned by GET.TOOLBAR(9) in a form that preserves the full array. The simplest method for doing so is to save the function's result as a name using SET.NAME. When you use SET.NAME to store an array result, you enter the formula as an array formula.

Now we can change the workspace settings using the WORKSPACE command and hide each of the visible toolbars with the SHOW.TOOLBAR command.

Changing Workspace Settings

Go to the area named ChangeWorkspace on EXEC.XLA. The following pseudo-code has been placed there for guidance:

ChangeWorkspace
remove scrollbar, status bar, formula bar
if there is at least one visible toolbar
for each visible toolbar
hide it
NEXT
END.IF
=RETURN()

Figure 7.39   ChangeWorkspace macro pseudo-code

Replace the pseudo-code with the completed macro instructions, as shown in Figure 7.40.

ChangeWorkspace
=WORKSPACE(,,,FALSE,FALSE,FALSE)
=IF(NOT(ISERROR(toolbarStatus)))
= FOR("barCount",1,COLUMNS(toolbarStatus))
=   SHOW.TOOLBAR(INDEX(toolbarStatus,1,barCount),FALSE)
= NEXT()
=END.IF()
=RETURN()

Figure 7.40   ChangeWorkspace macro code

Working with Custom Menu Bars

We've seen how to add custom menus to and delete custom menus from the standard menu bars. Replacing these menu bars with our own involves four simple changes to the techniques previously discussed:

1   Obtain a new menu bar ID number using the ADD.BAR function.

2   Add menus to the menu bar associated with this ID number.

3   Display the menu bar with the SHOW.BAR command.

4   When you are finished with them, free the memory occupied by these menu bars using the DELETE.BAR command.

Up until now, we have focused on customizing the built-in menu bars. You can also create and use entirely new menu bars in addition to (or instead of) the built-in menu bars. You create a new, empty menu bar with the ADD.BAR function, which takes no arguments and returns the ID of the new menu bar. To see this menu bar, you must display it by calling the SHOW.BAR command, which uses the syntax

SHOW.BAR(*bar_num*)

where bar_num is the ID number of the menu bar to display. Omitting this argument displays the built-in menu bar appropriate for the active window.

Microsoft Excel allows you to maintain 15 custom menu bars at a time. Menu bars require a good deal of memory, however, so if possible, you should create them as needed and delete them when you can, using the DELETE.BAR command, which uses the following syntax:

DELETE.BAR(*bar_num*)

Be aware that Microsoft Excel will not delete the active menu bar, so you must use SHOW.BAR to display another bar first.

Using Custom Menu Bars in the EIS Module

The Client Tracking System's EIS module uses a single menu bar with a single menu defined in the area named miniMenu, shown in Figure 7.41.

miniMenu	&File				
	E&xit	QuitMe		Exit the Executive Report Generator	

Figure 7.41   MiniMenu definition

This menu bar is created and displayed in a subroutine called ShowLittleMenu, which is called from the Auto_Open macro. The subroutine RestoreStatus, which is called at the time the user exits the EIS module, restores the built-in menu bars and deletes the custom menu bar.

A Subroutine to Display a Custom Menu Bar

Go to the area named ShowLittleMenu on EXEC.XLA. The pseudo-code shown in Figure 7.42 has been placed there for guidance.

	ShowLittleMenu
newBar	create a new menu bar
	add single menu with single exit command
	display the new bar
	=RETURN()

Figure 7.42   ShowLittleMenu macro pseudo-code

Replace the pseudo-code with the completed macro instructions, as shown in Figure 7.43.

	Show LittleMenu
newBar	=ADD.BAR() =ADD.MENU(new Bar,miniMenu) =SHOW.BAR(new Bar) =RETURN()

Figure 7.43   ShowLittleMenu macro code

Renaming Windows

One of the more egregious signals that an application was developed in Microsoft Excel is the file name that appears in each window's title bar. The EIS module replaces each report window's title and that of the main screen with the WINDOW.TITLE command, which uses the syntax

WINDOW.TITLE(*text*)

where text is the name that you want to assign to the title bar of the active window. By freeing you from the naming constraints of the file system, this command lets you do a number of things that would be impossible otherwise, such as including spaces in the title (illegal in the DOS file system) or showing no title at all.

The Auto_Open macro of the EIS module calls a subroutine named OpenFiles to open the report worksheets and main screen. The OpenFiles routine, in turn, calls the subroutine OpenReportWindow, the beginning of which is shown in Figure 7.44, passing it the name of the file to open and the text to use for its title.

OpenReportWindow
=ARGUMENT("aFileName") =ARGUMENT("aWindow Title") =OPEN(aFileName,0,TRUE) =ACTIVATE(aFileName) =WINDOW.TITLE(aWindow Title)

Figure 7.44   Beginning of the OpenReportWIndow subroutine

Working with Renamed Windows

Once you have renamed a window, you can no longer use the document and window names interchangeably. If you have changed the window title of the file EXEC.XLS to "Executive Report Generator," for example, the following formula will return a #NA error:

```
=GET.WINDOW(2,"EXEC.XLS")
```

This formula, however, would be unaffected by the change:

```
=GET.DOCUMENT(1,"EXEC.XLS")
```

because "EXEC.XLS" is still the name of the *document*, which is what GET.DOCUMENT expects as its second argument.

Microsoft Excel requires that the file names of all open documents be unique, but does allow you to rename multiple windows using the same name. If you take advantage of this feature, you'll need to use other functions such as GET.DOCUMENT to distinguish between the windows.

Restoring Renamed Windows

To set the window's title back to its original state, activate the window and call WINDOW.TITLE again, omitting the text argument. Microsoft Excel also resets a window's title when you create a second window from it using the NEW.WINDOW command.

Renaming Microsoft Excel

The biggest giveaway of Microsoft Excel, of course, is its own title bar. You can assign Microsoft Excel a pseudonym with the APP.TITLE command, which uses the syntax

APP.TITLE(*text*)

where text is the name you want to display in the Microsoft Excel title bar. The EIS module changes the Microsoft Excel title bar text to "Exotic Reports" during its Auto_Open macro, shown in Figure 7.45.

Auto_Open
=ECHO(FALSE)
=APP.TITLE("Exotic Reports")
=SaveStatus()
=ChangeWorkspace()
=OpenFiles()
=Show LittleMenu()
=RETURN()

Figure 7.45 Auto_Open macro code

Resetting the Microsoft Excel Title Bar

As with WINDOW.TITLE, you can revert to the default application title by calling APP.TITLE with the text argument omitted.

Making Microsoft Excel Think a Document Is Saved

Let's go back to the OpenReportWindow subroutine, shown in Figure 7.46, and examine a change we make to each of the worksheets as we load it.

OpenReportWindow
=ARGUMENT("aFileName")
=ARGUMENT("aWindow Title")
=OPEN(aFileName,0,TRUE)
=ACTIVATE(aFileName)
=WINDOW.TITLE(aWindow Title)
=RedirectButton()
=SAVE.AS(,0)
=RETURN()

Figure 7.46 Complete OpenReportWindow subroutine

The formula

```
=RedirectButton()
```

calls the subroutine RedirectButton, shown in Figure 7.47, to change the macro that runs when the user clicks the button labeled Close Report on each report worksheet. The buttons are linked to the HideThisReport macro on TRACKING.XLA that we assigned to them when we created them with the Button tool on the Utility Toolbar.

RedirectButton
=PROTECT.DOCUMENT(,FALSE,)
=CHANGE.LINK(thisPath&"\"&trackingAppName,thisMacroSheet,1)
=PROTECT.DOCUMENT(,TRUE,)
=RETURN()

Figure 7.47 RedirectButton macro (Windows)

RedirectButton changes the link on the sheet from TRACKING.XLA to EXEC.XLA, which has a HideThisReport macro of its own. If we did not do this, Microsoft Excel would load TRACKING.XLA the first time the user clicked the Close Report button. Normally, we appreciate Microsoft Excel demand-loading the Add-In, but not in this case. We just want to share the report worksheets between two different Add-Ins.

We change the link with CHANGE.LINK command, the equivalent of choosing Change from the Links dialog box that is displayed when you choose Links from the File menu. The CHANGE.LINK command is described in the *Microsoft Excel Function Reference*.

What is more interesting about the OpenReportWindow subroutine is that after it changes the file it sets it as though it has not been changed with the formula

```
=SAVE.AS(,0)
```

SAVE.AS, of course, is the equivalent of choosing Save As from the File menu, and its normal syntax

SAVE.AS(*document_text,type_num,prot_pwd,backup,write_res_pwd,read_only_rec*)

corresponds to the various options in the Save As dialog box. This is a special syntax of the command, however, that only pretends to save the file. When the file is closed, Microsoft Excel won't ask the user what to do about unsaved changes because it won't think there are any. We use this technique in the EIS module because the user may close the system by closing Microsoft Excel.

Leaving Microsoft Excel as You Found It

If you have taken the precautions of saving the original workspace settings, restoring them is a straightforward process. The EIS module resets the scrollbars, status bar, formula bar and toolbars in a subroutine named RestoreStatus, which is called from the EXEC.XLA Auto_Close macro.

The only snag here is that we must anticipate the two ways in which the user may exit the system—by choosing the Exit command from the File menu, or by choosing the Close command from the Microsoft Excel system menu. With the latter method, we can be sure that Microsoft Excel will call the Auto_Close macro. With the former, we must call it ourselves.

Go to the area named RestoreStatus on EXEC.XLA. The pseudo-code shown in Figure 7.48 has been placed there for guidance.

```
RestoreStatus

restore status bar, scrollbars, formula bar to the way we found them
if there were toolbars showing previously
  for each previously displayed toolbar
    display it
  NEXT
END.IF
show the built-in menu bar for current environment
delete the custom menu bar
=RETURN()
```

Figure 7.48   RestoreStatus macro pseudo-code

Replace the pseudo-code with the completed macro instructions, as shown in Figure 7.49.

```
RestoreStatus

=WORKSPACE(,,,scrollStatus,statusStatus,formulaStatus)
=IF(NOT(ISERROR(toolbarStatus)))
=  FOR("barCount",1,COLUMNS(toolbarStatus))
=     SHOW.TOOLBAR(INDEX(toolbarStatus,1,barCount),TRUE)
=  NEXT()
=END.IF()
=SHOW.BAR(IF(ISNA(GET.DOCUMENT(1)),3,1))
=DELETE.BAR(newBar)
=RETURN()
```

Figure 7.49   RestoreStatus macro code

Go to the area named QuitMe on EXEC.XLA. The following pseudo-code has been placed there for guidance:

```
QuitMe

turn off screen redraw
restore toolbars, status bar, scrollbars, formula bar to the way we found them
for each of the report windows
  activate it
  close without saving
NEXT
activate the EIS panel
change Excel's title to the normal
close EIS panel without saving
close add-in
=RETURN()
```

Figure 7.50   QuitMe macro pseudo-code

Replace the pseudo-code with the completed macro instructions, as shown in Figure 7.51.

QuitMe
=ECHO(FALSE)
=Auto_Close()
=FOR("reportCount",1,3)
=   ACTIVATE(INDEX(ytdWindow :outstandingWindow ,reportCount))
=   FILE.CLOSE(FALSE)
=NEXT()
=ACTIVATE(EISWindow)
=APP.TITLE()
=FILE.CLOSE(FALSE)
=ACTIVATE(thisMacroSheet)+CLOSE()
=RETURN()

Figure 7.51   QuitMe macro code

Go to the area named Auto_Close on EXEC.XLA. You will see within the body of the macro a call to RestoreStatus which has been commented out.

Replace the commented call to RestoreStatus with the actual formula.

Lesson Summary

In this lesson, we continued the creation of the Client Tracking System, a custom application. A macro for invoice writing was developed that displayed a simplified data entry dialog box, validated entries and handled user selection of Done, OK and Cancel buttons. Three menu command tables were introduced to define the different menus users should have access to depending on which module of our application was active (or if neither was active). The ON.WINDOW, GET.BAR and SET.NAME commands were used in macros to determine when to install which menu. We put the finishing touches on the EIS module of our application by writing macros that suppress or alter various features of the standard Microsoft Excel display while that module is active.

Dynamic Data Exchange

Dynamic Data Exchange, or *DDE*, is a protocol originated on the Windows environment through which programs may exchange data or execute each other's commands. With the advent of Apple Events on the Macintosh, available through System Software Version 7 or later, Microsoft has implemented the DDE protocol for its programs running under that environment as well. As of this writing, Microsoft Excel is the only application that provides DDE on the Macintosh, but other programs are expected to follow suit shortly.

The most obvious use for DDE is as a sort of private clipboard through which a document created in one application is linked to data from another and receives updates as the data is changed. An example of such a link is a report written in Word for Windows which includes data from a Microsoft Excel spreadsheet. In Word for Windows, this kind of document link is usually established without the macro language, by using the Paste Special command to create a LINK field.

DDE can do a lot more than just transfer data. It can also be used to execute another application's *commands*, so that different programs can work together as one integrated unit. Thus, the complete customization of Microsoft Excel made possible by its macro language may be extended to entire suites of applications.

You Don't Get All This Power for Free

An important consideration with any type of DDE communication, whether it be through document links or macros, is that both applications must be running in order to communicate. If your system doesn't have enough memory to run both programs simultaneously, you will not be able to take advantage of DDE.

As you explore DDE, you'll discover that other applications adhere to Microsoft's standard DDE specification with varying degrees of precision – what works in one program may not work in another, or may work in a slightly different way. Be prepared for some trial and error.

The final bump in the road to DDE mastery is that accessing one program from another often entails mastering both. The end reward, of course, is that this burden is lifted from users of your custom applications.

The DDE Protocol

The entire DDE specification consists of only a few messages which applications may send to each other. Before we discuss these messages and their equivalent Microsoft Excel macro functions, we need to understand the structure of a DDE conversation.

Clients and Servers

When a program initiates a DDE conversation, it is called the *Client*; the responding application is called the *Server*. These roles are maintained through the life of the conversation and govern the types of messages each application can send. Programs may be engaged in several simultaneous DDE conversations, acting as the client in one and the server in another. To insure that messages reach the correct parties, each conversation is assigned a unique channel number that remains active until the conversation ends.

Topics and Items

Each DDE conversation is established on a particular *Topic*, usually a data file, with the conversation thereafter limited to the data *Items* associated with that topic. If, for example, you want to get data from a particular Microsoft Excel spreadsheet, you need to initiate the DDE conversation with Microsoft Excel, specifying the spreadsheet's name as the topic. You may then use that channel to obtain the contents of any cell (item) within that spreadsheet.

If the sole purpose of your DDE conversation is to execute the Server's commands, a data file may not be an appropriate topic. In this case, Microsoft encourages developers to support a general topic in their applications called *System*. So that applications without prior knowledge of each other's topics may communicate, Microsoft suggests that each application associate a data item named *Topics* with the System topic. A program that follows this specification responds to a request for the Topics item by sending the client the names of all available topics, including the names of its open files.

DDE Messages

The following table summarizes the nine DDE messages and the way in which each may be accessed from Microsoft Excel macros.

Message	Description	Microsoft Excel Equivalent
INITIATE	Sent by one program to one or more other programs, indicating that the sender wants to start a DDE conversation.	INITIATE("App","Topic")
ACKNOWLEDGE	Sent by one program in response either to another program's INITIATE message or to some other DDE message during an ongoing conversation; indicates assent or dissent.	Not Available from Microsoft Excel macros
ADVISE	Sent by a client program to request continuously updated data from a server.	Not Available from Microsoft Excel macros
UNADVISE	Sent by a client program indicating that continuous updates of linked data are no longer required from the server.	Not Available from Microsoft Excel macros
REQUEST	Sent by a client program requesting a one-time transfer of data from the server.	REQUEST(Channel,"Item")
DATA	Sent by a server program in response to a client's REQUEST	Not Available from Microsoft Excel macros
POKE	Unsolicited data sent by a client program to a server	POKE(Channel,"Item")
EXECUTE	A string sent by a client program representing commands to be executed by the server	EXECUTE(Channel,"Command")
TERMINATE	Sent by either a client or server application to terminate a DDE conversation	TERMINATE(Channel)

A Typical DDE Conversation (Windows)

You create a LINK field by copying selected cells of a spreadsheet and pasting them into Word for Windows using the Paste Link button from the Edit Paste Special dialog box.

Suppose that you have created a Word for Windows document which contains the following LINK field:

```
{LINK ExcelWorksheet BUDGET.XLS GrandTotal \a \r \* mergeformat}
```

that references the cell named GrandTotal in a Microsoft Excel spreadsheet called BUDGET.XLS. The LINK field is used when the source of the data is an application which supports Object Linking and Embedding. If the application does not support OLE, but can act as a DDE server, the field would resemble the following:

```
{DDE Appname TOPIC.XXX ItemName \* mergeformat}
```

which specifies a link which must be updated manually, or

```
{DDEAuto AppnameTOPIC.XXX ItemName \* mergeformat}
```

which creates an automatic link. The flowchart on the following page illustrates the DDE message-processing undertaken by Word for Windows in calculating the LINK field described above.

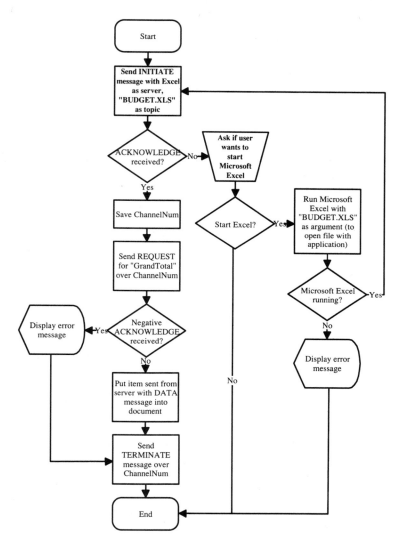

Figure A-1   Flowchart of procedure used to update a link from Microsoft Excel to Word for Windows

In this case, the name "GrandTotal" is the item being linked. If the selected cells had not already been assigned a name on the worksheet, the item would be the address of the selected cells as R1C1 text.

Linking From Word for Windows to Microsoft Excel

Let's see what happens when you paste data from a Word for Windows document into Microsoft Excel. If you copy a few words from a Word for Windows document and use the Paste Link command in Microsoft Excel to create a DDE link, you will see in the spreadsheet a formula similar to the following:

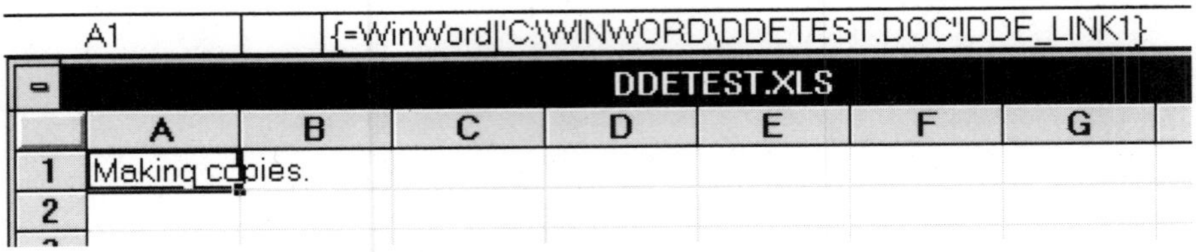

A1	{=WinWord|'C:\WINWORD\DDETEST.DOC'!DDE_LINK1}

	DDETEST.XLS					
	A	**B**	**C**	**D**	**E**	**F**	**G**
1	Making copies.						
2							

Figure A-2   Link from Word for Windows to Microsoft Excel

Microsoft Excel creates a link formula where the application name is separated from the topic (filename) and item by the pipe character ("|"). The data are divided into individual cells if the text from Word for Windows comprises several cells of a table or if the text contains tab characters and paragraph marks. Whether the resulting link is a single cell or multiple cells, the link formula is always entered as an array.

If you examine the Word for Windows document from which you copied the data, you will find that Word for Windows created a bookmark, in this case "DDE_LINK1," at the selection you copied. When Word for Windows is the source of a DDE link, the data item is always a bookmark.

What Other Data Can I Get From Microsoft Excel?

Programmers who venture into this territory often expect to find some way of requesting data other than the contents of cells from Microsoft Excel, such as the result of GET.WORKSPACE(2) or some other information function. They needn't bother looking—if Microsoft Excel is the server, the data item is a named cell range or its address as R1C1 text. To obtain the result of an information function, you must execute the commands to enter that formula into the cell of a macro sheet and then request the contents of the cell.

A Microsoft Excel DDE Macro (Windows)

The macros described in this section can be found in the file named DDETEST.XLM.

To illustrate the techniques you will need to develop applications with Microsoft Excel as a DDE client, we will examine a simple application, the Converse macro, which communicates with Word for Windows. While not intended as a useful application in itself, it does let us explore all of the DDE macro functions, and it illustrates many of the problems that confront developers who venture into this territory. The general scheme of our sample macro is illustrated in Figure A-3.

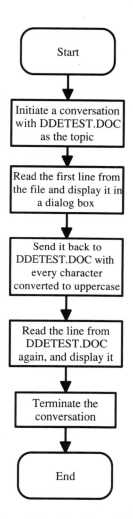

Figure A-3   Flowchart of Converse macro

We'll also display messages about the macro's progress each step of the way.

Talking to Word for Windows

The main macro for communicating with Word for Windows is shown in Figure A-4.

	Converse Ctrl-c	
ddeChannel	=InitiateConversation() =IF(ISNA(ddeChannel),HALT(DDEError(ddeChannel))) =Success()	Initiate conversation with Word doc returns #NA if initiate failed Show progress
tryToExecute	=ExecuteCommand(ddeChannel) =IF(ISNA(tryToExecute),HALT(DDEError(ddeChannel))) =Success()	returns #NA if initiate failed Show progress
bookmarkContents	=GetData(ddeChannel) =IF(ISNA(bookmarkContents),HALT(DDEError(ddeChannel))) =Success() =Show Greeting(bookmarkContents)	returns #NA if initiate failed Show progress
tryToPoke	=PokeData(ddeChannel,UPPER(bookmarkContents)) =IF(ISNA(tryToPoke),HALT(DDEError(ddeChannel))) =Success()	Send Greeting back in uppercase returns #NA if initiate failed Show progress
newBookmarkContents	=GetData(ddeChannel) =IF(ISNA(new BookmarkContents),HALT(DDEError(ddeChannel))) =Success() =Show Greeting(new BookmarkContents) =TerminateConversation(ddeChannel) =Success() =RETURN(TRUE)	returns #NA if initiate failed Show progress

Figure A-4   Converse macro code

Let's begin by looking at the general flow of the Converse macro and then explore the inner workings of each of its subroutines.

Status Messages

The Converse routine calls two general message functions for tracking the progress of the macro as it exercises each of the DDE commands. The first, shown in Figure A-5, is called Success and is used to describe the successful completion of each attempted task.

Success	
=ALERT(INDEX(MessageTable,globalMessageNum,2)) =RETURN()	display success message corresponding to globalMessageNum value

Figure A-5   Success subroutine for following activity of Converse macro

Before sending each DDE message, we place a value from 1-5 in a cell named globalMessageNum. The Success routine uses this value to index into the 2 x 5 cell range called MessageTable, shown in Figure A-6.

MessageTable

Unable to initiate conversation with Winword.	Conversation with Winword successfully initiated.
Unable to obtain data from Winword.	Data obtained from Winword.
Unable to send data to Winword.	Data sent to Winword and accepted.
Unable to execute Winword command.	Winword command successfully executed.
Unable to terminate Winword conversation.	Conversation with Winword terminated.

Figure A-6 MessageTable containing messages used by Success and DDEError subroutines

The first column of the range contains the error messages we want to display if we encounter failure during attempts to INITIATE, POKE, REQUEST, EXECUTE or TERMINATE, respectively. The second column contains corresponding success messages. The Success routine uses the ALERT function to display the message returned by the INDEX function. You'll recall that the syntax for the INDEX function is

INDEX(SourceRange,RowNumber,ColumnNumber**)**

so INDEX(MessageTable,globalMessageNum,2) returns the string in the second column of MessageTable that corresponds to the row value in globalMessageNum.

If the DDE message fails, we use a macro called DDEError, listed in Figure A-7:

	DDEError	
	=ARGUMENT("errorChannel",1+17)	
	=ALERT(INDEX(MessageTable,globalMessageNum,1))	*Show appropriate error message*
	=SET.VALUE(globalMessageNum,5)	
tryToTerminate	=TERMINATE(errorChannel)	*sever DDE conversation with Winword*
	=IF(NOT(ISNA(tryToTerminate)),Success())	*if actual terminate, say we terminated*
	=RETURN(TRUE)	

Figure A-7   DDEError subroutine

Like the Success subroutine described above, this subroutine displays the appropriate message from MessageTable to inform us of the type of error that occurred. It then terminates the conversation identified by the number passed as its errorChannel argument, and calls Success to tell us that the conversation has been terminated.

Let's return to the main Converse macro and see how all of this works in practice.

Detecting Errors

It is often necessary to disable normal error messages with Microsoft Excel macros to avoid alarming message boxes that might entice users to halt the macro. Microsoft Excel provides the ERROR function to enable and disable normal error handling and to replace the normal error handling with custom error handlers.

This sounds perfect for DDE macros, because we want to react appropriately when we are unable to INITIATE with a server, or when we REQUEST the value of a non-existent server item. Unfortunately, trapping for errors with the ERROR function will not protect us from all of the situations we are concerned about. If, for example, we REQUEST from a program the value of an item that does not exist, the macro cell will contain an error result, but not one that trips the ERROR function. Only later, if we try to manipulate the requested data, will a macro error occur.

The solution we show here requires more lines of code but flags the errors as they occur. Each of the subroutines that performs DDE commands is resonsible for setting globalMessageNum to the correct number. The routine then performs its given function and returns TRUE if successful, or #NA if not. The main Converse macro then uses these return values to respond appropriately, either by halting the macro with the DDEError subroutine or proceeding and displaying the success message.

The code shown in Figure A-8 illustrates how we use this to handle the attempt to initiate a conversation with Word for Windows.

| ddeChannel | =InitiateConversation() |
| | =IF(ISNA(ddeChannel),HALT(DDEError(ddeChannel))) |

Figure A-8   Checking for INITIATE error in Converse macro

Hello, WinWord?

The routine we use to initiate the conversation on the DDETEST.DOC topic is shown in Figure A-9:

	InitiateConversation	
	=SET.VALUE(globalMessageNum,1)	for lookup in message table
	=ERROR(FALSE)	avoid "Want to run?" message
docChannel	=INITIATE("Winword","C:\DDECLASS\DDETEST.DOC")	Opens program and/or document if closed
	=ERROR(TRUE)	
	=RETURN(docChannel)	return the channel number

Figure A-9   InitiateConversation function

You should place DDETEST.DOC in a directory of your choosing and change the path in the macro.

In the cell labelled docChannel, we attempt to initiate a conversation with "C:\DDECLASS\DDETEST.DOC" as the topic. If this succeeds, INITIATE returns a channel number over which the subsequent DDE messages can be sent. Before attempting the initiation, we first disable normal error checking to avoid encountering the dialog box shown in Figure A-10.

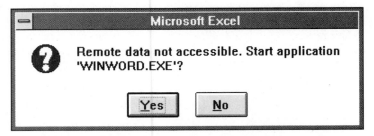

Figure A-10   An alert box we don't want users to see

With normal error handling in effect, you would see this message if either of the following is true:

- Word for Windows is not running

- Word for Windows is running but the DDETEST.DOC file is not loaded

When you disable standard error messages with the ERROR(FALSE) function, Microsoft Excel performs the default action, which in this case is associated with the Yes button: loading Word for Windows and the file. We return the channel number that is the result of the INITIATE function to the Converse macro, which uses it for all subsequent interaction with Word for Windows.

Executing the Server's Commands

OK, now we're talking. What we want to do next is to set the first line of the DDETEST.DOC file as a bookmark, so we can find out what is in it. To create this bookmark, we execute the WordBasic commands to select the first line of the document and insert a bookmark there. This is the purpose of the ExecuteCommand function, shown in Figure A-11:

ExecuteCommand
=ARGUMENT("executeChannel") =SET.VALUE(globalMessageNum,4) =EXECUTE(executeChannel,"[StartOfDocument][EndOfLine 1][InsertBookmark ""Greeting""]") =IF(ISERROR(previousCall),RETURN(#N/A)) =RETURN(TRUE)

Figure A-11   ExecuteCommand function

The EXECUTE function uses the syntax

EXECUTE(*ChannelNum,"[Command1][Command2]...[etc.]"*)

where each of the commands in "Command(s)" is delimited in some way defined by the server application. Microsoft encourages developers to support command strings in which multiple commands are enclosed in brackets ([ ]). This is the syntax supported by both Microsoft Excel and Word for Windows.

Just which commands may be executed depends on the server application. Both Microsoft Excel and Word for Windows allow you to execute their macro commands through DDE. Many other applications that do not have macro languages have still been designed to act as DDE servers, and publish the list of available commands in their reference guides. Still other applications accept keystroke sequences as command strings, so that you may execute commands through their menus.

Watch Out for Those Double Quotes

Examine the command string we send in the EXECUTE function in Figure A-11:

```
"[StartOfDocument][EndOfLine 1][InsertBookmark ""Greeting""]"
```

Notice the pairs of double quotes around the bookmark name. This is necessary because the WordBasic InsertBookmark command requires a quoted string as its argument and each literal quotation mark within a string argument in Microsoft Excel must be doubled.

Getting the Server's Data

Now that we have a bookmark, we can request some data. The subroutine which performs this for us is listed in Figure A-12:

	GetData	
greetingData *trimmedData*	=ARGUMENT("dataChannel") =SET.VALUE(globalMessageNum,2) =REQUEST(dataChannel,"Greeting") =IF(ISERROR(previousCall),RETURN(#N/A)) =TRIM(greetingData) =RETURN(trimmedData)	*Read contents of the first line* *Winword appends extra space*

Figure A-12   GetData function

In the cell labelled greetingData, we request that Word for Windows send us the contents of the Greeting item. The return value will either be the text of the bookmark or an error.

For some reason, the value returned from the REQUEST contains an extra space at the end, so we clean up the string with the TRIM function before returning it. We recommend that you allow for little mysteries such as these.

Showing the Result

The following is the macro we use to display the Greeting:

	ShowGreeting	
	ShowGreeting	
alertString	=ARGUMENT("aBookmark") ="The bookmark now equals "&CHAR(13)&""""&aBookmark&"""." =ALERT(alertString) =RETURN(TRUE)	*concatenate bookmark value in quoted string and show in ALERT*

Figure A-13   ShowGreeting function

Sending Data Back

With the function

=PokeData(ddeChannel,UPPER(bookmarkContents))

in Converse, we convert the greeting to its uppercase equivalent, and POKE it back to the Greeting bookmark, using the routine shown in Figure A-14:

	PokeData	
	PokeData	
	=ARGUMENT("pokeChannel") =ARGUMENT("aGreeting",2,pokeValue) =SET.VALUE(globalMessageNum,3) =POKE(pokeChannel,"Greeting",pokeValue) =IF(ISERROR(previousCall),RETURN(#N/A)) =RETURN(TRUE)	*Contents of bookmark in uppercase* *Replace contents of bookmark with it*
pokeValue	Hello From Winword!	*value to poke to Winword*

Figure A-14   PokeData function

Pay special attention to the form of the second ARGUMENT function. Why aren't we simply poking the value in the aGreeting argument passed by the caller instead of putting that value into another cell and poking it? We said it before, but now we'll say it louder: *in Microsoft Excel, data items are always cell ranges.* Not strings or numbers or function results or anything else.

And here's another thing to keep in mind. What gets poked is the text of the cell's currently displayed value, including numeric format, if applicable. If the sheet is set to display formulas (as is often the case with macro sheets) then the formula text is sent, rather than its result.

Finishing Up

We complete our main macro by requesting the data back from Word for Windows and showing it in the alert box. Finally, we terminate the conversation with the following routine:

```
TerminateConversation

=ARGUMENT("terminateChannel")
=SET.VALUE(globalMessageNum,5)
=TERMINATE(terminateChannel)
=RETURN(TRUE)
```

Figure A-15   TerminateConversation function

Those Important Details We Glossed Over

If you thoroughly test the macros described in this Appendix, you will find that if we attempt to initiate with Word for Windows when it is running but DDETEST.DOC is closed, Word for Windows loads the file, and then *activates itself*. We can avoid this problem by controlling the whole process ourselves, using the strategy shown in Figure A-16.

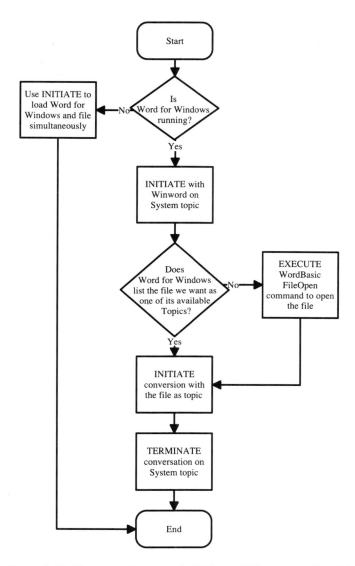

Figure A-16   Flowchart of strategy for initiating DDE conversation without activating Word for Windows

Determining if a Windows Application Is Running

The core components of Windows are three main DLLs: KERNEL, USER and GDI.

While there is no macro function for determining if a particular Windows application is running, we can call one of the functions that reside in the Windows dynamic link libraries (DLLs) to get that information for us. The function we need is called *GetModuleHandle*, and is part of the Windows *KERNEL* library. If you're in

Windows, then this library is guaranteed to be available, because Windows *is* its libraries.

The quickest method for calling this function is with the following command:

```
=CALL("KERNEL","GetModuleHandle","HC","WINWORD.EXE")
```

The codes for arguments to external functions are listed in the Microsoft Excel Function Reference.

where the argument string "HC", tells Microsoft Excel to expect an unsigned integer as the external function's result (data type "H"), and to pass a string to it as its argument (data type "C"). In this case, "WINWORD" is the module name that we pass as the argument to GetModuleHandle. When the macro evaluates this function, we'll either get a result of 0, meaning that Word for Windows is not loaded, or some integer greater than 0, which is the handle (unique identifier) assigned to Word for Windows for the current Windows session.

Our new, smarter INITIATE is shown in Figure A-17:

	SmarterInitiate
wordHandle	=CALL("KERNEL","GetModuleHandle","HC","WINWORD.EXE")
	=IF(wordHandle>0)
	= SET.VALUE(openIt,TRUE)
sysChannel	= INITIATE("Winword","System")
	= IF(ISERROR(previousCall),RETURN(#N/A))
	= MATCH("C:\DDECLASS\DDETEST.DOC",REQUEST(sysChannel,"Topics"),0)
	= IF(ISNA(previousCall))
	= SET.VALUE(globalMessageNum,4)
openIt	= EXECUTE(sysChannel,"[FileOpen ""C:\DDECLASS\DDETest.Doc""]")
	= END.IF()
	= TERMINATE(sysChannel)
	= IF(ISERROR(openIt),RETURN(#N/A))
	=ELSE()
	= ERROR(FALSE)
	=END.IF()
	=SET.VALUE(globalMessageNum,1)
docChannel	=INITIATE("Winword","C:\DDECLASS\DDETEST.DOC")
	=ERROR(TRUE)
	=IF(ISERROR(docChannel),RETURN(#N/A))
	=RETURN(docChannel)

Figure A-17   SmarterInitiate function

We begin by determining if Word for Windows is running. If it is not, we turn off standard error messages and use the INITIATE function to run Word for Windows and load DDETEST.DOC simultaneously. If Word for Windows is running, we initiate a conversation on the System topic and request its Topics item. If DDETEST.DOC is not among the available topics, then we execute the WordBasic command to open the file. After determining that DDETEST.DOC is open, we terminate the System topic conversation, and initiate a conversation with the document. We have also peppered the code with tests along the way, so that we can inform the calling macro if any of these attempts fail.

Most of this macro is straightforward, but the portion that examines the topics available from Word for Windows requires some explanation. With the code

```
=MATCH("C:\DDECLASS\DDETEST.DOC",REQUEST(sysChannel,"Topics"),0)
```

we search for the file we're interested in from the list of available topics. Notice that we're using the MATCH function to do the search, because Microsoft Excel interprets the result of our REQUEST function as an array. You can confirm this by running the SmarterInitiate macro and then entering the formula

```
=REQUEST(sysChannel,"Topics")
```

into a cell on the macro sheet. The result you will see will be the single value "System," regardless of the number of files open at the time. The actual result is a horizontal array of all of the files open in Word for Windows (including any templates upon which open documents are based), but because the REQUEST formula is entered as a normal formula into a single cell, Microsoft Excel only displays the first value in the array as the function's result.

To see all of the values, we would need to enter the REQUEST function as an array formula spanning several cells. We don't want to look at it, though; we just want to see if a particular value is within it. With a function such as MATCH, which expects array arguments, we can use the result of the REQUEST as the array to search. In this case, Microsoft Excel will search through the entire array and not just its first value.

There's Always Something

If we run Word for Windows, open DDETEST.DOC, activate some other file within Word for Windows and then run Converse, the following will happen:

1 We'll initiate a conversation with DDETEST.DOC, but the active window within Word for Windows will not change.

2 We'll create a Greeting bookmark in the first line of the *active* document.

3 We'll request the contents of the Greeting bookmark from DDETEST.DOC, which won't have a Greeting bookmark.

4 The macro will terminate, saying it was unable to get the data from Word for Windows.

It would seem that we need to execute the WordBasic Activate command to insure that DDETEST.DOC is the active document before we create the bookmark. This solution works, but produces an unfortunate side effect—Word for Windows becomes the active application. Another little mystery! Rather than spending any further effort perfecting the Converse macro, we'll just reiterate that you may find yourself breaking new ground when you integrate applications with DDE, and you should therefore expect the unexpected. As it is, Converse does put Microsoft Excel through a complete DDE workout and should serve as a good starting point for any Microsoft Excel macro that uses DDE.

Summary

In this appendix we have introduced all of the ways in which you may use Dynamic Data Exchange in Microsoft Excel macros. We began by defining DDE as a protocol through which programs can establish direct and ongoing communication, either for data transfer or to share program functionality. We examined the roles of client and server in DDE conversations. A macro called Converse was developed in Microsoft Excel for Windows, using the INITIATE, POKE, REQUEST, EXECUTE and TERMINATE macro functions to control Word for Windows and exchange data with it. We also examined the CALL function in Microsoft Excel, with which macros or spreadsheets may call functions that reside in Dynamic Link Libraries in the Windows environment, or Code Resources on the Macintosh.

Index

CROSSTAB.RECALC function 166
Customized Data Entry 194

D

Data form 144, 147, 161, 171-74, 189
   definition table 174
   dialog box alternative 189
DATA.FORM function 173, 175, 182
Database
   selecting 125-27
   sorting by fields 132-33
DDE
   Client 230
   definition 229
   errors 237
   executing commands 231, 239
   initiating conversation 231, 238, 244
   Item 230
   link formula 234
   Message protocol 230-231
   poking data 231, 241
   requesting data 231, 240
   Server 230
   System topic 230, 244
   terminating conversation 231, 242
   Topic 230
   Topics item 230, 244
Debugging 34, 40-41, 115, 118
DELETE.BAR function 221-22
DELETE.COMMAND function 110, 139
DELETE.MENU function 206
DELETE.TOOL function 122
DeleteSideBySideTool macro 123
Dialog Box
   as data entry form 189
Dialog box definition table 78-79, 87, 91- 92, 116
   order of entry 116
Dialog Boxes 77, 83-87, 89, 92, 94-95, 101, 189
   accelerator keys 89
   aligning items 83
   buttons 78-79, 82-83, 87-88, 92
   check boxes 92
   coordinates 77-78, 84
   copying to macro sheet 85-86, 95
   displaying 86
   dynamic 101
   focus 116-17
   group boxes 88-89
   initializing 94, 117
   list boxes 95-96, 98-99, 103, 132
     multiple-selection 103

   option buttons 78, 88-90
   previewing 115
   resizing 83-84
   results 87, 92
   trigger items 101-2
Dialog Editor 80
DIALOG.BOX function 78-79, 87
   results 87, 91-92
DIRECTORY function 75
Disguising Microsoft Excel 218
Display customizing 218
   Microsoft Excel title bar 224
   window settings 218
   window titles 223
DISPLAY function 28-29
DLL
   calling from Microsoft Excel 243
DOCUMENTS function 179
DoubleBorder macro 5, 7-8, 10
Dynamic Link Libraries, calling from Microsoft Excel 243
Dynamic Data Exchange—see DDE
Dynamic Menus 204, 213, 218

E

EDJ methodology 27
ELSE function 47, 59
ELSE.IF function 47, 59
END.IF function 40, 47
Error handling, DDE 237
Error checking 41, 75-76, 119
Event-triggered macros 212
Excel Startup Folder (4) 16-17
Excel Toolbars file 23
EXCEL.XLB 23
EXECUTE 231, 239
Executive Infomation System
   Auto_Open macro 224
Executive Information System 159
   customizing 167

F

FILE.CLOSE function 185
FOR function 68
FOR.CELL function 119
Format Cell Protection command 54
FormatBottom macro 62-63, 65-66
FormatWorksheet macro 68-69
Formula Create Names command 43
FORMULA function 120

Formula Paste Function command 28-29, 51, 55-56, 60
Formula Select Special command 36
FORMULA.ARRAY function 202-3
FULL function 183
Function Macros 51, 55

G

GET.BAR function 207
GET.CELL function 51, 177
GET.DOCUMENT function 42, 50-51, 223-24
GET.FORMULA function 120
GET.TOOLBAR function 123, 220
GET.WINDOW function 31-32, 118, 223
GET.WORKSPACE function 31, 220
GETMODULEHANDLE function 243
Global macro 3-4, 14-16
Global macro sheet 5-6
Group boxes 88-89

H

Hidden window
    saving 18, 51
HideAndSave macro 50, 53
HideThisReport macro 218, 225

I

IF function 32, 34, 40, 47
INITIATE function 231, 238, 244
INPUT function 71-73, 75
    type_num arguments 71-72
Invoicing 152, 155, 161-62, 190
    customizing 162
    line item dialog box definition 198
    line item formulas 163
    reprinting invoices 155
    reserved fields and 161
    WriteInvoices macro 192-93
    writing invoices 153
ISERROR function 75-76
ISNA function 180

L

Letter Template 157
Line Item dialog box definition 198
Links, changing 225
List boxes 95-96, 98-99, 103, 132
    multiple-selection 103

Loops 68
Lotus 1-2-3 4, 5, 11

M

Macro etiquette
    using Auto_Open and Auto_Close 111
    using SET.NAME 68
Macro Relative Record command 62
Macro sheet 5-7, 26, 34, 51-52
    differences betweeen worksheets and 6-7
    formatting 26, 34
    global 5-6
    saving as Add-In 51-52
Macro sheets
    editing 118
Macro toolbar 40, 113
Macros
    assigning to tools 19
    avoiding constant values in 176
    debugging 41
    event-triggered 212
Menu bars 107, 109-10, 221
    adding menus to 139
    custom 221
    ID numbers 109
    replacing 221
Menus
    adding to menu bars 181, 139
    command tables 108, 138, 209-10
    commands 107-8, 110, 138
    customizing 107-9, 138-39, 181, 206
    deleting 206
    dynamic 204, 213, 218
    menu bar 107
    removing commands from 110
    replacing 206
    replacing commands in 138
MESSAGE function 48
Microsoft Excel title bar 224

N

NEW.WINDOW function 224
NEXT function 68
NOW function 49

O

OFFSET function 65-66, 100, 127-28, 132-36, 203
ON.TIME function 48-49, 204, 213
OPEN function 180

OPEN? function 93, 95
OpenFiles macro 183
Option buttons 78, 88-90
Options Protect Document command 54

P

POKE function 231, 241
Preview Dialog tool 115
PRINT function 14
PrintSelection macro 12-13

Q

QuitMe macro 186, 228

R

R1C1 notation 61
RedirectButton macro 225
References
    circular 199
    computing with OFFSET function 65-66, 100, 127-
        28, 132-36, 203
    R1C1 notation 61
    recording 61
Renaming Microsoft Excel 224
Renaming windows 223
REQUEST function 231, 240
RestoreStatus macro 227
RETURN function 9, 14
ROUND function 56-57
ROUNDTO function macro 58-59
ROWS function 39

S

SAVE.AS function 218, 225-26
Screen unit 77-78
SELECT.SPECIAL function 36, 64-65
SELECTION function 38-39, 119
SET.NAME function 68-69, 94-95, 105, 216, 220
SET.VALUE function 94, 100, 102, 105, 198-99
SHOW.BAR function 221-22
SHOW.TOOLBAR function 220
ShowLittleMenu macro 223
SideBySide macro 118
SimpleDialog macro 86
Single Step Mode 41
SmartDataSort macro 127-28, 130, 138
SORT function 135
SPELLOUT function macro 55-56

Status bar, displaying message in 48
Subroutine 64-65

T

TERMINATE function 231, 242
ToggleGridlines macro 33-35, 44
ToggleRecalc macro 42-44, 47-49
Toolbar, Macro 40
Toolbar definition table 121
Toolbars 19-23, 120-22
    adding tools 20, 120
    assigning macros to 19-22, 120-22
    custom 20-22, 120-22
    customize dialog box 19
    Macro 40, 113-14, 121
    removing tools from 20, 122
    resetting 22
    shortcut menu 19
    where stored 23
Tools 21-22, 113
    adding to toolbars 21
    creating 21
    customizing tool face 21
    narrowing 20
TOOLS.XLM 113
TRANSPOSE function 203

U

UnComment macro 120
User interface
    Alert box 44-46, 48, 128, 130-31
    Dialog box 78-79, 87
    Dialog box with trigger items 101
    Input box 71-73, 75
    Status bar 48

W

WHILE function 68
Windows
    customizing 218
    renaming 223
    saving hidden 18, 51
WORKSPACE function 219
WriteInvoices macro 192-93

X

XLSTART 16, 51

Great Resources from
Microsoft Press

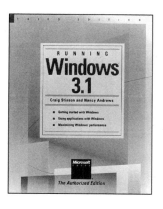

STEP BY STEP SERIES
The Official Microsoft® Courseware

Tried-and-tested, these book-and-disk packages are Microsoft's official courseware.
Complete with follow-along lessons and disk-based practice files, they are ideal self-study
training guides for business, classroom and home use. Scores of real-world business examples make
the instruction relevant and useful; "One Step Further" sections for each chapter cover advanced uses.
These courseware products are the perfect training guide for business, classroom, or home use.

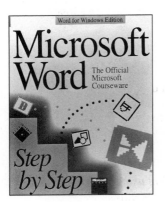

MICROSOFT® WORD FOR WINDOWS™ STEP BY STEP
Version 2

Microsoft Corporation

Learn to produce professional-quality documents with ease.
Covers Microsoft Word for Windows version 2.

296 pages, softcover with one 5.25-inch disk
$29.95 ($39.95 Canada)   Order Code WD2STW

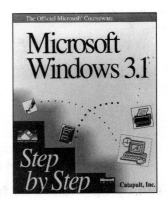

MICROSOFT® WINDOWS™ 3.1 STEP BY STEP

Catapult, Inc.

Learn Microsoft Windows quickly and easily with
MICROSOFT WINDOWS 3.1 STEP BY STEP.

272 pages, softcover with one 3.5-inch disk
$29.95 ($39.95 Canada)   Order Code WI31ST

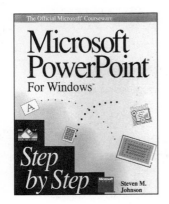

MICROSOFT® POWERPOINT® FOR WINDOWS™ STEP BY STEP

Steven M. Johnson

The fastest way to get up and running with Microsoft
PowerPoint! Covers Microsoft PowerPoint version 3.

300 pages, softcover with one 3.5-inch disk
$29.95 ($39.95 Canada)   Order Code POSBS
Available August 1992

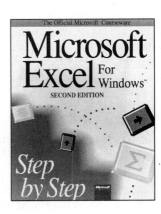

MICROSOFT® EXCEL FOR WINDOWS STEP BY STEP
Version 4

Microsoft Corporation

325 pages, softcover with one 3.5-inch disk
$29.95 ($39.95 Canada)   Order Code EXSTP2